# Earthkeeping

Gordon Harrison

# Earthkeeping

The War with Nature
and a
Proposal for Peace

HOUGHTON MIFFLIN COMPANY BOSTON 1971

FIRST PRINTING W

*For my colleagues*
*in the Resources and Environment Program*
*of the Ford Foundation*

# Preface

ENGINEERING THE NATURAL ENVIRONMENT for profit and convenience has been man's way up from the beginning. To
berate ourselves for the damage caused seems to me to make
no more sense than scolding a snake for biting. Furthermore
it is beside the point. Environmental wounds so evident in
befouled air and water, uglified landscapes, poisoned birds
and fish, ever-spreading deserts (some subdivided) have not
been the result of carelessness or irresponsibility or even ordi-
nary stupidity; they are direct consequences of an unduly
prolonged state of war with nature.

The primeval human habit of mind that regarded the
world outside the tribe as an assemblage of hostiles has disastrously persisted into a time when man is incomparably the
most powerful force on earth and his world is the home not
of his enemies but of himself. In such a world we can and
must make peace. What follows is an analysis of the origins
and characteristics of our long war with nature and some
tentative suggestions as to how that war might be ended in
time — that is to say, before we have won it.

An effort to survey so large a subject must owe large debts
to many friends and experts. The Ford Foundation, where
I have been working on environmental issues, provided my

basic education and then generously allowed me time off to read and write. I appreciate Vice President Mitchell Sviri-doff's understanding and tolerance during the year and a half of split time between the office and the typewriter. My col-leagues in the Resources and Environment Program, to all of whom this book is gratefully dedicated, shouldered the burden of my absences and kept my work and their own going. For such devotion beyond the call I especially thank William E. Felling and Edward A. Ames.

Janet Koch not only typed and retyped the manuscript but worked with me during the revisions, checking facts and references and discovering errors and ineptitudes.

C. S. Holling during years of close association has helped me to understand what ecology means. He reviewed and criti-cized the manuscript, saved me from some mistakes, deepened some interpretations and generally made the book better than it would have been without his counsel.

Joseph L. Fisher also gave me the benefit of his special knowledge and friendly but critical eye. Allen Kneese read and commented in detail on an earlier version of Chapters Sixteen and Eighteen which, in part because of his criticism, were completely rewritten. I am grateful to them, though none will wholly approve the result.

It would be impossible by name to acknowledge my debt to all the people whose wisdom I have been exposed to in the course of eight years' traveling in the field of conservation, and it would be invidious to single out a few. I believe they will recognize their contributions and know how much I ap-preciate them.

It is only slightly less difficult to properly document the facts and notions I derived from reading. In general I have tried to credit all ideas that I know I did not think of first to the writer who did. But as I make forays into a variety of special fields in which I am an amateur it is also obvious that no more than some of the syntheses and more skeptical comments can be strictly my own.

Footnotes are in the back of the book, keyed by page number and citations from the text. This is to avoid the superscript numbers in the text which I find especially annoying when references are not on the page. The footnotes contain a minimum of supplementary information, except in Chapters Five through Seven. Read with the notes, these chapters are intended as a summary of federal environmental improvement programs through 1970. However, readers who do not care about completeness may disregard the notes and not miss anything essential to the essay as a whole. In similar spirit the rest of the back matter may be disregarded. It is there for those who may ask, "Is that so?" or "Where can I find more?" I hope there are some.

GORDON HARRISON

*New York City, January 1971*

# Contents

PREFACE     vii

PART I — SITUATION REPORT

1. The Environmental Crisis    3
2. An Agreeable Revolution    16
3. How to Get Less by Multiplying    26
4. Numbers, Space, and Time    37
5. Deferred Maintenance    49
6. The High Cost of Waste    55
7. To Kill a Goose    70

PART II — THE ANTAGONISTS

8. Natural Systems    81
9. The Coexistence Process    88
10. The Nonconforming Species    104
11. The Agricultural Revolution    116
12. Country Ecology    126
13. Home Is the City    139
14. The City Means Business    149
15. Are Slums Necessary?    157
16. A Passion to Consume    170
17. American Dreams    186

PART III — EARTHKEEPING

18. A Price on Everything                    199
19. All There Is                             207
20. The Meek Take Heart                      215

NOTES                                        233

INDEX                                        267

PART I

# Situation Report

# CHAPTER 1

# The Environmental Crisis

ABOUT EIGHT YEARS AGO, when I first became professionally interested in the impact of modern technological man on the natural environment — the issue was then badly labeled conservation — I used to be asked daily how many redwood trees I had saved that day. To most of the hard-headed men of affairs conservation then was a whimsy of nature lovers, who seem always to have been considered odd. I used to worry over my inability to get intelligent people to understand that the evident signs of environmental deterioration, in dirty air and water and, yes, in thousand-year-old forests cut down for the moment's profit, were symptoms of something radically wrong with the way we were living and managing our affairs. Other "conservationists" whose concern was longer than mine and whose understanding was deeper worked harder to get the message across. They had some success. The literature of concern mounted steadily during the sixties. The issue was blessed by two presidents. Congress was stirred to remedial legislation beginning about 1963 and accelerating thereafter. Angry citizens in increasing numbers and with some astounding success challenged the despoilers. Embraced at last by President Nixon as the issue of the decade, environmental quality has achieved the dangerous respectability of being everyman's love.

New success had some of the old warriors more worried than old failure. A few no doubt resented the loss of their patent on the crusade — especially to upstarts. Some perhaps had become so fond of the noble shabbiness of a hopeless cause that they shrank from fashion. But many cited more substantial cause for concern. They noted two disturbing facts: first, the intemperance and impatience that characterized the new crusaders, and, second, the lack of convincing signs that the nature of the problem was better understood now that it was on every reform agenda than when it was generally written off as a sentimental worry over wild things.

This is a rhetorically violent age: We declare (though we scarcely wage) war on poverty and hunger; we cope (or fail to) with the revolution of rising expectations; we shake before (or stop our ears against) the population explosion; we face (or turn from) the environmental crisis. Perhaps the violence of each definition bears some Freudian — or merely hypocritical — relation to the parenthetical reservations in action. It could be that we talk big to scare ourselves out of otherwise immovable lethargy, to achieve at least a minimum alertness, like the fabled mule whom the psychologist had to whack over the head with big lumber in order to get his attention for the subtle persuasion to come. It could be too that by hyperbole we subconsciously mean to define the problems as so unmanageable that we need not seriously try to cope at all. Or maybe the violence in speech is just another outlet for frustrations that also erupt physical violence in a world increasingly unresponsive to the needs and wishes of the private man.

Whatever the reason, the practice profoundly discourages rational analysis and effective action. We are continually knocked off our mental pins by the newest blowup (now population or ecology or some hyper-explosive amalgam of the two). The net result is successive bewilderment with ever-decreasing sensitivity. We get inured to a world of exploding manhole covers as we would to a world of popping champagne corks. The reaction mainly induced is a wish to have the annoyance go away, and even that wish grows feebler until at last, fully adapted to rhetorical buffeting, we succumb to a weary complacency that will make real explosions or collapses in time inevitable.

Even if apocalypse is at hand (and who can possibly be sure?), to try to conjure up the flames for early warning can produce only terror or despair. Neither is useful. What we have to fear is not ultimate catastrophe (which, if you make ultimate long enough, is inevitable anyway) but drift into ways of life that do not suit human needs and that impoverish human potential. One of the objects of this book is to draw the shades against apocalypse, not in order to comfort but in order to see by a less blinding light what the problems really are that could be dealt with rationally and whose solution would preserve a better world for people. This is not to express any deep faith that we will in fact either see them or solve them. I do not know any optimists among those who have looked long and steadily at man in the environment. I do know some wise men to whom I have talked and whose books I have read and whose separate insights it is my chief hope to collect and focus on the problem which, after all, President Nixon was not wrong in calling the issue of the 1970s. It might even be around a bit longer.

Generalizations are difficult at best once one gets in any field close enough to see some of the facts, their complexities and their ambiguities. On issues as large as those that this book addresses few if any general statements can be more than approximations (or even perhaps first guesses) at truth.

Nevertheless they are obviously indispensable for understanding and to qualify them continually would be tedious. Little learning takes place when pronouncements of the experts are impeccably accurate and everybody else is happily asleep.

So let me begin with some broad and possibly unpopular statements, which it will be the business of the rest of the book to define, modify and I hope illuminate:

**The population problem — the potentially disastrous rapid increase in numbers of people — and the problems of environmental degradation are separable and should be kept separate if we are to both solve them rationally and live through the solution.**

The connection between numbers of people and the difficulties of feeding them, housing them, transporting them and disposing of their wastes is too obvious to argue. Clearly in that sense those who would control population and those who would preserve the environment should join hands. The danger and delusion, however, lie in an assumption (which is often made explicit) that the way to save the environment is to cut down the birthrates and the way to make people slow their insane rates of reproduction is to show that the resources of earth simply cannot support any more. Both of these propositions are demonstrably false: At zero population growth the environment could continue to degrade and in conditions of increasing affluence at an ever-accelerating rate. There is no evidence that the earth cannot support much larger populations in reasonable comfort and cleanliness (even though there is equally no evidence that more would be in any sense better). Reasons to halt population growth by rational action to control births and do it now are legion. Among them is certainly the fact that with fewer people more resources and energy could be devoted to enhancing the conditions under which all live. The argument is not that we should have more people but that we should give quite independent attention to managing the environment properly.

**If by environmental crisis is meant an imminent and catastrophic failure of natural systems under human abuse resulting in mass starvation or mass deaths from poisoned air, food, or water, there is no convincing evidence that we now face an environmental crisis.**

Many scientists recently have publicly been predicting various environmental disasters in terms and on grounds they would not consider using to address their professional colleagues. No one of course can prove or disprove prophecy, but any man's use of evidence is open to assay.

Take just one well-publicized warning: that carbon dioxide, an inexorable result of burning anything, is building up in the atmosphere at such a rate that in a relatively few years it will warm the global climate enough to melt the polar ice caps and inundate the great sea-level cities of the world. That vision is stark and simple enough to catch any imagination, and it rests on certain stark and simple facts. We are generating and consuming ever more energy; its production delivers carbon dioxide to the air faster than green plants can use it or oceans absorb it. Hence concentrations of $CO_2$ in the atmosphere steadily increase. In air $CO_2$ acts rather like the glass on a greenhouse; light passes through on the way from sun to earth but heat radiated back from the earth is partially blocked and reflected. Despite the tumultuous variations in weather from day to day familiar in Mark Twain country, average temperatures over decades are remarkably stable in various climatic regions. When those long-run averages do shift even by a degree or two the effect can be cataclysmic — a new desert, wholesale extinctions of species, or melting or formation of ice sheets.

But there are other relevant facts. Much combustion produces fly ash, soot, particles large and small that also accumulate in the air if they are put up faster than they can settle out. These particles can make the air measurably more opaque and literally darken the sun. The less radiation from the sun reaching the surface of the earth, the less heat can be reflected and the colder we become. In fact since 1945 worldwide temperatures on average have gone down a little. Also temperature is affected by how wet the air is and vice versa. The air circulates in patterns poorly understood and this circulation is also in part caused by temperature and moisture differences that it in turn affects. In short the weather systems are so very complicated that science speaking scientifically can only say that changes in the amount of carbon dioxide must at some density have some effect on climate but they cannot be sure just what.

Prediction is difficult and hazardous at best, as good scientists know. They use it as the final proof of a hypothesis already exhaustively tested by experiment, not as the first leap into print from a set of incomplete and ambiguous data. All, or nearly all, current apocalyptic statements about the environment are in this sense thoroughly unscientific. They gloss over the real complexity of fact that makes all simple predictions suspect; worse, while deploring the reckless ignorance of those who are engineering the environment, they in calling for a halt pretend to superior and certain knowledge, which in fact they do not have.

**There is less truth than plausibility in the frequent assertion that since pollution and other adverse effects on the environment have resulted from the impact of advanced technology, it is up to still more advanced technology to repair the damage, and it can.**

In no simple, direct way is technology the cause of our troubles. It is of course obvious that if we did not have paper factories we would not have paper wastes polluting the rivers or burning newsprint polluting the air. Subtract civilization from the human condition and we would be minus its costs. But given civilization it is by no means self-evident that the primary responsibility for pollution should be laid to technology itself, nor that improved or better-directed technology would eliminate it. In fact to debate the role of technology at the start is to come in at the wrong door, asking questions to which the best possible answers, while touching truth, will miss the heart of the matter.

Technology does us in (so far as it does) because we have placed it at the service of false values. But the problem is really more complicated than that. In the nonatomic world where everything, as in the old song, is connected, and in which the whole is a process, a creator is always in part his own creation. Technology serves the values it helps to develop. Since each reinforces the other and both have evolved for a long time together a reformer is not likely to get far by trying to beat one at a time into new form. To suppose that the environment can be taken care of simply by shifting machines to a new task is to embrace an illusion comparable to the perennial dream of some day investing some of the billions now spent on war in rebuilding the cities and bringing justice to the poor. That dream builds on an assumption that war is merely a misfortune and temporary diversion from the norm of peace. It ignores the plain fact that wars reflect a society's priorities, that the relative allocation of resources between war and civic justice derives from a scale of values that makes quite inconceivable the turnabout to vast schemes of social improvement. In fact peace is more likely again to be followed by a search for new wars or fresh justifications to prepare for them, as it always has in the past, unless both the institutions of war and their value systems can be dismantled together.

So with the environment, it is idle to suppose that a technical correction in the normal processes of production and consumption will suffice to remedy the ills. That supposition equally is built on the belief that environmental degradation is a misfortune visited on us by our own carelessness, or somebody else's wickedness. In fact we are in the mess that we are in because our economic, political, and value systems, operating very well, are producing mess as part of their normal output. If this book has a single theme, that is the theme.

Prophets of disaster can be good at scaring people and it can be good to scare people when, blind to a clear and present danger, they need to be aroused in time to avoid it. But prophecy by its nature carries a relatively high shock voltage and relatively little convincing information. Doom is of course inherently incredible if only because it never happened before. More seriously, futurology (which is essentially the art of continuing curves in the direction they seem to have been going) can at best only say certain developments are likely if there are no changes other than those the forecaster has elected to consider. But since everything is more complicated than anyone thinks, that invites the retort: How do you know you have considered even the right things, much less all that is relevant, in reaching your conclusion? To prove you have is impossible; much that is relevant has not even happened yet. Historically the record of prophecy does not inspire confidence. The unexpected is always turning up, or more accurately change in a system always inspires further change whose nature and direction are not predictable. No system progresses or regresses steadily in one direction; all tend to oscillate. What the future looks like at any one moment partly depends on where one happens to be among the waves and troughs of oscillation, looking up or looking down.

But if where there is life there are no straight lines and no inevitabilities, there are changes that may have definable trends in the past and measurable rates at present. The significance of such changes is not where they might ultimately lead if they run on unchecked, but whether they have so far produced desired results, whether an extension of the trend will continue to produce desirable results, and whether the rate at which change takes place is compatible with the ability of man and nature to adapt.

*Science* magazine recently reported the sad history of the reckless, greedy exploitation of Galveston Bay, Texas, which has brought a precious economic and esthetic resource to the verge of total destruction. The despoilers were many. They were not part of a conspiracy; they were scarcely known to each other and they preyed separately upon the common resource for their own purposes. They had no plan but for immediate profit and no understanding of what they did except that it made them rich. One lot dredged up the great reefs of oyster shells that used to cover about a fifth of the bay's bottom. These reefs were, in the words of a congressman who struggled to save them, "nursery ground for myriads of marine organisms" near the beginning of the food chain that ultimately nourished large marine fish like channel bass and spotted sea trout. But the shells were also useful for the manufacture of cement. The reefs therefore were destroyed, ground up and used to pave highways. Other fish and shellfish nursery grounds are being destroyed by an Army Corps of Engineers dam, constructed primarily to make the lower end of the Trinity River navigable. It will inundate some 20,000 acres of salt marshes. If those marshes produce shrimp and fish worth as much as $60 an acre, the annual costs of the dam will be greater than its estimated benefits. In fact biologists of the Department of the Interior believe the marshes' productive capacity is five times that great.

Engineers have been busy building other dams to divert water chiefly for fast-growing Houston industry that uses it and returns it with dissolved and suspended filth to the bay. The disturbance to the bay system occurs at both ends of the process: As the freshwater input is reduced, the bay becomes too saline to be usable by many marine organisms, which are adapted to early life in brackish waters; and of course the pollution particularly in the tributary rivers and at the edges of the bay can be lethal to all marine life. Fish kills have frequently driven people from their bayshore homes to wait out a lessening of the stench. The Houston Ship Channel, into which oil refineries, chemical and paper plants and the city of Houston dump untreated wastes, "ranks as one of the filthiest stretches of water in the United States," according to *Science*. It is all but biologically dead and its bottom is lined with two feet of putrid sludge.

On top of all this a major power plant is under construction that had originally planned to draw a billion gallons of cooling water a day from the foul ship canal and dump it into the bay. Under strong conservationist protest that plan has changed, but the plant will still increase the load of pollutants and also raise the temperature of the bay. Many fish are notably sensitive to even small temperature differentials and warming a body of water (though not certainly or universally damaging) is a profound disturbance of the system, whose results are difficult to foresee.

The story of Galveston Bay is notable just because it is not at all unusual. The bay's difficulties are more massive and more varied than those visited on many other estuaries but they are of the same kind and spring from the same indifference not merely to nature but to the needs (and even the specific economic advantage) of people. One can project the Galveston story some years ahead to a point where the bay will die, its capacity to sustain life (including human) will be exhausted, and Houston and Galveston will live beside a stinking corpse. But the real horror is here now; one does not have to tick off the soothsayer's years to the doom to come. The bay itself, like the once beautiful bay that charmed and fed the first settlers of San Francisco, is a reproach against a way of life that not only wastes its assets but works itself into a cul de sac of steadily decreasing opportunities of all sorts.

Galveston Bay is a natural system. I will have more to say in detail on the properties and functioning of natural systems. Here it is enough to note merely the connectedness of every living thing within the bay and every physical property of the bay and the dependence of the whole on what is delivered to it or taken from it by its own surrounding environment. Raise its mean temperature and it will not necessarily be made better or worse; it will inevitably be different in *all* its parts and functioning. Some forms of life will do better in the warmer water and tend to supplant those that do less well, with ramifications throughout the marine food chain. The bay's influence on its climate will change and the climate in turn (more or less rainfall, for instance) may alter the water intake and hence the salinities and the composition of the biological communities sensitive to such changes.

Small changes generally will have small effect — often scarcely measurable — and one will say, "Well, that didn't make any difference." But many small changes not only add up to big change but can reinforce each other (synergism). Higher water temperatures, coincident with increased sewage, can produce a lethal effect that would not have come from either insult by itself. Quantitatively very small changes can have large effect if in kind they are not assimilable by the system.

In Galveston Bay the changes are very extensive — massive dredging, huge volumes of pollutants, large-scale water diversions. Some of the pollutants are highly toxic and would have caused significant damage even in small quantities. Alterations have been made in a few years — a pace that on the time scale of evolution (still the time scale on which natural communities order their affairs) is instantaneous. That is to say, the disturbed system has no chance to settle in and find a new, viable way of life because it has constantly to absorb fresh blows.

Why did it happen? Because each exploiter of the bay was let in as if to Treasure Island with license to seek and take whatever bit he fancied. No one ever considered that the resource was not bits of the bay but the bay itself. Society had (and has) no common vantage point from which to see the common resources whole and no agency to manage them for common benefit. Leaving to the mercy and profit of individuals resources that must sustain all people is not merely of dubious morality and justice; it does not work. So long as each individual is moved to extract all he can from his exploited piece, the sum of every man's exploitations is bound to exceed the capacity of the system as a whole, and it will collapse.

The people of Galveston do not need foresight to look at the bay and ask themselves whether they like it. It takes no more than a sense of history and a sensitive awareness of the present to realize that we have been extraordinarily destructive of natural resources, with results already visible in disturbed, polluted systems whose capacity to produce and sustain life has already been impaired.

People in the Galveston Bay region, like people almost everywhere in industrial nations, have looked and smelled and decided, at least officially, that they do not like it. They have begun to clean it up. Nationwide this is a herculean task, whose size is usually grossly understated. One can be hopeful nevertheless that we will clean up at least to some minimum housekeeping standard. What is a good deal more problematic is whether we will face in time the sources of our difficulties in attitudes, values, and behavior, which can only be changed slowly but have to be recognized to be changed at all.

# CHAPTER 2

# An Agreeable Revolution

EDWARD TELLER, in championing recently the use of nuclear explosives for excavation — the piously named Ploughshare program — deplored what he feels is conservation carried too far, that is, to the point of obstructing "progress." As progress seems to mean to Dr. Teller improvement of technology he is right in fearing the conservationists. For if they have an enduring contribution to make to mankind it will not be in saving a marsh here and there but in making the point that technological sophistication and human betterment are not synonymous.

"Progress," Dr. Teller writes, "cannot be and will not be stopped." Either that is a tautology or it is a declaration of war against the new spirit that appears to be informing man's view of his world. Progress in the sense of growth and change is of course unstoppable. Progress in the sense of unlimited development of technologies is not. It could be stopped by a moderating decision in favor of other human needs not met by faster airplanes, foamier soap powders and bigger bombs. Dr. Teller is wrong in identifying his chief enemy on the right among reactionaries "who seem to believe that everything that is good lies in the past." The significant spirit opposing unlimited technology is young, revolutionary and —

if it turns out to be what it seems to be — new to the world.

I know of no friends of the environment who would seriously argue that we should begin to dismantle our technological civilization and return to the good old wild, nor even any who would urge that we stop looking for better ways of doing the manifold things that as creatures of culture we have discovered a taste for doing. Their position is rather defined by a series of questions addressed to those children of the scientific and industrial revolutions who have never seen fit to ask these questions. Does the particular gadget for doing something better answer a real need for better performance or is it rather the product of a momentum of science? Is it promoted by manufacturers unreasonably for profit or by bureaucracies for occupation? Does it chiefly flatter national pride or man's sense of his own cleverness? Regardless of motivation, what does it cost and whom does it cost? Admitting a genuine need to be met, are there alternative responses? Do the evaluated costs include the consequences of the new technology in creating demand for more? If satisfying one need only establishes a new demand more importunate than the first, if consumer hungers grow by what they feed on, then frustration inheres in the process and we had better face up to it sooner than later. It is mad to direct human aspiration toward goals that by their nature recede as they are approached.

These questions move from a doubt as to the self-evident goodness of the particular invention to a general skepticism of the values underlying the Teller view of progress. It is important to underline that they do *not* question or in any way disparage the contributions technology has made in our time to the welfare of people and the advancement of civilization. It would be absurd to pretend to regret the long way up that science has brought us to lives of greater comfort and variety than man ever knew before. But it is no less absurd to insist that therefore we must continue forever in the same direction getting more and more of the same. A silencer for those who grow restive under the tyranny of money and things is to ask where we would be today if such eccentric views had prevailed two or three hundred years ago. That is an impertinence, for what was quite right yesterday may be quite wrong today, and in defending a critical view one does not have to prove it has always and universally been true.

What is new in the new environmentalism is precisely the dawning perception that the human condition is now importantly different in all sorts of critical ways and that therefore our traditional attitudes and behavior need radical revision. We are different for one thing because we have command of technical skills so much greater than even seemed possible fifty years ago that they must be considered a new kind of power. It is a power that conveys the idea and at least part of the substance of total control over the environment. The technical progress of the past few decades is not just an extension of the developments of the preceding millennia. A threshold has been crossed. Victor Ferkiss has called it the existentialist revolution, to suggest that man's technological potential has now become real. In fact the actual power of man over the environment — to navigate space, change weather, rewrite the messages in genes — may be less revolutionary than his growing confidence that that power is indeed limitless. In any event both the facts and their impress on the mind are unprecedented and demand a fresh look at technological progress and its costs.

Fifteen years ago John R. Von Neumann observed the technical feasibility of deliberately altering the reflectivity of the polar ice to plunge the world into a new ice age or new tropical interglacial period. He did not recommend it. Reported seriously under consideration in the Soviet Union is a scheme to turn south three rivers now emptying into the Arctic Ocean. Since the rivers contribute about half of the total fresh water entering the Arctic, the diversions might increase the ocean's salinity enough materially to lower its freezing point and thus set in chain a series of global climatic changes. Engineers in this country have seriously proposed in effect replumbing the entire continent to bring water to where people choose to be, with side effects that neither they nor anyone else has examined.

Whether any such comprehensive projects of global redesign are ever tried or not, it is becoming increasingly difficult to avoid increasingly massive interventions in the natural systems. The existence of very powerful tools always urges their use. The Ploughshare program of nuclear excavation is a genie in search of a master. Since it cannot consider small jobs it will discover large ones regardless of social priorities. So it goes generally in our world. The inconveniences we are moved to fix grow larger, in part because we have run through most of the lesser ones, and in part because the numbers and proximity of people tend not to permit either local disturbance or local adjustment. In the effort to feed the world we cooperate in providing ever larger dosages of fertilizer and pesticide, whose influence is significantly disturbing for the first time because of the sheer quantities that the biosphere has to cope with. We look to managing the weather and continental hydrology because these, as it were, are the order of problem our sophistication has reached. Finally we are so generally and constantly meddlesome that our separate interventions tend cumulatively to overwhelm the recuperative powers of natural systems, as we saw in Galveston Bay.

One obvious consequence of giant engineering is that it raises risks. Adverse side effects, if incurred, will be more serious and affect more people. Less obvious, but at least as alarming, is the tendency to imprison man more and more totally within an artificial world and to remove him from that direct struggle with environment that has always been his way of getting along, evolving and prospering, as it has been the way of all other creatures. Individuals and species have always been tested and shaped in constant interaction with the environment. Man until very recently has been no exception. Although the environment is not of course hostile in any anthropomorphic sense, it has generally been so represented by man. Classic art and legend are filled with heroic men who battled nature and defeated her. But the victories were ephemeral, assuring only another opportunity to fight.

Today they are in a new sense final. Not only do we seem to approach something like a total victory, but the outcome of each successive struggle is to insulate man from further challenge. Few members of industrial society ever test themselves against natural adversities or against any other creature than another man or woman. They are thus removed suddenly from the basic process of action and reaction within the whole life system that shaped them for the first million years. The experience must be traumatic and there is suggestive evidence that it is. Some time ago Charles DeCarlo, then director of education for IBM, perceptively remarked that the plays of Samuel Beckett, speaking most eloquently to the anomie of modern urban man, contain little reference to the physical world. As striking is the withdrawal of the modern painter from the classic tradition of landscape and nature painting. Abstract canvases assert the irrelevance of environment, the self-sufficiency of the inner man. Typically they are as remarkable for reducing the old man-environment confrontations and conflict to a feeble esthetic tension among forms as they are for conveying a spiritual bleakness, whether tortured or complacent. Resurrected realism in pop art has not returned to nature; it lingers among the artifacts of industrial man and handles even these as blandly as possible.

But one does not need to rummage among symbols to find the essential discontent nor the reasons for it. City man still dreams of nature and normally takes his vacation when he can where nature is. The folk wisdom is still filled with the axioms that nature is healthily tough and civilization sickly effete. We provide for our children a chance to try themselves in the wild in such experiments as Outward Bound or the Student Conservation Association as well as in the more traditional routines of the Boy and Girl Scouts and countless other outdoor youth organizations. Moreover, these groups grow and the demand for places in them grows still faster. Adult demand for outdoor recreation has been increasing much faster than population. The national parks in 1956 had 20 million visitors; in 1967 they had 40 million. Since World War II, visitors have increased at an average rate of eight per cent a year, as compared to a population increase of 1.1 per cent.

A capacity to change the environment massively and to insulate man from nature is one big change in the human condition that requires new attitudes. Another in the phrase of Marston Bates, is the "prevalence of people." I have asserted that population pressures are not the *cause* of environmental degradation. Nevertheless a certain abundance and distribution of people clearly does affect both the nature and the severity of the problems. Concentration of people in a metropolis for one thing multiplies the overlap of interests. More and more individual activities cannot be carried out in a crowd without in effect becoming public actions inviting and requiring some public constraints. In short, density of people tends to enlarge the commons which, as I have noted, require public protection and correspondingly shrink the realms of private right. Concentrations of people (and to some extent absolute numbers) also multiply the size of potential disasters and so increase the risks of mismanagement. If you turn out to have been wrong in a great irrigation work to make millions of acres productive and the land is destroyed, the millions who came to depend on it pay a large price for the blunder. Finally, the fact that the world is now filled, that there are no longer fertile areas unsettled or even substantially under-exploited, means that one can no longer escape environmental damage in one place by moving to another. This is but another reminder that every tendency of our age is in fact to make this one world, and that one large consequence is to reduce the opportunities to make small mistakes.

"Environment," said Walter J. Hickel, former secretary of the interior, in January 1970, "is one of the hottest issues going on in Washington. Politicians are suddenly aware of the fact that support of environment, like support of motherhood, is good politics."

In part the politicians were reacting in the normal way — late and with verbal anguish — to problems that had long since roused their constituents. But they reacted with abnormal unanimity and enthusiasm. They thought they saw a political miracle — an issue to unite left and right, black and white, young and old, in a common struggle for the common good. Each party dreamed of capturing this unanimity for itself. In a nation sick of the corrosive divisions over Vietnam, race, generation gaps, and law and order, the environmental issue was not only a miracle but providentially timed to relieve both headaches and tired blood. A surrogate for motherhood, Mr. Hickel called it. Still more beautiful, it had the look of a crusade without infidels, an agreeable revolution, in which one could find the exhilaration of *Sturm und*

*Drang* without anyone's head being broken. Does that sound unreal? It is.

Under the environmental banner were marchers with as many different thoughts as in any other parade. Probably most numerous were those for whom an attack on environmental problems meant little more than an effort to clean up water and air. This is, of course, not disputed as a goal. Sanitation has such a secure place in the American pantheon that it needed only someone to notice the filth in order to make us all shudder. Everybody, now including most of the industries that have been, and remain, heavy polluters, agrees that the nation must get out the brushes, roll up its sleeves and get to work scrubbing. This agreement — even the passion of virtue that makes it ring — reminds one of a comparable unanimous endorsement of peace for which one can get as many hearty testimonials in the Pentagon as on the campuses. Everyone wants peace ultimately more than anything else except, of course, for those things which in his view are prerequisites to peace, like justice, security, and national honor. For these unfortunately it is often — indeed always — necessary to fight. Men fall out not over the issue of peace or war but over what kind of peace and how to achieve it, or (what is the same thing in mirror image) what kind of war and how far to wage it. So, quite probably, with environmental purity. Oil companies earnestly regret the recent leakages from drilling in the Pacific and the Gulf and will pay to clean up the mess. Would they as cheerfully surrender the right to drill? Owners of the *Torrey Canyon* paid for their irresponsibility in jeopardizing the public interest for private gain, so far as money could compensate, without protest. Yet no one has seriously suggested a halt to the construction of ever bigger oil tankers or even the development of devices to cope with spills if they occur. No environmental issue rouses more citizen indignation than dirty air. Yet the mayors of big cities make no move to deprive the citizen of his right to drive his car as much as he likes, or as he can, through congested streets, pouring into the urban air the bulk of the pollutants that cause smog. On all such issues the arguments over trade-offs between cleanliness and comfort or profit could be expected to be long and bitter. It is not in that country that mother-hood politicians are inclined to seek their fortune.

Among supporters of the environment were some who have a conservative, sentimental or idiosyncratic distaste for change; some who just wished to keep civilization from spoiling the hunting and fishing; some who would defend nature essentially as a preserve of privacy (and sometimes privilege); some — and perhaps a very large number — who had very little interest at all in the issue but saw ways to exploit its popularity to get votes or grants or power. Finally at the opposite end of things for some, and particularly the rebellious young, the environment was the one banner big enough to embrace all the causes of their discontent. Stephen Cotton, one of the student organizers of the environmental teach-in on Earth Day, April 22, 1970, protested what he felt was the official view of the environment as a "pacifying" issue. "The issue," he said, "is not just 'sanitation.' The issue is the envi-ronment — what it's like to live in this country in 1970 — the defense-oriented economy, the whole question of priori-ties on hunger, housing, income . . . the problems we've been concerned with all along."

There is a sense in which this too could be viewed as an opportunistic use of a popular issue to further other ends. But even if it is partly that, the shoe fits. Environmental problems are at bottom behavioral; therefore they do call into question the society's way of life and sense of priorities. It is fair enough to look at our abuse of nature for the sake of private gain and ask "what it's like to live in this country in 1970," with all that implies in fundamental, revolutionary criticism. Both the symbols and the facts are consonant in the parallel protests against the greed system as it poisons the air or moves to deny space on the planet to any but man.

While the gentle delusion lasts that all men are environmentalists and before we begin to dispute the particulars of who is to blame and who should pay, there is a brief interlude at least in which to stay with the question in something like Mr. Cotton's framework. How bad are the troubles we face? And how did they come upon us, not just here and now as the sudden curse of the newest age but as consequence (for they certainly are) of how we as people and we as Americans have evolved and learned to live? These are the questions to which the remainder of this book is addressed.

# CHAPTER 3

# How to Get Less by Multiplying

BARBRA STREISAND on June 17, 1967, gave a concert in New York City's Central Park and 135,000 people crowded onto the Sheep Meadow to hear her. After they left, scores of sanitation men spent three days cleaning up the trash spread inches deep all over the ninety-acre field. Moralists were shocked at the revelation of mass man as the careless vandal. Conservationists swore to keep the park henceforth safe from culture. But at issue really were more than manners or park policy. An audience sophisticated enough to appreciate Miss Streisand and her music had otherwise behaved like the small bands of protohominids who millions of years ago hunted vast plains, dropping their wastes onto nature's continuous reassembly lines where they would nourish over months and years a myriad of interdependent organisms feeding incessantly on each other. The wastes deposited in the park could in time have gone the same way, but in the process they would have smelled and drawn rats and flies to a small piece of ground that happens to be in the middle of the living room of one of the biggest cities in the world.

It is not intrinsically rude or dirty business to toss chicken bones over the shoulder; it is simply behavior inappropriate to the living room. Persistence in the city of the behavior of man in nature may be viewed as a kind of failure in adaptation, and one can ask why we have not adapted better.

The failure is broad. The Indian's campfire imparted a transient fragrance and color to the air dangerous only if an enemy was about. Industrial furnaces in Pittsburgh all but choke the city with soot. One can dig a hole in the woods to bury remnants of a meal, but when cities overspread the land the remnants become mountains and there is no place left to bore even small holes. So with the capacity of streams and lakes to dilute waste, and so in time it could be with the oceans, to which some harried sanitation departments are now looking as to the ultimate town dump.

Why are we trying to live in cities with the habits and attitudes toward waste acquired in an unpeopled planet? One reason is that we have ignored, often conscientiously, the implications of size. Bigger is not better. Bigger is not even just bigger. Bigger at some point pushes populations over a threshold into a new environment in which the rules for successful behavior are necessarily different, the problems new (not just worse). We are well across that threshold.

The implications of numbers of people and their relationship to the quality of life have to be confronted at the beginning, not — let it be said again — because environmental problems are at bottom only population problems, but because population size, distribution, and rate of increase establish the basic conditions in which man's collective relations with the environment have to be worked out. Each of the three demographic facts — absolute numbers, distribution, and rate of growth — have distinct impacts and it is important to see how and how far each may affect the problems of earthkeeping independently as well as in harness with the others.

*

The world now contains about 3.6 billion people, and the population is growing at the rate of almost two per cent a year, which would double present numbers in 37 years. In fact United Nations projections estimate a substantial slowing down. By the year 2000 the UN demographers predict a world population of at least 5.4 billion and at most 6.9 billion, depending on various assumptions. In the past, population projections have almost always proved to be underestimations — sometimes, in the recent past, very substantial underestimations. One expert in 1950 predicted the world would have 3.3 billion people by the year 2000 — a total achieved in less than 20 years from the time he spoke rather than the 50 he expected. Since, however, projections do not reckon the possibility of catastrophic increases in deaths by war or famine, Paul Ehrlich thinks there is a possibility that this time around they may be too high. What seems as nearly beyond question as any prophecy can be is that barring universal thermonuclear war, the world will have (and cannot avoid having) two or three billion more people two generations hence than it has today. The United States, although growing more slowly than the world average (1.1 per cent a year as compared to 1.9 per cent) will also inevitably add substantially — probably about 100 million — to its present 200 million by the end of the century.

The population upsurge in the twentieth century is by far the greatest and by far the most critical humanity has ever known. But it is not the first. On a relative scale comparable jumps occurred with the invention of agriculture perhaps ten to twelve thousand years ago; with the improvement of agriculture, first in about 3000 B.C., again in the Middle Ages, and again in the seventeenth and eighteenth centuries; and then finally with the coming of the Industrial Revolution. The phenomenon on each recurrence was essentially the same: a sudden advance in technology materially enlarged the capacity of the environment to support people; more people could thus live longer and did because births, tuned to higher mortality rates, continued in greater abundance than was necessary to maintain an equilibrium of numbers in the new safer system. That has happened again in our time chiefly through the control of disease.

In European industrialized nations birthrates have fallen since the mid-nineteenth century. With some fluctuations in time and differences among nations they have remained low, though generally higher than needed to replace deaths. In the unindustrialized worlds of Africa, Asia, and Latin America, birthrates have risen or remained as high as they have had to be to balance the traditionally high mortality rates (particularly of infants) in peasant societies. Modern medicine and public health meanwhile have cut mortality to rates comparable to those of Europe and North America. The result is population growth in many nations of around 3 per cent a year.

In time, of course, a new equilibrium will be found either by fewer births or more deaths or probably both. Like other species, man could not have survived without population control mechanisms that adjusted his numbers to the available food. In all successful species, moreover, the controls must become effective *before* the food supply runs out. Clearly, if a population grows to the point of total exhaustion of its food supply it will either become precipitously extinct or be subject to such wide swings in numbers as to be at the mercy of other hostile forces such as competition, predation, or disease. There have to be early warnings of approaching disaster that affect the physiology or behavior of the individuals in such a way as to make them thin out their numbers. Among animals these mechanisms are various and sometimes almost miraculously complicated, or just as miraculously simple — as with flour beetles (Tribolium) who may eat their own pupae when they come across them in the flour. The more beetles or pupae, or both, the greater the number of fatal chance encounters. What could be more straightforward? More devious are the fabled lemmings, who are driven into mass migrations by complex glandular changes apparently set in motion by the stress of crowding.

Analogous self-regulating mechanisms must have existed among primitive human populations; some still exist and have been described, though there has been curiously little systematic study. A few controls may be physiological in men as in other animals. For instance, women who undergo stress during pregnancy from malnutrition or various kinds of emotional disturbance have been shown to have a significantly larger number of mentally or physically malformed children than the norm. The malformations curiously tend more often to be lethal to female than male children. It is tempting to interpret the phenomenon as a two-way population control: it cuts down the number of mothers in the next generation and also reduces the hunting efficiency and hence survival chances of the next generation's predatory males.

Among more obvious regulators is epidemic disease, which is an increasingly effective killer the more dense are the populations it attacks. Certain diseases, like smallpox, attack children selectively and so are tuned into the system to intensify their depredations as births increase. More subtle but probably extremely important controls are a wide variety of cultural practices, customs, taboos that seem to function to restrict numbers. If, for instance, a society demands that a boy and girl must first have land and a house of their own before they can marry — as many peasant societies do — then marriage and childbearing will be delayed in something like due proportion to the difficulty of finding unoccupied land. G. Evelyn Hutchinson has suggested that the common requirement of dowries and elaborate weddings may mean that a disproportionate number of spinsters are girls from large families; thus both the genes disposing to fecundity and the tradition of large families would tend to be reduced in succeeding generations.

Whatever the mechanism, typically it has a delayed impact. It takes time — sometimes a generation or even several generations — for the message, "We are now too many," to trigger the controls and elicit the correction. Pests need time to sense their opportunities to attack people in a crowded city and to mobilize to exploit them. Pressures on the mother mold the offspring. Possible institutional reactions can be even slower and several generations may be needed to reshape attitudes toward marriage, sexual practice, ideal family size and so on.

The problem mankind faces today is that while we were able by technical ingenuity (i.e., disease control) to upset in a few years the adapted relationship between death and birth rates we find ourselves unable so far to establish a new equilibrium. Research into new contraceptive methods is essentially an effort to achieve a compensating adjustment by technical means in recognition of the fact that the normal evolutionary processes of adaptation involving changes in human behavior are too slow. The two big questions are whether the technological fix will be found in time to avoid major calamities and whether once found it will be effectively used.

When population growth escapes from self-regulating (homeostatic) control, two characteristics make it both explosive and intractable: it is exponential and it has a kind of systemic inertia. An annual increase of 2 per cent adds 20 people in one year to a population of 1000, and if 20 people were added in each successive year the population would take 50 years to double. That would be arithmetic increase; in fact population grows exponentially, as a constant rate is applied to a constantly increasing base — as in compound interest. The resulting acceleration is dramatic: Instead of taking 50 years to double, the original 1000 becomes 2000 in less than 35 years. In the case of capital growth at compound interest, one could elect to slow it down by regularly pruning out the accumulations or — as in fact has happened historically — by regularly depreciating the value of the increment (by inflation, for instance). Clearly no such options are open to check population increase. Since control by compensatory execution is ruled out, one must struggle to bring the birthrates down. This is not only inherently difficult, for all sorts of familiar reasons, but even with success it would take generations to reverse the growth and bring about either a stable or a declining population.

Suppose a Washington czar decided to hold the American population at its present 200 million. The command affecting births, demographer Tomas Frejka has figured out, would have to prescribe as follows: Because of the disproportionate number of women now entering childbearing age as a result of the war and postwar boom, they would have to cut their families far below replacement rates, in fact to precisely 1.2 babies each for about the next twenty years. Then, as their own abnormally sparse offspring came of age, the rates of procreation would have to be stepped up gradually to about 2.8 children per family in the period 2030–35. Thereafter the numbers could decline gradually to the maintenance rate of 2.1.

Clearly human behavior cannot be manipulated in that way except by dehumanizing controls. Even if it could, moreover, the consequences of violently and continually varying the age structure of the population would be to set up correspondingly violent shocks in all other human systems. For instance, the number of children of school age (5–19), constituting 28.1 per cent of the 1965 population, would drop to only 17.7 per cent of the 1990 population, increase to 22.4 per cent in 2040 and slide back to 18 per cent in 2065. We would need inflatable schoolhouses and remarkable recruiting and pensioning systems for teachers. Similarly, the economic system would be rocked by the suddenly changing proportions of producers and non-producers. Those over 65, totaling 10.4 per cent of the 1965 population, would almost double in the first 50 years thereafter, then in the next 50 decline to a midpoint of 15.7 per cent.

What that means is that even if one could now suddenly halt population growth it would be irrational to do so. A rational policy is to accept continuing growth at gradually reduced rates, aiming at a plateau sometime early in the next century. From there theoretically one could maneuver a slow descent without dire consequences. In practice it seems highly unlikely that any species, however numerous or enlightened, would ever deliberately reduce procreation below the replacement rate. To choose the path toward extinction, even if meaning to go only a short way, would be to challenge the one universal command of life. (The governments of both Japan and France have already shrunk from first consequences of having brought births down close to the numbers needed for replacement. Too few young men and women are now entering their work forces to sustain high rates of economic growth. Both governments, moved perhaps by nationalistic as well as economic fears, called for more children.)

Many who most passionately urge population control begin by asserting that the world is already seriously overpopulated and that even the minimum projected increases in the next thirty years will put an unbearable strain on the world's resources. Both propositions may indeed be correct, but no one should be deluded into thinking that population control is a possible solution. The practical alternatives are simply and exclusively these: (1) even if birth controls work eventually, we will have something like six billion people in the world before growth stops and we will have to find ways not just to feed, clothe, and house them but to keep open for them opportunities to live like human beings so that they will endure the human condition; or (2) we will not be able to do so and billions will sink into subhuman lives or rend the fabric of society and destroy it; or, finally, (3) we will fall into a great war — one can no longer think of possible acts of God sufficiently grand to serve — that will relieve us of up to, say, two thirds of the burden, and the rest can more happily divide among them what is left.

While my own view is that pessimistic prognoses are almost always the more probable ones, there is nothing impossible about the first alternative. The case for asserting present overpopulation used to rest chiefly on the facts of present hunger in the world and Malthusian extrapolations proving that not only could food production not keep up with population increase in the long run, but it was already losing the race.

Then with a remarkable and startling suddenness came the "green revolution" — the development of new prolific strains of rice, wheat and maize, which with appropriate fertilizer, water and pest control, are capable of multiplying the grain yields in the underdeveloped countries anywhere from two to twenty times. Many countries which, like Pakistan, were candidates in the early 1960s for imminent famine, have achieved since 1965 or are about to achieve surpluses of wheat or rice or both. The U.S. Department of State has estimated that if people eat no more apiece than they did in the years 1955 to 1957, the world by 1975 will have a surplus above current consumption of 40 million tons of wheat and 70 million tons of rice. (That assumes no increase in the rice and wheat production of North America, which is still under official and economic rein, and no increase in European wheat production.) Even in 1969, 15 per cent of the world's total wheat crop remained unsold. While that is not to say, of course, that it could not and should not have been consumed by hungry people, the fact of large surpluses, even if partly artificial, plus the fact of continuing rapid increases in production even in the hungry nations, suggests that the specter of general famine is at least further away than the doomsayers of just a few years back were saying.

There is every reason to believe that food production will continue in the foreseeable future to stay at least one jump ahead of people production. How many years of grace we can expect is anyone's guess. But the best guess is that the first limits of grace are not food at all but the capacity of organized societies to absorb the multiple strains imposed by increasing numbers. Signs of the strain are visible everywhere and stand out with special clarity in industrialized nations that are well fed, but for the perennial differential hunger of the poor that has nothing to do with total numbers. The breakdown of public services, the deterioration of education, the unresponsiveness of huge bureaucracies, and perhaps the diverse and ominous manifestations of individual and group hostilities — all of these, although they are complex phenomena with complex causes, signal a failure of systems devised for a less crowded world to adjust to the very rapid growth imposed upon them. It is at least possible, moreover, that institutions have a critical size beyond which they will simply not function. Communication among their component parts may be so weakened that the whole no longer articulates; the task of management may become too large and complicated for managers to grasp.

If the adaptability of institutions is in fact less elastic than the means of producing food, then the limits of adaptability will impose the effective limit on population size. Since those limits so far as I know are impossible to measure, prediction as to when (or even whether) any given institution can be expected to fail by inanition or collapse is also impossible. Therefore we do not know how much time we have to hold the world together while bringing population again into balance. The easy optimism of some of the fathers of the green revolution becomes irrelevant. On the other hand, if we were convinced that city government, schools, and transportation systems were really on the point of breakdown, we could resolve to shift energy and resources to their rescue which would not only buy time for population control but begin the adjustment to the larger numbers of people that are inevitable anyway. That is one prospect that offers hope, but not much, in the light of current preoccupations and what one knows about traditional political priorities.

# CHAPTER 4

# Numbers, Space, and Time

SO FAR THE DISCUSSION HAS treated the population problem as one of total numbers pressing on total resources. In fact, of course, the pressures are exerted very unevenly and the points of pain and danger are where the pinch is greatest. As demographers put it, distribution at least in the short run is more significant than absolute numbers. Crowding is essentially a local phenomenon and it is also a peculiarly difficult one to define. The Netherlands, with an average of almost 1000 inhabitants to the square mile, is not considered one of the world's overcrowded countries — and it is not. Japan, with a far smaller proportion of inhabitable land, nevertheless prospers with an average of 700 people on each square mile. India with only 400 to a square mile is grossly and manifestly overcrowded. Manhattan packs in densities of 75,000 people to a square mile; these are elbow-in-eye concentrations and often arouse appropriate animosities, and yet the city is far more nearly viable than Calcutta, of a similar density.

To be meaningful, density in human populations as in animal populations has to be related to the carrying capacity of the environment. Calcutta is grossly overcrowded because there are vastly more people in it than the city as a generator and purveyor of goods and services can support. All the signs

are that the great cities of the developed world are now reaching a similar environmental limit, even though it is expressed
less in lack of jobs, food, and shelter than in crises of transportation, education, municipal services, and social disintegration.

There is a third consideration affecting the definition of
density: the demand or consumptive capacity of the population. The United States as a whole with only 55 people per
square mile (or about 67 excluding Alaska) is comparatively
uninhabited by world standards. Even if one subtracts unin-
habitable acreage, the average density remains extremely low.
Even if one isolates the 600-mile-long eastern megalopolis of
some 40 million people, still the concentration in that sliver
of the continent alone is less than in the whole of the Netherlands. But each American consumes many times more
energy, land and resources than does the most urbanized and
sophisticated of Europeans. The 31-county New York Metropolitan Region, as defined for planning purposes, is almost
the same geographical size as the Netherlands (about 13,000
square miles). It contains about half again as many people
(19 million as compared to about 13 million), but four times
as many automobiles. Dutch average per capita incomes are
$1500 as compared to more than $4000 for the U.S. Dutch
incomes are almost precisely the average for fourteen Western
European nations, which along with North America, Australia and New Zealand are the wealthiest in the world. Most of
mankind earns closer to the $100 per person or less estimated
for India and China; these people, of course, make comparably small demands for resources and energy.

If one American has something like fifty times the pur-
chasing power of one Indian, our 200 million consumers are
in some sense the equivalent of 10 billion Indians — a comparison that makes India's actual population of 450 million

seem like much the lesser of the two population explosions.

One American may make an even heavier relative demand on the environment than those figures suggest. Energy to run the underdeveloped countries is predominantly food to fuel human bodies. In our technologically sophisticated society calories take a back seat to kilowatts: food is the least source of the total energy used. With 6 per cent of the world's people we, driven by an insatiable passion to consume, burn 900 gallons of oil per person (about eight times the world average), use more than a third of the world's tin production, a fourth of its inorganic fertilizers, half of its newsprint and synthetic rubber, a fourth of its steel, a fifth of its cotton. Into the American industrial maw also go many scarce materials drawn from all over the world whose exhaustion is likely to hamper or at least increase the cost of manufacture for everybody.

America is not only consuming its own substance at a faster rate than any other nation; it is consuming the common resources of the planet in grossly disproportionate shares. While we talk about (and some people work hard and earnestly at) raising the standard of living of the rest of the world more nearly to our own, the best conceivable effort can hardly deliver more than a comparative crumb. It is easy to calculate that three and a half billion people with U.S. incomes would consume in one year more than the known reserves of most critical minerals. Moreover, as usual the rich grow richer much faster than the poor improve their lot.

To sum up, population growth in India is at the expense of India's capacity to prosper; population growth in the United States may be at the expense of the world and its future. A Chinese leader might rationally conclude that China's chance for a place in the sun requires the annihilation of the United States. Though less realistic, it would be no less reasonable for African, South Asian, and Latin American leaders to feel the same way and to nourish a legitimate resentment even if they cannot toss a bomb.

Within most countries, including the less developed, the great drift of people into the cities — so long a fact of our times — seems to be accelerating. Kingsley Davis has calculated that if the process were to continue at the current pace, within eighty years everybody on earth would be living not just in cities but in cities of over a million population — the largest having 1.4 billion people. The end point is of course an absurdity, but the process meanwhile is real and, as every mayor knows, profoundly disturbing.

The nodes of greatest concentration are the pressure points of population growth where the crisis is felt in all its impacts and where, correspondingly, the warning signals are sounding. The city is not only bedeviled by increasingly intractable problems of finding food and shelter, educating, disposing of waste, keeping order, and above all providing minimum human satisfactions; it is resonating its own despair through the society. A curious sense of alienation, not only from each other but from past and future, seems characteristic of the day and surely owes something to that ever-growing indigestible urban lump in the nation's innards. Even many of the urban planners and other professional urbanists seem in various ways to have given up on the city. On the one hand, they wish to break it up into smaller, self-contained new towns, or do away with it altogether on grounds that vastly improved communications are making unnecessary the face-to-face confrontations that cities exist to facilitate; and on the other, they point out the apparently irresistible growth of conurbations or urban regions which, if viable at all, will shape quite different ways of life and have to be managed quite differently from the traditional city.

If the city has no future, how do you minister to its current agonies? It is hard enough to provide physically decent living conditions for the poor in great cities (it has never been done) when one can at least imagine a remade city that might work and enrich men's lives. Now imagination fails. Perhaps the most positive statement in recent years that the city is good and has a future has been that of Jane Jacobs. But Mrs. Jacobs essentially sings the organic city, product of evolution. Though she does not say so, that city, even if all planners and builders were as sensitive to human values as she would have them be, almost certainly could not survive expansion so rapid that evolution really has no chance and change inevitably comes by instant mass development. Her vision in short is honest and attractive, but it probably does not help much; there is no time for the slums to evolve into something better, and there is little faith that the something better would turn out to be what anyone wanted. If we could slow population growth we might have the time and find the imagination and the city might have a future.

Historically, local overcrowding has occurred in a world that in whole was underpopulated. It was only necessary, therefore, for local crowding to cause enough economic pain or psychological unrest to overcome the cultural inertia to migration. Then people, like lemmings, were on their way either to new worlds or into marginal lands made accessible by greater need, tighter social organization or improved technology.

The patterns, of course, were not simple, and migration and dispersion are clearly not simple responses to pressures at the center. Charles Elton has observed in animal populations a tendency to peripheral drift as animals probe for food which he suggests helps to forestall overcrowding rather than to relieve it. Joseph R. Birdsell believes that among prehistoric hunters migration was also not a means of relieving population pressure but of keeping populations small; he argues that when men were constantly on the move in pursuit of game their women would abort or kill infants to avoid the inconvenience, even danger, of taking them along. Nevertheless dispersion is an obvious and quite general response of populations when they increase beyond the immediate resources of home. So it happened notably in Europe in the seventeenth and eighteenth centuries. Typically, the relief then was marginal; that is, the pool from which the migrants were drawn remained full if not overfull.

Geographer Oscar Horst has studied the process among a community of Indians who inhabit impoverished volcanic uplands in the western part of Guatemala. These Indians, the Mam, historically have produced children at the yearly rate of 49 to 61 per thousand population. (In contrast the estimated worldwide "natural" rate prevailing where contraception is not practiced is 35 per thousand, and the current U.S. rate is 17.) Before 1950 death took an average of 30 or more per thousand and the tribe was periodically decimated by smallpox and flu. Since 1950 births have stabilized at about 50/1000 but deaths have dropped to 20/1000. The dramatic banishment of disease now permits the population to grow at almost 3 per cent a year. A Protestant clinic established in 1952 and a Catholic counterpart in 1963 stand guard against a possible return.

Thus protected, the Mam have expanded well beyond the capacity of their fields to grow the food to feed them. That fact is spectacularly reflected in land prices: Now an acre capable of yielding 15 to 25 bushels of wheat commands $400 to $500, or more than twice the average family's annual income. While the economic squeeze is a clear signal to move, the

NUMBERS, SPACE, AND TIME 43

Indians, adapted to the altitude and cool climate, have stub-
bornly resisted the only way out — descent into the tropical
coastal plain. Now they can no longer help themselves. Some
are forced out but in such small, reluctant numbers that the
ancestral upland home remains desperately impoverished.

Migration, though still barely possible for the Mam, solves
none of their problems except to keep a few more of them
alive, which may be a purpose sufficient for animals but not
for humans. Migration may offer temporary escape for a few
more years or even decades in a few countries like Indonesia or North America that are still relatively thinly peopled.
But except in the dangerous metaphors of the booster, the
frontiers of the world are now closed. The walls of home no
longer move out as new boarders move in. The limits of environment are palpable everywhere, and whatever biological
or cultural pressures local crowding puts on men will henceforth be an inescapable fact of existence to which he must find
some adjustment where he is — or not find it.

The possibility of adjustment turns for one thing on slowing the rates of growth. While eventually growth must be
reduced to zero, and sometime should perhaps ideally go below zero, the immediate need is simply to damp the runaway
pace. Those who argue, usually without data, that we are
overpopulated now (or that we are not) argue a relatively
trivial question of values, even of taste. How many seems just
right? But what threatens civilization immediately is not the
numbers who are here now nor even the numbers to be expected tomorrow; it is the *rate* at which they crowd upon us
and make their necessary demands on existing institutions for
food, shelter, education, justice, liberty. For instance, a
school of several hundred students could comfortably grow at
the rate of two or three a year. The increase would gradually
demand more classrooms and teachers, but if held steady over

generations those demands could easily be anticipated: the teachers could be trained; the space could be built; the expansion could be readily financed. But step up the increase to 50 or 100 a year, and classes immediately burst their familiar bounds. Even the relatively short time lag for planning and constructing new classrooms becomes all but unbearable in terms of deteriorated education and attendant disintegration of morale and discipline. The instant exorbitant demand for teachers cannot be met at all. So one resorts to television and programmed instruction (which also take significant time to install). These alter the whole character of the educational process, perhaps for the better, perhaps for the worse. No one has had time to find out. The large amounts of money needed also in a hurry to finance the expansion compete with other demands simultaneously generated by the rapid increase in numbers of people. All of them simply cannot be met at once. The consequence is the desperate series of losing battles being fought by nearly every school system and municipality in the United States today. Institutions, like organisms, have evolved rates of evolution; to drive them suddenly faster assures failure and risks collapse.

It is a good bet that population growth will be checked in this century. It is not such a good bet that the check will be a deliberate and rational control of births rather than a substantial increase in deaths. To ask what are the chances of rational control is to step into an arena where the arguments among demographers, population biologists and other cousinly experts are both intemperate and difficult to sort out.

Optimists believe that felt pressures of overpopulation will feed back to parents and make them want fewer children. To assure that fewer children are born it is only necessary to supply these parents with cheap, convenient and effective contraceptives. Most family planners believe also in the power and need of education to reinforce the message from the crowded environment. The argument is essentially this: a stable population is a rational goal; people are rational; therefore, if people can be shown the goal they will want it and take appropriate steps to achieve it.

Pessimists have several reservations, of which two are probably key: Unless overpopulation, whatever it may mean in whatever context, is perceived as a threat to personal welfare, it will not signal to parents that they should have smaller families. The number of children rationally wanted by each couple has to add up to just the number needed by the whole population to replace deaths, and there seems to be little reason why it should. (Strictly speaking, birthrates must be slightly higher than death rates for stability since otherwise, accidental deaths in excess of the average would inexorably drive the population to extinction.)

Overpopulation is not perceived throughout the world even as an external fact, much less as a fact of personal significance. Farmers in the less developed countries still by and large want large families, not only because children are useful labor but because they are social security. Many developing countries continue to feel that population is power and that conversely birth control propaganda from the outside is an attack on them by the prejudiced and the privileged. Revealed irrationality in this country is even more discouraging, since it has resisted the full force of education. A Gallup poll taken in January 1969 reported that a third of college-educated Americans believed that it would *not* be necessary even "at some time" to limit population even to maintain present living standards.

If one is to rest population control on voluntary individual action, the key question is how many children people want. It is peculiarly difficult to get reliable answers, and demographers bitterly dispute the validity of various surveys and their meaning. That there is no simple correlation between parents' ability to prevent conception and numbers of children born is indisputable. Sociologist Lincoln H. Day told Congress recently that it is the well-off and presumably well-informed who as a class contribute proportionately the largest number of excess children. He was talking not about "large" families (which are rare among the upper classes) but about the difference between two children and three, which is the difference between a population replacing itself and one doubling in about 40 or 45 years. A recent survey among undergraduates, graduate students, and faculty at Cornell University dismayingly confirmed that education and even alleged awareness of the population problem do not seem to make people want the "right" number of children. Although 84 per cent of respondents agreed that families should be limited, almost two thirds (65 per cent) said they themselves wanted to have three children or more. The surveyors threw up their hands: "What are we to make of the educated youth growing up among us that is either unconcerned about population growth or, at the very least, unable or unwilling to apply to itself the simple arithmetic of compound interest?"

Clearly this does not argue that family planning efforts are no good at all. If all people were able easily to prevent the births they do not want, substantially fewer children would be born. One third of first-born children in the U.S., according to a recent U.S. survey, were conceived out of wedlock. Presumably most were unwanted and might have been prevented. The spread of contraceptive information and devices and the research to find better, easier ways are amply justified as the most immediately feasible and promising attack on the problem. They may be — indeed they almost certainly will be — insufficient.

Education may reinforce the messages of pain from a crowded environment to slow population increase. But until the message is individually brought home, individual behavior cannot respond to the collective need. Humanity's interest in limiting *my* family to the size needed for equilibrium may not coincide at all with my own rational reckoning of how many children suit my personal well-being. The well-to-do who decide to have four or five children observe that they can afford them, and that these children may enjoy unusual advantages; some may quietly congratulate themselves on giving society second and third helpings of exceptionally well endowed new citizens. Others may choose large families rationally enough because they like large families and hold that love is more important than money to grow on. Since parents do vary widely in their fitness (however defined) to have and raise children, decisions of this kind can be deliberate and, from the individual view, sound.

What could make hundreds of millions of parents, separately deciding how many children to have, come out with a total that just replaced themselves? Some observers have despaired that persons acting freely on self-interest could ever collectively arrive at a result that served the common interest, and have therefore warned that coercion is in prospect. But mechanisms acting individually for the interest of all are common throughout nature; indeed that is the usual form of population control. The special difficulty as regards man is that we have insulated ourselves against the signals of crowding with technology to stretch the environment, affluence to upholster it against the squeeze, medicine to stay the pruning hand of death. In consequence the signal has to be that much louder to be heard. Crowding may therefore have to go far beyond the point where it is rationally seen to be inimical to human welfare before enough individuals are hurt sufficiently to trigger the controls. Whether that is a pessimistic prognosis or, compared to the threat of coercion, an optimistic one would be hard to say. Whatever the final solution, there seems no question that large and still-growing populations will press harder on dwindling environmental resources (living space above all) for many decades to come.

# CHAPTER 5

# Deferred Maintenance

"THE BATTLE FOR the quality of the American environment," said presidential candidate Richard Nixon on October 18, 1968, "is a battle against neglect, mismanagement, poor planning and a piecemeal approach to problems of natural resources." If that is so (and it *is* so), the accumulated consequences of neglect and mismanagement over many generations can be expected to be so large as to require both a massive public program of reparation and heroic efforts to reverse the processes that brought us here. In fact both conclusions have been resisted.

There have been various attempts to estimate the cost of "restoring the quality of the environment" (as one well-known government report of 1965 put the problem). None is satisfactory. Price tags can be pinned only to physical works (water treatment plants, sewers, sanitary landfills, smokestack precipitators, automobile afterburners and so on). Even here all sorts of guesses have to serve for missing facts. Manufacturers, for instance, do not like to disclose, even when they know, the quantity and quality and present treatment of their factory wastes. By and large one has to guess the costs of a cleanup according to techniques now known; but these may be supplanted by other means better and cheaper; they may also prove ineffective. For some problems there is no technical solution yet in sight (as for instance the run-off of fertilizer and pesticide from farms that is a major contributor to the pollution of rivers and lakes). Beyond the many difficulties of reckoning what a physical earthcleaning plant might cost, there would be wholly unknown (but probably very high) costs involved in changing patterns of production and consumption to check continuing deterioration. What is apparent from all appraisals of the possible costs of physical maintenance so long deferred is that the total is to be reckoned not in a few hundreds of millions of tax dollars but in a substantial percentage of the gross national product, that is to say, many tens of billions. If that is the order of magnitude, precise calculations of how many millions may be needed here and there are rather the second than the first step: First the society has to face the overall magnitude as clearly demanding an economic and quite possibly social revolution.

Needless to say, the United States has not faced any such thing, and most of our political leaders are facing the other way. That is not surprising. The law of the political minimum holds that when confronted with public outrage the government should do only as much as necessary to keep voices down. In any case establishments are not easily persuaded of the need for revolution, and Americans traditionally have viewed even the worst of troubles as no more than temporary setbacks to business as usual.

But if minimal response is customary, in this case it carries unusual risks. It answers as a matter of urgency the nonurgent half of the two-stage problem: straightening up and keeping straight. With some local exceptions we could get along safely (if not ideally) with air, water, and land no more befouled than they are today; what we cannot accept is the pace at which all are getting less fit for human use.

A more than exponential growth of people in the United

States is accompanied by growth in wealth and technology at rates even faster. The extra 100 million Americans who will probably join us by the end of the century may make demands on resources at least equal to that of the 200 million here now.

Demand for energy is a good measure of how fast the economic production-consumption machine is turning over. In the mid–nineteenth century the United States each year was using energy (in all forms except food) equivalent to the heat produced by burning 90 million tons of bituminous coal. A hundred years later consumption equaled 1341 million tons. Between 1940 and 1967 the electricity generated annually in this country rose fivefold from 1200 kilowatt hours per person to 6100 kilowatt hours. Continuing spiraling demand requires the power industry to increase its installed capacity by about 6 or 7 per cent a year. In recent years the industry has not been keeping up.

Most of the energy that animals and primitive man use comes from food. An American requires forty-five times as many calories to maintain his culture as to maintain his body. Total demand for energy is increasing by about 3.3 per cent a year or about three times as fast as population. In California since 1940, gasoline consumption has gone up one and a half times faster than population; power consumption 2.2 times faster. And in California population has been increasing at almost double the national rate.

Where does the energy go? A large part performs no useful work at all. About 90 per cent is dissipated as heat to the environment. Much of the energy delivered in usable form moves us around, keeps us warm or cool, and recombines and rearranges the materials found on earth into goods, so called because we find them useful. Almost all the latter convert rapidly into waste, so called because we find it useless.

Accumulation of waste as a measure of economic progress

and prosperity tells the same story. The amount of waste sent to one scrap heap or another by each living American has gone up 60 per cent since 1918. The current consumer and industry infatuation with packaging promises to step up that rate and deliver wastes in forms increasingly difficult to dispose of. In 1966 the United States made, sold and threw away 46 million tons of packaging (12 per cent of the total domestic and industrial refuse) and it looks as though the 1976 total might be about 64 million tons. In a single year at the end of the sixties we were producing 48 billion cans and 26 billion bottles and jars, each with metal or plastic cap. More and more of the cans are partly or wholly of aluminum, comparatively nondegradable, and the bottles of glass and plastic, nonreturnable.

These numbing statistics can be made graphic in a number of ways. If New York City's trash and garbage for the next thirty-five years were burned, compacted and piled in Central Park it would make a mountain with vertical sides 600 feet high. (No wonder the city's sanitation department is beginning to worry about finding enough graves in which to bury this mountain.) One of the costs of living high on the hog is that one has to keep so many hogs and other edible creatures around. Agricultural wastes are becoming one of the major and most intractable of the disposal problems. Animals on ranch and feedlot and chicken coop convert fodder into manure at the rate of 50 billion cubic feet a year, which is more than enough to cover Long Island one foot deep. One average automobile, traveling at 60 miles an hour under normal climatic conditions, discharges three liters of nitrogen oxides a minute; to dilute that to an acceptable concentration harmless to health (i.e., .05 parts per million) requires as much air as 10 million people might breathe in the same minute.

But if the size of the waste problem is impressive, it is the rate at which it grows that is alarming. Delay in bringing it under control may ultimately cost more than money. To clean two rooms may take twice as long as to clean one, and each dirty room added thereto for a while may lengthen out the chore by simple addition. But at some point there are more rooms than one can handle and the processes soiling them move faster than the fastest broom. Thereafter if one still wishes to keep house, different policies and tactics have to be tried. One must somehow intervene at an earlier stage in the disintegrative process (everybody pick up his own clothes) or bring to bear new forces (sanitary police, perhaps) or change the management objectives (a little dirt and disorder are good for you).

Precise and complete measures of how we stand in the grandiloquently styled "battle" against pollution do not exist. Monitoring the environment to find out how good or bad it is for people and how much better or worse it is getting would seem basic to any program of environmental care. Yet after a decade of official concern, monitoring is still hardly more than an aspiration. In the absence of systematic data the best indication of how we have been doing is the shape and size of federal programs. What happens or does not happen in Washington, though only a part of the national effort, fairly reflects how seriously and effectively the nation is facing up to the whole problem.

During the sixties Congress enacted legislation that in sum marked out a new role for the federal government as guardian of the great common resources of land, air, and water. The role has impressive potential but remains so far ill-defined. Though everyone talks environment, no federal agency and no federal program confronts environment. The problems faced have been solid waste disposal, air pollution, water pollution, ocean pollution, pesticides, parks and recreation, fish and wildlife. How land is used and how various public services, such as highways, utilities, airports, and so on, affect land use — the most important and basic single environmental issue — is not the concern of anyone anywhere in the federal establishment or, for that matter, anywhere at any other level of government.

Environment takes in such a large proportion of human affairs that overlapping authority within the government is to some degree inevitable and desirable. But even so, redundancy has been overdone. A recent analysis by the staff of the Senate Interior Committee indicated that 63 agencies within 13 executive departments as well as 16 independent agencies in 1970 had environmental responsibilities. Such diffusion demanded coordination, and coordination was the business of 24 interagency committees and presidential councils.

The establishment at the end of 1970 of the Environmental Protection Agency (EPA), with status just short of an executive department, was a step toward rationality: It put together the federal pollution control responsibilities (or the major ones). If EPA turns out to be more than another departmental tent for warring tribes, it could for the first time address the single problem of waste production and disposal, which hitherto has been split according to where the nuisance occurred, on land, in air, or in the water. On the other hand, EPA is strictly a pollution control agency, not an environmental control agency; it is thus set up to deal with the symptoms and consequences of trouble in our society, not the causes. Moreover, it cannot make a big difference unless it gets money sufficient for the big job. Realistically, on the record of federal niggardliness in the past, it is not likely to.

# CHAPTER 6

# The High Cost of Waste

BEFORE 1965, when the Solid Waste Disposal Act was passed, more than half of American cities and towns with populations of over 2500 disposed of trash and garbage by dumping it in a relatively convenient hole. Almost no one was officially trying to do better. The Public Health Service had a research program, but in fiscal 1964 it spent only $430,000. In the prevailing wisdom trash was a local problem in any event.

Under the 1965 Act, Washington recognized that localities and states needed help, and has since developed a program of research and technical assistance. Most of the research and demonstration supported has been to develop and test methods of disposing of wastes. Typically Washington has responded to the need as defined traditionally by home towns; help us get rid of a nuisance. Behind that view was the pervasive sense of waste as not only a useless residue but a filthy one. Excrement and garbage send twin shudders of revulsion through city people, who no longer have to handle them. Scavenging proverbially is subhuman behavior. Ragpickers and junkmen have traditionally been beyond the pale as individuals, and even now in corporate garb collecting and processing wastes strike many as disreputable occupations. Possibly tongue in cheek, a Rutgers University professor recently suggested that waste be packaged and fired into the sun. The notion has charm as a parody of man's exploitative career culminating in digging up pieces of the only ground he has to stand on and hurling them into space.

At last in 1969, upon being told to do so by Congress, the Bureau of Solid Waste Management admitted a more basic need to work on recycling and new methods of collection and transport. Both needs are yawning. Recycling is bound to be largely neglected in an economy that has access to abundant raw materials and in which waste disposal is a charge on the public generally and not on the producer. With considerably less excuse, even less attention has been paid to an improved technology of collecting and handling, which remains for the most part at the motorized wheelbarrow level of sophistication and which accounts for four fifths of waste disposal costs. With new and more sensible priorities, the Bureau regrettably got no more money.

Comparatively few used products are now reclaimed for further use. Outstanding is the recovery rate for automobile hulks — about 80 per cent — which, however, still leaves a lot to rust in the countryside. No other salvage and recycling effort is comparable. Although the secondary materials industry does a five-billion-dollar-a-year business with about nine thousand processing plants, the best record of reuse is in the iron and steel industry, which processes about 45 per cent scrap. Despite some advances in salvage techniques (as, for instance, in the shredding and cleaning of automobile hulks to make high-quality scrap), technological progress appears overall to be reducing recovery and reuse. Ever more complicated gadgetry binding together paper, plastics, and ferrous and nonferrous metals makes salvage more difficult and expensive. Wastes mixed at the source in factories and households are not easily separated, and since increasingly high labor costs are involved, less and less is done. On the farm the concentration of animals in feedlots has turned manure into net waste; the costs of redistributing it to the land that badly needs it seem prohibitive.

Since solid wastes are for the most part out of sight and scent of the people who are most articulate and influential in society, the handling of them has had far less public attention than air and water pollution. Yet finding ways to avoid the fate of some ancient cities, such as Ur, that literally buried themselves in garbage, may actually be the most critical of our pollution problems. Ironically, it becomes more serious as the attempts to clean up air and water become more success-ful: cleaning air and water means simply removing from them alien solids which then have to be put somewhere else.

Fifteen years ago air pollution was already officially recog-nized as a matter of "growing public concern." What are still the classic incidents of multiple deaths from poisoned air in the Meuse Valley (60 deaths), Donora, Pennsylvania (20 deaths) and London (perhaps 4000 deaths) had occurred. Los Angeles smog was one of the wonders of the automobile age, and Los Angeles had been working to eliminate it for years.

In 1955 Congress passed the first federal air pollution con-trol law, authorizing $5 million a year for five years to sup-port research, training, and technical aid to the states. But in the next eight years the only substantial nationwide progress was to document the seriousness of the problem and reveal how little was being done about it.

In response to growing public pressure, the Clean Air Act of 1963 stepped up support for research, authorized grants to states and local agencies for control and even looked toward "federal action to abate interstate pollution problems."

Nevertheless, under the prevailing philosophy that states should do their own housekeeping, Washington formally ignored the apolitical ambience of air and federal action remained minimal. (A notable exception was to set standards for motor vehicle emissions in accord with authority granted by the amendments of 1965.) Research and development fared hardly better. Despite expenditure of some $60 million in the twelve years ending 1967, congressional experts reviewing the record in 1968 found that "progress toward development of new methods, processes, and technology was negligible."

In recognition of these shortcomings and of the worsening problem Congress in 1967 passed the Air Quality Act which, like the Clean Water Restoration Act of the previous year, tried to establish a national policy, which the several states would then be ordered to carry out freely and separately, subject to an occasional federal prod. Thus the Secretary of Health, Education, and Welfare would delineate regional airsheds in which effective controls could be established, but the states were to set air quality standards and enforce them. The federal government would review the standards and act against polluters only if the states did not. The new law authorized much more money for research and demonstration as well as for abatement and control.

Because air monitoring is so recent and still so inadequate, it is impossible to know precisely what is happening to the quality of air. There is a nationwide network of sampling stations (Continuous Air Monitoring Program — CAMP), but since it has been taking only one reading in most cities the data are highly suspect. The perils of a single sample are nicely pointed up by a scientist who in studying air pollution data in California was surprised to find that one station in Santa Clara County consistently reported the highest pollution levels at night. He investigated and found that the intake pipe gathering air samples was in a parking lot. In the cool of the evening lovers parked under the pipe with car engines running to warm them.

There are other difficulties of interpretation. In a few cities that have records over a period of years, curves typically show an overall increase in those pollutants chiefly emitted by automobiles (carbon monoxide, hydrocarbons, nitrogen oxides) up to a point where they seem to level off. The reason seems to be not that controls are working but that each major city has by now as many cars on its streets as the streets can take. Los Angeles did report that hydrocarbons in the city air were 6 per cent less in 1968 than in 1967. In New York the sulphur dioxide content in the continuing smog was substantially reduced during 1968 and 1969 by the shift to low sulphur fuels in the city's power-generating plants.

It is characteristic that to report on the state of pollution control one has to collect such fragmentary data and be content with scoring very small relative gains to our credit so far. Actually even these gains are misleading because air pollution, if less intense here and there, is spreading. While some city dwellers may be a little better off than they were five years ago, many more Americans are exposed daily to dirtier air.

Some air control officials, while admitting that city air is at best not improving rapidly, take some comfort in the fact that potentially dangerous pollution occurs only now and then under special weather conditions. These are the so-called temperature inversions in which abnormally warm air at 500 feet or less above the ground blocks the usual vertical circulation. The pollutants enter a stagnant mass that thickens during the day and, as shown by a dramatic time-lapse film taken by Walter Orr Roberts of the National Center for Atmospheric Research, sloshes about like a saucerful of coffee on a train.

Inversions may last for days, and though generally thought of as abnormal, they are in fact of common occurrence in some parts of the country, ranging from an average of one hour out of every ten to one hour out of every two. Unfortunately the topography that favors temperature inversions tends also to attract people — the coasts, valleys, and comparatively windless inland areas. Thus 97 per cent of Californians live where smog frequently impairs visibility, and 80 per cent where it is serious enough year round to cause plant damage.

Because inversions, though frequent, are usually predictable and become serious only when they persist, some large cities (Los Angeles and New York, for instance) have emergency plans on which they depend to alleviate the worst consequences. The Air Quality Act also authorizes the Secretary of HEW, whenever he finds that an inversion emergency exists, to ask the attorney general to enjoin polluters. Such vigilance is admirable. The trouble is that no city has a plan to control the private citizen's automobile, and as of now few could. Los Angeles, almost wholly lacking in public transport, has no present hope of reducing automobile traffic, much less halting it in an emergency. Lawyers doubt that a class action enjoining motorists could be sustained. In any event it is hard to see how it could be enforced.

No action taken through 1970 to abate air pollution carried assurance of success. The standards for automobiles were only a stopgap. Even if emission control devices were to reduce pollutants coming from each car by 80 per cent (a figure much higher than the rated efficiencies of devices installed on 1968 model cars), they were applied only to new cars. Since the average car is driven ten years it would take at least ten years to achieve that reduction. That assumed that the devices would be kept in repair and perform at tested efficiencies for the life of the car — an assumption that hardly squares with what we know about machines, mechanics, and drivers. At the end of 1970, against the opposition of the Administration and to the anguished protests of automobile industry leaders, Congress passed the Muskie bill requiring a 90 per cent reduction of hydrocarbons and carbon monoxide emitted from cars manufactured after 1975. But how rigorously will or can this tough regulation be enforced if the manufacturers continue to claim the requirement is technically unachievable? Even if effective controls are developed, enforcing their proper use against the negligent owner will remain a key problem, which no one has yet addressed.

The long-run answer would seem to be a substitute for the internal combustion engine or still unproved methods of achieving more nearly perfect combustion. In 1970 the Administration announced a federally assisted crash research program to find a mechanical paragon. The quest comes very late. And at the most optimistic it will take time — perhaps five to ten years. Even then a new engine, whatever it may be, is likely to replace the old only over another ten-year period.

The prospect of living for at least another generation with air that quite probably will be as polluted as — or more polluted than — it is now may be merely unpleasant or it may be serious. No one knows. It took twenty years or so for scientists to demonstrate and the public seriously to accept a correlation between cigarette smoking and health. Yet that was a simple problem in epidemiology as compared to establishing whether or not breathing any one or a combination of dozens of air pollutants has an adverse effect on any one of scores of bodily functions. Such poor evidence as we have, however, raises warnings.

Nationally the death rate from pulmonary emphysema (a

disease that destroys the air sacs in the lungs) increased more than fivefold between 1950 and 1960 — from less than 1.5 per 1000 to a little under 8 per 1000. The increase has been disproportionate in cities. The rate in New York between 1960 and 1970 rose a colossal 500 per cent, according to the New York Tuberculosis and Health Association. Impressive and scary as these figures are, they are shaky evidence against air pollution. Reporting of the causes of death contains large errors of ignorance and caprice. Without autopsies, doctors frequently cannot be sure what happened. Once recognized and named, a new disease inevitably is more frequently reported even if it is not more current. Finally, no causal connection between emphysema and any air pollutant has been shown. Conversely, the findings clearly do not support complacency.

The Public Health Service almost ten years ago had statistics indicating that deaths from lung cancer in cities with more than three million people were twice as numerous as deaths in rural areas. Moreover, the death rates seemed to vary directly in different areas with observed concentrations in the air of benzene-soluble organics that are known cancer-causing agents. In the laboratory bronchial cancers have been produced in rats who breathe heavy concentrations of either sulphur dioxide alone or sulphur dioxide in combination with one of the carcinogenic organics. Again, the evidence, though far from conclusive, is ominous.

Flatly one can say that dirt in the air does not make man healthier. Almost as flatly one can say that polluted air lowers resistance to other disease and thus, if not a killer itself, may often be an accessory.

The data we have speaks only to possible correlations between present pollution and present disease rates (these latter measured in grossest form by differential mortality). We know virtually nothing about less than lethal effects of long exposures, though at least one research project is now underway to study the effect on monkeys and guinea pigs of prolonged breathing of sulphur dioxide, sulphuric acid mist and fly ash in low doses comparable to those city people breathe. While awaiting results from such studies, we unfortunately cannot hold our breath. Prudence would therefore recommend that we take seriously present intimations of danger and not wait for proof before acting.

Clean air might be defined as air that is safe to breathe. If, then, we could be quite sure of what was safe to breathe, we would know what the demand for clean air means. But what is clean water?

Polluted water may be a threat to health even in technologically advanced nations that by and large have eliminated the organisms in water that cause such epidemic diseases as cholera and typhoid fever. Increased cancers of the bladder, for instance, have been observed in areas where water supplies are drawn from the Mississippi-Missouri-Ohio river systems; these may be related to wastes put into the rivers upstream. High nitrate concentrations resulting from the seepage of excess fertilizers into ground water are known to cause the blue-baby syndrome in infants (methemoglobinemia). And there are other relatively minor dangers.

Fears for health, however, are not articulated in the public demand for clean water. The motivation appears rather to be esthetic: as a society we seem to be saying we want clean rivers because we are offended by dirty ones, offended by the sight and smell and perhaps still more by the outward signs of a swinish neglect. There is a sense in which "clean water" has become a modern grail in pursuit of which we might repudiate the materialistic ethic and purge ourselves of affluence and arrogance. If so, there is no use asking how clean is clean; nothing would do short of absolute purity. Yet obviously any such demand is a practical absurdity. Pollution of water is inseparable from use of water. Although theoretically the impurities of use could be removed (by distillation if need be), to expend energy in that way would be a waste of resources that only a quasi-religious obsession could rationalize.

Clean politically means cleaner — enough cleaner to pacify, if not satisfy, the politically effective demand. Responsible government officials in the past five or six years have been making some rough, unstable, and generally unsatisfactory guesses as to how clean that must be. Their basic ground rule is that clean water demands, as a minimum, secondary treatment of municipal and industrial wastes.

When in preparation for the legislation passed in 1966 to clean up the nation's rivers Congress asked the Department of the Interior to estimate costs, the experts confined their attention pretty much to secondary treatment, in large part because when they got beyond that the unknowable yawned even wider than the unknowns. They ignored removal of inorganic chemicals, some highly toxic. They took no account of pollution by excess heat, possibly an increasingly significant phenomenon. Since there were and are no techniques to cope with run-off from farmlands, no costs could be reckoned for keeping fertilizer, pesticide residues and animal manure out of water, though these are major threats to the continuing health and abundance of fish and birds dependent on rivers, lakes, and marshes. Even with this limited definition of the problem, the economists predicted a bill of $26–29 billion for capital and operating costs through 1972. From what one knows of the art and history of estimation a safe second guess is that the figure is much too low. Moreover, many experts now doubt that secondary treatment leaving plant nutrients (phosphates and nitrates) in the effluent to fertilize algae and weeds will achieve even the modest goal of politically acceptable water purity.

In effect, what experts say about the cost of clean water is that the minimal steps to achieve it will be very expensive and probably in the end will prove insufficient. All calculations set the cost of clean water at some substantial per cent of the gross national product, indicating that paying the bill when we get around to it is likely to hurt.

Equally clear is the fact that we have not got around to it. The federal Clean Water Restoration program, hailed by then Secretary of the Interior Udall in 1967 as "the turning point in the war on water pollution," suffered thereafter such an economy squeeze that it is probably not even checking deterioration of our rivers much less beginning to clean them up.

The General Accounting Office, checking up for Congress, reported in early 1970 on antipollution fights on eight river fronts in different parts of the country. All, GAO found, were being lost. While municipal treatment plants had reduced somewhat the domestic pollutants dumped in the streams, the improvements were overwhelmed by continuing massive wastes from industry.

The failure, as the GAO noted, was due in large part to the lack of money. But even the amounts spent had been applied relatively inefficiently, because they were scattered in a kind of political lottery. Under the law the Federal Water Quality Administration has allocated funds to the several states by formula in response to state initiative. So long as the state has an overall plan and its proposals for specific plants conform, FWQA has not been authorized to evaluate their probable effect on stream purity. As often happens with grant-in-aid programs, the political and administrative machinery settled down to providing the means (sewage treatment plants) and lost sight of the end (clean water) — or more precisely water as clean as the society may wish and be willing to pay for.

Questions of cost effectiveness are especially important for water quality control; the need for sewage treatment plants is not as overriding as some enthusiasts have made it appear. We could rationally choose to befoul some rivers if the cost of keeping them clean were exorbitantly high. Clearly society has to weigh the relative urgency of clean rivers and other social goods that compete for limited budgets. If, for instance, the choice were between cleaning up the Hudson River and improving living conditions in New York ghettos, people who care about people would not hesitate to let the river go. By any reckoning we cannot afford investments in water purity that in fact do not make a real difference — expensive sewage plants whose net contribution may be to upgrade water quality from the unacceptable to the unsatisfactory.

Some of the economic conflicts involved in pollution control and some of the political embarrassment they cause have appeared dramatically in oil spills. Leakage from an improperly cased well in the Santa Barbara Channel beginning January 28, 1969, doused some of the best and most-used beaches in the country with thousands of barrels of oil, killed birds and fish, disgusted people, and led to a considerable stirring in Washington, ostensibly to prevent a recurrence.

On the face of it the regulations laid down under the Outer Continental Shelf Lands Act already provided the requisite safeguards, including orders to take "all reasonable precautions" to keep the wells under control and a specific order against polluting "the waters of the sea." Nevertheless the Secretary of the Interior amended these rules specifically to put upon a polluter the costs of cleaning up any mess that might result from his drilling and to reiterate that in addition he was liable to suit for damages. In fact, the state of California has joined Santa Barbara and other affected jurisdictions in a damage suit that asks "no less than $500,000,000."

These actions seemed tough but did not grasp the issue. The Department of the Interior has not in the past been able to enforce its regulations and there is little reason to expect that the new Environmental Protection Agency will do so in the future. While the risks of having to pay for cleanup may be perfectly acceptable to the oil companies and so not limit their activities, damage, when it occurs — particularly the destruction of fish and other wildlife — may not be compensable at all. Milton Katz has observed that the courts reviewing the state of California's huge claim for compensation must consider that it "could be devastating for the particular defendants, and might tend beyond the immediate case to discourage exploration and development of the mineral resources of the continental shelf." There, of course, is the heart of the matter: the central issue is whether the nation — as distinct from the oil companies or the government — profits more from oil drilling or from other competitive and incompatible uses of continental waters. That clearly is not an issue for the courts.

It is not easily confronted, much less resolved in the welter of conflicting jurisdictions. Drilling is on federal lands but the major damage from accidents occurs inshore on state, municipal, and private lands. The Department of the Interior in different bureaus has been responsible both for awarding leases, which bring in hundreds of millions of dollars in annual revenue, and for controlling pollution — a schizophrenia not unlike selling weapons to the Mafia in order to pay the police force. Bureaucratically that conflict may be resolved by the 1970 reorganization. But government still has warring interests that someone must mediate. It is not now clear who will. All in all the arrangements seemed to guarantee inadequate — even impossible — compromises. In the Santa Barbara Channel drilling went on. So did the sale of leases in other coastal waters.

On March 10, 1970, a well in the Gulf of Mexico sprang a leak, from which oil gushed out at the rate of 600 to 1000 barrels a day. For more than two weeks the well was out of control. By the luck of the wind the slick was kept offshore. Damage to fisheries has not been assessed. The evidence of company carelessness (not to impute anything worse) was even more flagrant than at Santa Barbara. Inspection by the Geological Survey turned up 347 alleged violations of the regulations that condition licenses to drill. Secretary Hickel asked for a grand jury investigation, reportedly because the company was not cooperative. No move was made, meanwhile, to halt drilling or suspend licenses.

Nominally the political response to oil pollution by tankers on the high seas has been more realistic. After many futile attempts Congress in 1970 passed a law holding the oil companies responsible for tanker spills, whether as a result of negligence or accident (barring "acts of God"). Liability for damage not the result of negligence was limited to $100 per gross ton — precisely the limit set by cooperative insurance established after the *Torrey Canyon* disaster by the International Tanker Owners Pollution Federation, Ltd. The law will not be easy to enforce; opportunities and temptations will abound for political as well as legalistic maneuvering. By limiting liability for accidental spills, moreover, Congress missed a chance to dampen the new, reckless enthusiasm for giant tankers whose breakup at sea could easily cause damage on a scale to render a few millions of compensation virtually irrelevant. The *Torrey Canyon*, which spilled its oil in the

English Channel on March 18, 1967, had a capacity of 119,000 tons. The cost to the British government alone of cleaning up the mess it made was $3.84 million out of pocket, reckoning nothing for the lives of shore birds or lost tourist revenue or forgone pleasures of natives. *Torrey Canyon's* owners paid more than $7 million in damages. In mid-1969 more than sixty tankers of 150,000 tons or more were on order and some of up to 800,000 tons were planned. Numbers, moreover, have increased along with size. The world tanker fleet in 1955 comprised 2500 vessels; it had 4300 in 1968. Neither the American government nor any other has chosen publicly even to notice the escalated risks. Without careful review of all potential costs and in the absence of any technology whatsoever to control oil spills in emergencies, the current law may turn out to be hardly more than a crying towel.

# CHAPTER 7

# To Kill a Goose

AMONG THE SAD HISTORIES of human abuse of this earth, DDT has written the classic case of environmental manipulation directed so narrowly at eliminating a particular nuisance that it failed disastrously to reckon with the complexity of the systems disturbed.

Only a nature lover who was also a people hater could contend that malarial mosquitoes should be spared, lest killing them cause some birds also to die. Nor for that matter is the plight of the eagle with DDT in its system the heart of the case against the policies that have turned a boon to mankind into a menace. The count against DDT (or rather against the way it has been used) is that technical efficiency (namely spectacular insect-killing power) has beguiled people into a simplistic view of both the problem and the solution. Even the immediate goal is not to kill pests, but to control them; and the overall purpose is not just to control pests but to create a more productive environment. In the short run chlorinated hydrocarbons are extraordinarily efficient in killing many crop pests and vectors of disease. In the longer run most insect populations can and do develop immunity. In the small view getting rid of the bug that eats the crop is all, and whatever does that is good. In the large view exterminating useful creatures, among which are natural enemies of our enemies, represents a substantial cost of doing business with DDT. Whatever may be said about the use of chlorinated hydrocarbons during the past twenty-five years, we have clearly arrived at a point where the revealed costs are high enough to warrant the urgent development of better and socially less costly techniques.

In May 1970, after heavy, prolonged public pressure marked by a number of court suits, the U.S. Department of Agriculture was ordered by the District of Columbia Court of Appeals to suspend the licensing of DDT or "show cause." Four states meanwhile had issued their own proscriptions (Arizona, Michigan, Wisconsin, and California). But Agriculture chose to dig in its heels. It was willing to ban certain "nonessential" uses but contended that DDT is necessary to control major crop pests and vectors of disease. The Department failed to point out that they will also soon be difficult (or impossible) to control *with* DDT as immune populations develop. The time to push all out for substitute methods of control is now. That will be done only if bureaucracy and industry are forced to do it by prohibition of the easier and more profitable course.

Even with such a ban a turnabout might be slow. To date the federal record of enforcement does not inspire confidence. The Pesticides Regulation Division of the Department of Agriculture (PRD) (shifted in 1970 to the Environmental Protection Agency) has been responsible for testing, licensing and policing the use of all pesticides under provisions of the 1947 federal control act. PRD has been the nominal watchdog over a billion-dollar-a-year industry marketing more than 45,000 products containing 900 different chemicals. But the congressional watchdog, the General Accounting Office, looking into PRD in 1969 was sharply critical of its performance.

For the first thirteen years, despite repeated industry violations, it filed no criminal prosecutions. Though it had frequently seized potentially harmful chemicals, it took only
those it found and made no effort to round up others or even
broadcast warnings. Between 1964 and 1969 public health
officials objected to 1663 proposed registrations. Not one of
these disputed cases was referred to the Secretary of Agriculture as the law required. Health officials' objections were
overruled (without that adjudication) in 185 registrations in
1969 alone. The lack of vigilance was on occasion comic: In
May PRD approved a fly and roach spray whose label warned
that it should be used only in "well-ventilated rooms." In-
structions on the container began: "Close all doors, windows
and transoms . . ." Collusion between the regulators and
the powerful petroleum industry, though not established, was
powerfully suggested.

As DDT and other hard pesticides begin to be excluded
from use in the industrialized nations — Sweden, Denmark,
and Great Britain have also taken steps to ban it — the chemical companies remain free to cultivate markets in the less developed countries. There the need for pest control is pressing, the farmers' ignorance of the dangers of DDT is all but
total, and official attitudes range from indifference to a
booster conviction that the quantity of pesticide (any pesticide) applied per acre is itself a measure of agricultural sophistication and progress. Since pesticides get into the oceans
and the upper air and travel around the world, their use anywhere is automatically a concern everywhere. We will have
gained little if DDT instead of being outlawed turns out only
to have been exiled. The best defense against the danger is
for governments and scientists to cooperate as a matter of urgency on developing alternative pest controls. That urgency
has not caught on yet.

*

The physical basis for community is land, though we do not commonly regard it so. How a society disposes its lands, what provision it makes for the communal interest in living space, are measures of how the society regards its own goals, reality, and importance. To those outside the conservation movement the preservation of land as natural habitat or as parks for people has generally seemed peripheral to more serious concerns for an unpolluted environment. Conservationists on the other hand have always tended to regard preservation as absolutely essential — not only to save places where their hearts are but to define their view of the world as a natural system of which man is but one dependent part. In that view a society has no duty more compelling than to cherish nature in order that it may itself survive in humane form. The United States historically has accepted that duty only now and then.

The bulk of public land set aside for public enjoyment — the national parks and national forests — are remnants of the public domain, reserved under a variety of laws, programs, and public pressures during the past hundred years. (Yellowstone National Park, our first, was established in 1872.) Use of federal money to purchase park, forest, and other natural lands is of recent vintage. Two laws of the 1930s provided small funds to the Department of the Interior for purchase of land to protect game. The Forest Service has long been permitted to use fee revenue to buy inholdings within existing forests and to acquire land east of the Mississippi which is important for the protection of water supplies.

In 1964, Secretary Udall, despairing of getting appropriations to add to the national park system, persuaded Congress to set up a Land and Water Conservation Fund for which certain federal revenues were to be earmarked, including new park-user fees, receipts from the sale of surplus federal property, and taxes on motorboat fuel. The fund, administered by the Bureau of Outdoor Recreation (BOR) in Interior, would distribute roughly half the money to states on a matching basis and the rest to the Park Service, the Forest Service, and the Bureau of Sport Fisheries and Wildlife for federal acquisition according to agreed priorities.

The Land and Water Conservation Fund came fully into operation in fiscal 1966. In 1968 the enabling act was amended to provide that if the revenues nourishing the fund fell below $200 million (as they regularly had) the difference would be made up out of money from offshore oil and gas royalties. Through 1969, appropriations from it have totaled only $492 million, of which about $256 million was granted to the states for both acquisition and park development.

Up to 1970 nearly 850,000 acres of land had been bought by the several states and federal agencies. Since 1960 the federal government has established 4 new national parks; 8 new national recreation areas; 9 new national seashores and lakeshores; almost 100 new wilderness areas, national monuments, and historic sites; a system of wild, scenic and recreation rivers; a national system of trails.

Although these are large figures representing an unprecedented commitment of resources to recreation, they measure a response at least as inadequate to the need as the responses to pollution just reviewed. Federal agencies now estimate that they need more than $400 million in the next five years just to round out acquisition in already designated park and recreation areas, some of them authorized by Congress ten or more years ago. These backlog needs substantially exceed current rates of spending and allow nothing for new parks, for which the need is certain to become more pressing. In 1960 Marion Clawson of Resources for the Future took a forty-year look ahead and guessed that to provide our rapidly multiplying population with outdoor recreation adequate by current standards would require federal, state, and municipal parks costing possibly $85 billion.

Besides the Land and Water Conservation Fund, the Department of Housing and Urban Development has an Open Space program, from which states and localities can get matching funds to buy land. Although HUD gives priority to open space in and around cities and in general has tried to spread its investment in a lot of relatively small areas, its program parallels and partly overlaps BOR's. By the end of fiscal 1969 more than 300,000 acres of open space had been bought and set aside for public use at a cost to the federal government of $220.8 million, somewhat less than half the total cost.

A close look at government actions shows the immense gap between the rhetoric of total commitment and the reality of a miscellany of generally unimaginative and uncoordinated programs regularly starved for funds. The simplest analysis reveals that the scale of the federal programs is so much smaller than that of the problem as to make them almost irrelevant. One informed guess, for instance, has set the annual cost of controlling air and water pollution and disposing of solid waste at $13.5 billion. For the same purposes Washington in fiscal 1969 appropriated $320 million. The real shortfall is of course considerably less, since one must add state and local spending. Yet it is large enough to raise the question of whether we as a society are really serious about wanting even to clean up the dirt, much less go on to creative housekeeping.

Since the federal budget has had no category for environmental protection it is difficult to know the whole size of the federal effort for and against the environment. The budget has segregated spending for "natural resources," including in that category most of the relevant water and air and other

Interior Department programs along with others (like the dams of the Corps of Engineers and the activities of the Bureau of Mines in the service of extractive industry) that for our purposes are not relevant. This overall figure a little more than doubled in the ten years between 1960 and 1970 (from $1.8 billion to $3.8 billion), but as a per cent of total federal spending it remained precisely the same. That steadiness in priorities during a decade of unprecedented public agitation and political rhetoric, remarkably testifies to the inertia of institutions.

Aside from parsimony, the government's approach has suffered from fragmentation, partly bureaucratic, partly philosophic. That is not easy to remedy. The new Environmental Protection Agency is not an answer. While putting together major waste management responsibilities, it may encourage an always latent disposition to treat the earthkeeping job as a task for kitchen maids: a nasty cleanup following an inevitable making of messes. The very existence of an EPA seemed to suggest that environment is not the concern of the Department of Transportation, for instance, or the Federal Power Commission, any of whom could make decisions having an impact on the environment that would cost EPA billions to rectify, if indeed it could be rectified at all.

In any event reshaping an organization chart to the newest fashion or even to new perceptions of order is essentially a trivial response to human problems. At most the revised groupings may achieve slightly greater, or slightly less efficiency. They will not in themselves put more energy to the task, much less produce the supervisory overview and harmony in action that perennially haunt the tidy mind.

Recognizing that fact, Congress and the Executive have sought various ways to unify activities under a comprehensive environmental policy. The National Environmental Policy

Act of 1969 and companion measure (the Environmental Quality Improvement Act of 1970) grasped the nettle and proclaimed simply that it was United States policy to care for and enhance the quality of the environment (whatever that might mean). All federal agencies were charged to act accordingly. A White House Council for Environmental Quality was set up to see that they did. It was rather like building a windmill to control the wind.

To seek unity through policy is to look in the right direction, but to conceive such policy as an addition, a fresh overlay on present federal agency missions, to be harmonized or compromised as necessity or expedience dictates, is to miss the essential nature of the problems. A federal policy on the environment cannot be considered realistic unless it begins with an examination of the policies explicit or implicit in the missions and operational guidelines now in effect.

The quality of the American environment has been deteriorating because official policies embodying the traditional economic and political wisdom support the systems that are doing the damage. If we really want to do better we have to redefine not just environmental objectives but concepts of human welfare, including the costs we may be willing to pay in the sacrifice of certain goods for certain others. That the deferred costs of bad housekeeping are so large is not just a fiscal fact; it points to the more basic shift of resources out of production and consumption into maintenance. That cannot happen without a policy decision, ultimately expressing the public will to accept a different scale of values. It is the search for such values that has to concern us above all.

# PART II

# The Antagonists

# CHAPTER 8

# Natural Systems

ENVIRONMENT IS the stage for life but it is also in large part the product of life and of the particular forms, proportions and distributions of living things in different places on earth. Some cosmologists speculate that the cooling and crusty earth may have been born some three billion years ago in a gaseous caul of ammonia, methane, hydrogen and water vapor. In such an atmosphere, it has been shown experimentally, electrical discharges can assemble protein molecules, the essential stuff of life. In an environment of relatively simple proteins more complicated ones could be joined. Biologists have worked out plausible scenarios of how, through increasing complexity, feeding and reproducing organisms might have arisen out of the larger molecules, although no one, of course, can ever know how in fact it happened.

Whatever the starting point, evolution must have proceeded by continuously interacting changes of both organism and environment, each change the precondition of the next. First life began literally remaking the world for itself and its progeny, and that new world welcomed new forms that would have been impossible before. At some point this restless process (acting as if it aspired because it was continually finding and preempting the opportunities of change) created the prototype of plants — organisms not dependent on finding ready-made proteins in the environment but able to make their own out of inorganic materials and energy from the sun. One might regard this event as the first of the great thresholds in world history commonly called revolutions, for it opened the way to the infinite variety of animal forms feeding on plants and on each other. With the arrival of photosynthesis green plants consumed carbon dioxide and respired oxygen, cycled nitrogen and moisture, and thus began to transform the primitive atmosphere into that sovereign mixture of oxygen, nitrogen, carbon dioxide, and trace gases that we regard as the indispensable support of life, often forgetting it is the gift of life, dependent itself on the continuation of life processes.

The fact that organisms and their environment are parts of a single interacting and continually evolving system can be observed where that ubiquitous process that ecologists call succession goes on. Neglect to mow the lawn and season by season an ever-changing mix of vegetation will replace the fescue and bent. What in fact is happening? Seeds of other grasses, shrubs, and trees are laid down by the wind or passing birds or animals, and if they find the soil and moisture and other physical conditions to their liking they will grow and in growing compete for the limited energy and nourishment to be found in this particular place. Grasses, as we all know, are crowded out first by various scrub plants. Once these are established they greatly alter their own environment and produce one favorable ordinarily to certain species of tree. The trees taking hold grow and further change the environment to one less favorable for the bushes, more favorable to various shade-loving plants. The environment that the first forest growth creates, moreover, may be less favorable to its own offspring than to the seedlings of other species, which will then come in and crowd out their hosts. The changing vegetation also creates a changing habitat for animals and a succession of animal life parallels the plant succession. The Kirtland warbler, resident in the cutover, burned-over lands of Michigan, cannot survive if those lands are left alone and allowed to grow back into pine forest. On the other hand, of course, the rich fauna of the forest, from the squirrels in the branches and the owls that feed on them to the microorganisms that live in the leaf fall, depend entirely on the special environment that the trees create.

Where does succession end and the resident community of plants and animals become settled? Strictly speaking, never. The alterations in any natural system are unceasing, even if it is spared catastrophic disturbance by nature (fire or flood, for instance) or by man with axe, plough or bulldozer. Ecologists, however, do speak of a climax state — a so-called virgin forest, for instance — in which inheres a degree of permanence and stability. Stability is a complicated concept and an important reality about which I will say more shortly. Here it is sufficient to note that in nature there are no static states, only oscillations of varying magnitude and pace. A primeval forest is called stable because within it the changes in kinds and numbers of creatures are relatively small from year to year and alterations in the physical environment are comparatively slow. As for permanence, that is a notion corresponding rather to the limits of consciousness than to the duration of anything outside.

The intimacy of organism and environment means more than that they evolve together. They are indeed so close that the difference between them can often be the point of view. Charles Elton, the great English ecologist, once examined a wood mouse and found a large community of specialized wildlife that made that mouse home: tick larva on one ear, adult tick sharing the fur with 14 mites and 11 fleas; and inside a roundworm, a tapeworm and a flatworm occupied the stomach and small intestine along with flagellates, a ciliate, an amoeba and coccidians; blood and kidney boarded a ciliate, a spirochete and trypanosome. This was a mouse, but this too was environment. The three-toed sloth inhabiting tropical forests wears a meadow of algae on his fur, in which graze the larvae of the sloth moth, which makes the animal its lifelong home. A recent book regards man in the same light as habitat of a host of microorganisms, transient and more or less settled, some friendly and helpful, some greedy and competitive.

Even with reference to a particular organism it is impossible to delimit precisely and scientifically where organism begins and environment leaves off, simply because there is not in fact and could not be any such frontier. Marston Bates, observing the probable origin of life in the sea and the fact that protoplasm is largely water, has called organisms leaky packages of sea water. That is not very precise either but it makes the point — all-important to a discussion of man's relations with his environment — that the materials of the environment are in us and the environment is constantly receiving materials from us. An organism, even the most solid-seeming, is full of holes, and inside we are packaged in semipermeable membranes that do not so much separate us from the environment as discriminate between what part to let in or out and what not to. Life is better thought of as a process continually cycling matter in and out of more or less organized systems, rather than as an aggregation of discrete, skintight individuals sustained by various media collectively called environment.

The organism-environment system, or process, runs on energy and the use of energy and its flow through the system is highly organized, if not very efficient. Green plants capture radiation from the sun and use it to bind together molecules of carbon, hydrogen, oxygen, and various minerals in very complex organic compounds out of which the plant tissue is made. From the plant's point of view one can think of energy being consumed to produce living tissue out of inorganic chemicals in soil, air, and water. But from the point of view of the whole system of life, tissue is not an end product but a device to conserve energy temporarily by converting the transient radiations of the sun into more durable chemical bonds. This energy (or more accurately a substantial part of it) then becomes available to animals who feed on the plants. These animals convert the plant proteins into their own kind of protein, using the energy locked into the chemical bonds. Some is dissipated in the process; some is preserved in chemical bonding in the animals' tissue, and is used by the animal itself in growth and activity, or passed along sooner or later to carnivores or parasites and, ultimately, to the detritus feeders who take over only after death. At each link in the food chain a portion of the energy originally fixed from the sun is "used up" in the processes of chemical recombination involved in metabolism. The energy is not, of course, "lost"; it is scattered as heat and made biologically unusable. At the final stage, when through the action of microorganisms the organic compounds are separated again into the inorganic components, the usable biological energy has all been dissipated and the cycle must begin again as plants drawing further upon sunlight recombine the elements in new tissue. The two important facts to be observed about this system are that energy passes through only once but materials are cycled over and over without loss.

The world is running down. There are many ways of saying that and of regarding it. The fanciest formulation is to say that entropy increases. Imagine a community, perhaps a suburb, growing old. No one moves in or out. Residents become more and more alike, and as they do they have less to say to each other. Without communication or reason to communicate the structure of the community dissolves like a clay house in the rain, and the people, entities in a system running down, become increasingly indistinguishable and inactive. This is essentially a single process of aging, not a sequence of causes and effects. So viewed, it can stand as a metaphor for entropy. Entropy is a measure of disorganization or of probability and lack of information content. The second law of thermodynamics, which itself can be stated in hundreds of different ways, asserts the universal fact of observation that in any transaction involving exchange of energy a portion of the total is unavailable to do work. This is the unarguable answer to perennial dreams of perpetual motion. One cannot construct a machine that will deliver exactly as much usable energy as has been put in and will therefore keep itself running.

Since all process involves exchange of energy and since the universe is process, the universe in time will run out of usable energy and stop. Note that this does not say that energy is lost (which the first law of thermodynamics asserts to be impossible); it only says that in the end energy will not be exchanged. A state of maximum entropy is a state in which absolutely nothing happens or could ever happen because there are absolutely no distinctions between the parts of the whole. By definition that must also be a state of maximum (i.e., 100 per cent) probability and zero information, for among identities there can be no exceptions, no accidents (i.e., no improbabilities), no events to talk about. German cosmologists with a nice irony have called that eventual state of the universe "heat death (Wärmetod)." An important corollary of the running-down process is that time is thus given direction and history becomes irreversible. That can be a sobering thought even before the approach of death.

The world is running down (so slowly that no one really has to worry about it) but it is not running out of materials. Life expends energy, making a portion of it thereafter unusable, but it does not consume matter. It is worthwhile contrasting this fact about the natural world with the usual formulation of man's problem: that while he has energy to burn (the nucleus of the atom is surely an inexhaustible source) he has increasing difficulty in finding and making the things he needs and in getting rid of the things he has used and needs no longer. Since the natural world obviously is man's world too, the discrepancy lies not in the fact but in the formulation which is a recent delusion of our culture.

Life makes use of available energy very inefficiently. In a laboratory under ideal conditions a green plant has proved able to use 3 per cent of the sunlight falling upon it in photosynthesis. In the field the actual efficiency is probably not one tenth of that. It seems likely that only about one ten-thousandth of the solar radiation striking the earth's surface is captured to fuel the biosphere, that is, the interlocking system of living things. And the bulk of even that tiny fraction is dissipated along the food chain as organisms that become food for others pass on only about 10 per cent of the energy they used to grow.

On the other hand mature, stable systems — those that have reached the so-called climax state of succession — are usually remarkably conservative of minerals. One ecologist calculated that a certain New Hampshire forest, using about 365 pounds of calcium per acre to nourish life within it, lost annually only about eight pounds per acre by run-off. Of this, three pounds was replaced by rain and the other five by fresh weathering of rock. Incidentally, it was observed that when the trees were cut vastly greater quantities of calcium washed away.

# CHAPTER 9

# The Coexistence Process

THE PREDESTINED END of the world is neither a bang nor a whimper but perpetual repose in an exhaustion that makes no difference. Entropy is time's arrow. We are all ultimately headed for the ultimate mediocrity. But before we get there — now and for any predictable future — the apparent direction of life is just the opposite. Life is essentially the organization of energy and life appears to evolve in the direction of ever-greater organization. This does not mean that a man is more highly organized energy than an amoeba, though there is certainly rather more to him. There does not appear to be any consistent tendency for life to take ever-more-complicated forms. The simplest "living substance" known — the virus — is also notably one of the most successful. But there *is* a tendency of life forms to proliferate. After a lifetime of studying the phenomena of evolution, George Gaylord Simpson concluded that the only general progressive change since the beginning of the world has been the radiation of living forms into all available niches in the environment. Wherever it has been possible for a creature to make a living, some creature has taken up residence. Life evolving acts as if it wished to fill up the world and take possession of every cranny.

Some observers have been so impressed with this apparent exuberance of life that they have insisted that the appearance must be a reality, that life does in fact *wish* to behave this way, that in short there is some vital force that compels living things toward some sort of upwardness, onwardness and fulfillment. (Teilhard de Chardin is the most prominent modern proponent of this view.) It may be so but it need not be so on the evidence, for the observed trends of evolution are just those made likely by the nature of the process itself.

In succession, as we have seen, a simple community of a few species progresses to a complicated one of many by bringing in outsiders. In evolution complications are continually invented by the interaction of species with each other and with the physical environment. One universal mechanism is competition. Creatures seldom enjoy a monopoly of their own way of life. There are nearly always others who could exploit it if they had a chance. And the chances are frequent. Invasions by one population of another's territory are commonplace and the threat of invasion is an all but universal condition of life for everyone. This rivalry, actual and potential, among species that could make use of the same resource — either food or territory — early became the key image in the "struggle for existence" among popularizers of evolution. In fact the "struggle" in nature has little in common with war or even with a direct confrontation of rivals. Competitors appear not as enemies to be annihilated or driven off but as elements in the environment requiring adaptive reactions. While the outcome may be — and often is — the defeat and extinction of the species less fitted to occupy the niche effectively, the process, unlike war, does not simply assure the replacement of a succession of losers by a succession of winners. At least as important for evolution are the adjustments the species in occupation or those invading or both make to the competitive situation, all acting as though they would rather endure than triumph.

Adjustment is normally by specialization either of form or

behavior or both, which has the effect of splitting a hitherto single environmental niche or of opening up a wholly or partly new one. Robert MacArthur studied four species of warbler that were thought to be competitive in the Maine woods. He found that in fact each nested and fed at different altitudes and so in effect had divided the wood among them in storied layers like an apartment house. Richard Miller observed a different kind of accommodation among four species of prairie gopher, each of which in the absence of the others occupies the same habitat. In competition one species took over the bulk of the territory that all favored because it was the best equipped of the four to exploit it. The other three made do with nesting and feeding grounds less satisfactory. If one is inclined to the military or laissez-faire view, the three peripheral populations look like losers and outcasts and in a sense of course they are, having failed to maintain themselves where they preferred to be. From the evolutionary view, however, they proved a superior ability to adapt to conditions less than ideal for them and conditions in which the fourth "fittest" species actually could not live at all.

John J. Christian has proposed that such dispersion is a possible mechanism of speciation. Suppose a single population of gophers is in occupation of the favored grounds. As the population approaches the limits of environment, competition becomes acute. It does not take the form of warfare. Instead it is regulated by a peck order; the dominant gophers monopolize both food and mates. The subordinates may starve, fail to reproduce, or migrate; in fact they are likely to do all three. Those that migrate to less happy hunting grounds are likely not to survive. However, since all individuals differ, the probabilities are that in a population large enough — and the subordinate animals will greatly outnumber the dominant — some will be different (mutant) in just the way needed to enable them to live away from their ancestral home. Once established, these mutants are likely to find life more difficult than the stay-at-homes and consequently their populations will undergo more rapid evolution than those who, having made it in the best of all possible worlds, have no need to change.

Evolution, proliferating life to fill all niches in which life is possible, involves a familiar paradox; its agency is death — death for individuals and death for species. Obviously populations can adapt by selection only as generations succeed each other, which is to say as parents are successively removed to make room for their children. New species arise out of competition and dispersion, the normal price of which is extinction of the old. Ancient survivals — oysters, horseshoe crabs, ginkgo trees — are excessively rare. Extinction — relatively rapid in the time scale of evolution — is the rule.

But the rule is extinction of *species*. It is far more common for genera to persist in geologic time and still more common for families, classes, and orders. The largest groupings of organisms, the phyla, appear so far all but immortal. Taxonomists recognize from 20 to 40 animal phyla, depending on how basic they deem certain distinctions of form to be. Each represents distinct major evolutionary pathways that divided hundreds of millions of years ago. Once having taken these turnings into certain groups of environmental niches, life stayed with them. In George Simpson's reckoning only one of the major animal phyla has become extinct, and its right to the status of an independent phylum is not clear.

Speciation, as indicated, is the mechanism for fine adaptation of creature to the environmental niche. Responsive to the relatively rapid diversification of environment on a small scale and over short spans of time, it is by nature an instable process: A species by definition is only a temporary solution

to a passing problem. But the process of change is also necessarily cumulative. New species arising from old retain many
of the specializations and limitations of their origin. These
cumulative changes establish a history that is irreversible.

From an Olympian view life pushes into the unoccupied
crevices of the environment like a rising tide encroaching on
the land, flooding the low-lying plains, reaching here and
there into narrow valleys, everywhere filling the cracks and
holes of opportunity. Yet for each of those tidal fingers the
opportunity becomes also a probable trap and dead end. The
smaller and more remote from the main bodies of water, the
more likely the branch is to be cut off by the slightest shift in
the lie of the land. But since no one can ever tell what
changes in the environment will occur, all species are vulnerable precisely to the extent that all species are specialized.
The judgment that a creature became extinct because it was
overspecialized is always a tautology after the fact; specialization can be shown to have gone too far only when it kills the
specialist.

Among the many ways in which man has become a threat
to the survival of his fellow creatures is his power to alter
those small environments to which a few highly specialized
organisms have become adapted at the cost of having lost
their adaptability, their capacity to push in other directions
into other ways of life. With the exception of a few animals
that have been literally hunted to the verge of extinction, the
rare and endangered species now as always are those that have
been crowded into a tight environmental niche — a limited
territory, a finicky taste for a few foods, an unusual sensitivity
to climate. Man has greatly accelerated the processes by
which these specialists have been cut off and left stranded out
of the tide by his propensity to make more and more of the
planet suited to his own specialized uses. For man is the first

species in the history of life to alter the terms of evolution: he has learned to adapt the environment as a supplement to and partial substitute for adapting himself.

In opposition to a new dam or highway or power plant, conservationists often warn against upsetting the balance of nature. The metaphor, though reflecting a glimmer of truth, is on the whole misleading. To be in balance is to achieve near immobility on a point of ideal adjustment. Balance is the egg on the toothpick on the nose of the juggler. Living systems are in constant motion in only one direction — the direction of time. "Balance of nature" implies fragility and brinksmanship — the egg forever in danger of a smashing fall. Most communities of creatures are notably tough and resilient. They have to be. It is one of the things life learned from evolution in an environment always subject to change, and often violent change, long before man came. A forest burned to the ground — by lightning at least as often as by a careless campfire — will ordinarily grow again in a few years and the populations of animals and birds chased by the flames will return as soon as the home is rebuilt. In severe drought northern trout streams may dry up in August; yet next season the fish will again be there to bite. Individual organisms are easily killed, but species succumb only to adversities prolonged over time and spread widely over the habitat.

It is true that some systems are more sensitive to disturbance than others and may have less capacity to recover. It is true, and all-important for environmental management, that all systems have an elastic limit beyond which they cannot snap back. But none totter on the head of a pin. Rather they are forever reacting to adversity and opportunity, continually reshaping themselves defensively or offensively (if terms implying purpose are understood to impute no such purpose to nature) within an environmental container that is never quite the same from moment to moment, season to season. The important fact is not a presumed ideal arrangement of parts in balance but the capacity of the whole to stretch, shift, reshape to shifting circumstance — the capacity to adapt.

The capacity of a species to adapt is a composite of the tolerance of individual members and the range of tolerances represented by all individuals. No organism is so rigidly programmed to a particular environment that it cannot live in another slightly different. Daily and seasonal variations in temperature occur in virtually all habitats. A serpent sunning himself on a rock must be able to survive the cooling of his blood by a passing cloud. Rabbits in the north temperate zone get along in August heat and hardly less well in winter snow. Adaptation to temperature change is by a variety of mechanisms, physiological and behavioral, that tend to stabilize the internal temperature of the animal within its own limits of tolerance. In general these mechanisms are tuned to compensate for the extremes normally encountered. Because water temperatures vary less than air, aquatic creatures are generally less tolerant of extremes of heat and cold than inhabitants of the land. Plant communities tend to be more sensitive to variations in mean annual temperature than do communities of animals, and this is both cause and result of their tendency to inhabit geographically restricted areas.

In a population of the same species, individual variations are compounded by variations among individuals. No two are just alike. If sexually reproduced, the probability of exactly duplicating any one combination of genes (except in identical twins) is so near zero that it can be ignored. Moreover, the copying mechanism, by division and reforming of immense molecules of DNA, inevitably makes mistakes. Most of the mistakes are lethal but a few survive, as mutants, and mutants are the material for evolution.

In an uncertain world all individuals have some capacity to bend to circumstance. But many often have too little to survive. The fate then of a population will depend on those who can and their ability to pass along to succeeding generations the special adaptive talents by which they endured. A species over time adapts to its environment by natural selection, which preserves for breeding a preponderance of those best able to exploit their environment and so gradually assures a preponderance of those characteristics that fit the individual organism for the life he leads. Natural selection depends, thus, on the fact that no two individuals are alike and that the differences among them tend to give each of them more or less capacity to survive under differing conditions. Note that this does not say that some individuals are stronger or even in any absolute sense more fit than others. Fitness has meaning only in relation to the environmental challenge. For selection the important requirement is variety, since the nature and direction of environmental catastrophe are never prefigured. Cotton pests in Louisiana were not constructed to anticipate chlorinated hydrocarbons. But a few happened to have unusual genes that made them exceptionally resistant. The extermination of those bearing the "normal" genes cleared the habitat for the "aberrants," which proceeded in the usual way to populate the available niches with their offspring. In that way populations have acquired resistance by selection, unnatural in this case but exactly comparable to the selective process in nature, except that the artificial process may be partly reversible. If one stopped spraying, the resistant insects would lose their advantage and might find themselves less fit with regard to other challenges.

Populations, the species group, do not of course live by themselves but in intimate interaction with other populations in natural communities. Membership in a population is determined by who is sleeping with whom; membership in a community, as Marston Bates observed, by who is eating whom. The community of plants and animals is as a whole still more adaptable to environmental change than individuals or populations, since within it more than one species can ordinarily play the essential roles that integrate the community and make it work.

Some ecologists have argued that stability in a natural system (defined as its relative likelihood of extinction) is directly a function of the number of links in the food (or trophic) chain. The hypothesis is plausible if not proved. Imagine a community of just chestnut trees, squirrels and owls, and suppose the squirrels could eat nothing but chestnuts and owls nothing but squirrels. Blight in these conditions would in a single season wipe out trees, animals and birds. But in a real woodland, disaster would be avoided by alternative food supplies. Even if no chestnut trees resisted the blight, a few squirrels would try seeds or acorns though they had never tried them before, and some owls would discover an unexploited skill for catching field mice and an untutored taste for them. The more alternative ways there are of eating and being eaten, the less likely it is that damage to one population will leave the others without sustenance and so the less likely those precipitous feast and famine oscillations of instability. Even though in a mature system each species will be specialized out of the others' way so that each can make a living, the variety of feeding possibilities has the effect of building potential redundancy into the system, which as any engineer knows is the best insurance against breakdowns.

Diversity is associated with stability as both cause and effect. Once life discovered ways to vary individuals, evolution was headed inexorably into increasing diversity. This is so because diversity feeds on itself: The more difference in the environment, the more opportunities for different organisms to specialize and find special advantages; the more different kinds of organisms, the more varied they make the environment and the greater the opportunities and challenge for further change. Provided the potential for variation persists, variance will increase, subject, of course, to environmental inhibitions. That is really another way of saying that in evolution whatever is possible will almost surely happen; the more abundant the possibilities, the more numerous the happenings. Relative equilibrium will occur when the potential for variation or specialization can profit one population only by eliminating another.

The precise relationship between diversity and stability is a question of great scientific interest. For our purpose, however, a rough approximation of probable truth will suffice: In the absence of constraints life tends to specialize for the most efficient exploitation of food sources, and therefore diversity tends to increase toward the limit of absurdity when each individual would be its own species. What is certain is that when succession reaches climax in conditions especially favoring life (where there is a maximum available energy) as in a tropical rain forest, a highly stable system results that contains a bewildering variety of resident plants and animals.

In a one-and-a-quarter-acre section of a rain forest in North Queensland, Australia, ecologists counted 1261 trees belonging to 141 species. Marston Bates, who spent some years in the tropics studying yellow fever, identified 150 species of mosquito within ten miles of his laboratory in Colombia. By contrast only 121 species are known in all of North America. This does not mean, of course, that one's chances of being bitten are necessarily fewer up here than down there. For, characteristically, species multiply at the expense of each other so that each population contains fewer individuals. So universal is this phenomenon that Darwin, among others, has observed that "rarity is the attribute of a vast number of species."

Here is another of the many paradoxes in the organization of life. A species like the black-footed ferret must always be rare because he occupies so special a niche among the prairie dogs on which he preys. His rarity puts him in greater risk of extinction than the dogs but at the same time it testifies to the maturity and adaptive stability of the system of which he is part. The paradox may be resolved by shift in point of view: Rarity is indeed a danger to species but a requirement of a community of species. So, in contrast to the rain forest, an arctic tundra with only a few months a year of warmth and sun typically reiterates individuals of a relatively few species and each appears abundant. But each is excessively vulnerable, for the arctic is subject to just those alternate plague-like explosions of prey and predator populations and sudden catastrophic declines that signify instability and continually force major readjustment and rebuilding.

There is another paradox to observe. When a natural community contains as many different species of plants and animals as can live there it has achieved its most highly organized state — in technical terms a state of least probability, greatest information, and least entropy. It may thus be as far as one can get on earth from the warm death that is the ultimate fate of all. We say of this state that it is stable because it stands apparently firm against sudden change. But in some larger and longer view it is highly unstable, even illusory. So far as living things diversify and associate in ever more highly organized systems they run against the tides of time. In the end that is a losing game. But we have always known that. In the short view stability in natural systems remains real, and as valuable in maintaining the production of the earth as instability is disastrous.

As life is process it is inconceivable without history. A living system is always shaped by — indeed in a sense it is — its own past. The extraordinary variety of forms of life in a mature community and the subtle and complex relationships among them were not first detailed in blueprints and then set out to work as prescribed. They resulted over very long periods of time by unplanned but nevertheless controlled interactions and adaptations. These of course never cease. In maturity, however, a community acts as though it wished to stay as it is. The fact that a forest primarily of oak and hickory year after year remains recognizably a forest of oak and hickory invites analysis as of a finished product. The fact that one can — however imperfectly — see how it works may misleadingly suggest a machine that could be instantly reproduced, for time does not obviously appear in the analysis. (The dream of "genetic engineering" — at least in its more naively grand formulations — embodies this fallacy of a living system constructed without time.)

While history of course needs time, the mere passage of time does not make history. In history not only must things happen; they must happen nonrepetitively. The nitrogen cycle by which plants and soil bacteria continually reshape nitrogen in organic and inorganic forms requires time but it does not belong to history. To make history there must be some organized system (alive or not) that is capable of learning, that is to say, able to sense external phenomena and alter its own responses accordingly. Machines in this sense may be capable of learning — a computer, for instance, that is programmed to perform difficult tasks depending on how it perceives a particular set of facts. The state of such a machine at any point in time would have to be defined in part by its history.

All living systems have that characteristic: All are conditioned by their past experience. That introduces an interesting complication that is critical to understanding and resolving environmental problems. Every living system reacts to the impacts of the present with the lore and learning and adaptive skills acquired by coping with problems in the past. While problems past and present may or may not be similar, they can never be precisely the same.

Ecologists speak of time lags in the system. Very long lags correspond to the evolutionary history of the organism or community of organisms. Hostility among men (biologists call it "intraspecific aggression") and their jealousy of home and nation ("territoriality") have been referred back to hominoid origins in the plains of Africa. In fact the evidence for such origins is quite insufficient and the uses of what evidence there is have often been naive. Nevertheless the presumption is reasonable that in some form the learning of the jungle persists, genetically if not culturally, in modern man and in some ways, no doubt too subtle ever to be precisely defined, influence his responses to current stimuli.

More significant in defining how a living system can and will react are the shorter-term histories: community succession through stages of mutual adaptation that take many generations and may last many hundreds of thousands; the differentiation of individuals attributable to the experience of their parents (the generation bridge); variant states of mind and body of any one individual depending on what has just happened to him — whether, for instance, he is fed or hungry. C. S. Holling has observed that for each of these histories, the system has a "memory," not of course a conscious recollection, but rather a particular setting of its controls that will shape its response: Has the community ever before tried to metabolize DDT? Has the horse been conditioned to start at the sight of a moving object without waiting to define the danger? Does the mantis seek a meal or has it just had one? The whole set of time lags means that in large part the past writes the programs that the present tries out.

History thus stiffens the system, as it were, and in one sense steadies it, just as a body of law and custom tends to steady human societies against momentary caprice. Through learning, systems become adapted to the most probable of the conditions they have to deal with. By the same token, however, time lags condemn them to a rigidity and often an irrelevance when faced with a less probable challenge. It is a familiar complaint of youth that Dad cannot really handle the present because he is living in the past with a lot of superannuated ideas. So are we all, even youth. The crux is in how much past we have and how different is the present. Freud among others observed the incongruous persistence into adulthood of behavioral controls once set in reaction to childish events.

If a community of living things is in some sense a momentary organization of history, it is organized and exists in space. The kind of space, how it is occupied, what is happening at any one moment in one portion or another — these are critical to the ability of that community to adjust its relationships harmoniously.

In general each species of plant and animal tends to occupy as much of the earth as it can get to and live in, subject to the competition of other plants and animals that have similar tastes. Furthermore, every community of plants and animals tends through dispersion and specialization to make the maximum use of the energy and nutrients available to it. By these two broad principles the spatial patterns of populations in the environment are cut. Thus in deserts grass tends to lose out in competition with shrubs, cacti and other larger plants that need less water, can capture more or are capable of storing it. These in turn tend to be relatively widely spaced, each requiring a considerable catchment area for the meager rainfall. But in climates only a little less arid than those of the true desert, grass can and does take hold. Its slight competitive advantage, however, is easily destroyed when, for instance, grazing animals keep it too closely cropped. Then scrub growth wins out and monopolizing moisture prevents the return of grass. In a rain forest, as already noted, individual trees of each species may be as widely spaced as the cacti or creosote bushes of the desert; that is also the result of competition. But here the competition has been won by the intervening plants that occupy the interstices, because they are specialized to make more efficient use of their particular microhabitats: Even though the forest is vastly more productive than a semi-arid grassland, the spatial arrangement of its residents represents an accommodation by competition that is also relatively stable only so long as it is not drastically disturbed. The farmer who tries to replace trees with corn and beans quickly discovers that the abundant productivity of the tropical forest cannot be simply rechanneled out of wood into crops.

Animals develop exactly similar patterns in space even though they may move their personal space around and alter their demand for it from season to season or year to year. The primary space an animal needs, of course, is the area sufficient to raise the food to support him. In competition with others those animals will survive who can find and keep for their own use just that much space. Thus the spatial arrangements of animals in stable communities are equally shaped by competitive accommodation and maximum exploitation.

It is not surprising, therefore, that animals have evolved sensitivity to their space needs and various mechanisms to assure that the needs are met. The defense of territory in almost all birds and in many other animals is one mechanism that apparently acts to regulate competition and keep populations below the density that would exhaust the food supply. Wynne-Edwards has argued that dispersion is another. John Calhoun, John Christian and others have shown experimentally that rodents respond to crowding by changes in the endocrine systems that in various ways inhibit reproduction. Dogs, as all city owners know, record their presence in a territory by urinating at checkpoints, apparently to forewarn of possible overcrowding.

Mechanisms of this sort, limiting numbers to the carrying capacity of the environment, ecologists call density-dependent. They are triggered by a feedback. It is as though the population has a thermostat setting for a certain density against which it continually presses by competition and reproduction. But when exceeded, the switch is tripped and either more animals are driven out to die, or fewer are born, or both, until the spatial equilibrium is restored.

All stable natural systems have those switches. But not all populations do. People as noted have none now working and appear to have jammed those they had earlier evolved. Pests have none. Indeed, one definition of the plaguing pests such as locusts, Colorado beetles, or rats, is that they are animals whose population size is regulated externally and directly by the availability of food without any mediating mechanism sensitized to density. Pest species of this kind reproduce enormously more young than can be normally supported and thus suffer enormous infant mortality until a good year comes or some obliging farmers put in thousands of acres of their favorite food. The resulting plague can be thought of as a sudden massive reduction in infant deaths. It does not take a misanthrope to observe the parallel to man: "the species that explodes is by definition a pest and the latest addition to the ever-growing list of injurious pests is, of course, man himself."

# CHAPTER 10

# The Nonconforming Species

ONE WOULD NOT write a book about ants or elephants and the natural system. It is assumed that ants and elephants (and indeed all creatures other than man) are inextricably parts of the system and cannot be thought of as standing in opposition to nature. Man can. The literal — and ultimately all-important — observation that man too belongs in nature papers over the immediately more significant fact that he is a partly nonconforming member, like a very bright, creative, obstreperous child in a school all of whose rules and procedures are hallowed by a tradition so ancient that it is written in the genes. Moreover, the creativity and obstreperousness of man are unique in nature in ways that this and following chapters intend to explore.

It seems reasonable to start the inquiry at the beginning, that point in evolution when man became man. But when was that? In looking for the origins of man, one seeks to identify that turn in evolution which pointed the progenitors of man in the direction that made them so. When can one say of what primate that he has undergone just the change that separates him from his cousin in such way as to put him and not his cousin in the direct line of succession leading to *Homo*? The experts guess it might have been some 10 to 50 million years ago. While all estimates can be radically altered from one archeological find to another — so great is our ignorance — the basic uncertainty is that we do not and cannot know what we mean by beginnings.

One can talk of beginnings only from the vantage point of a development that has already occurred or from the springboard of a plan or purpose. (Logically the procedure is identical, since a plan is just an imagined history projected as the probable or desired course of events to come.) Beginnings, in short, are always referred to ends and take meaning therefrom. In the process of evolution, which has no plan, or projected ends, beginnings can be marked only after ends appear, that is, after a set of changes has taken place in an organism to produce a particular configuration that we find distinctive and interesting.

The "ends" specified in this analysis are of course just as arbitrary and without objective reality as the "beginnings" sought. Language betrays thought. When one examines a process the starting point for the examination necessarily appears as culmination: one wants to know what led up to it. In the study of life, ends are an analytic convenience, the most important aspect of which is that they do not exist. But man does, and he is such a highly distinctive biological organization, so fascinating to himself, that he wants very much to believe both that he is culmination and that he had an appropriately distinguished start, even if not necessarily by special creation.

Some decades ago there was a lot of misleading popular speculation about a missing link, as though between the clearly ape and the clearly man there existed somewhere an intermediate form bridging the two. The search falsely assumed that man was descended from apes and that the descent was by a definable single path well marked by palpable milestones. In fact hominid evolution *diverged* from pongid (ape) evolution presumably from a common starting point. The divergence moreover was probably neither single nor straightforward. Evolution does not put out one line and then develop it; rather the process is one of continual branching, with natural selection acting as the pruner determining which branchings will leave the most descendants. Missing-linkism as a game has been pretty much swallowed in scholarly disputations over the meaning of variations in the forms of molars and bicuspids which command little public attention.

From a technical point of view the fine-grained examination of evolutionary steps is important to elucidate the process, but it is not going to come up with a simple answer to when and how human destiny took off. No modification of the protohominid animal predestined it to the path leading to man. There was no path. Any change could have become a takeoff for some quite different development. That is one capital difficulty in finding where man came in. Another is that the more closely one examines a continuous process, the smaller become the differences between one step and the next until at last, if the microscope reads fine enough, steps disappear altogether and change itself (not the stages through which it passes) is seen to be the ultimate reality.

Nevertheless the admission that one cannot say where man became man is not to suggest that the distinctions between man and his hominoid forebears are indistinct. For purposes of analysis man began when he became recognizably man; he became recognizably man when he possessed just those human qualities that have significance for the investigator in the light of what he is investigating. If there are uncertainties and circularities here bordering on vertigo, never mind: we can still find some relative truths that are solid enough.

The human qualities relevant to this inquiry are those patterns of behavior that gradually enabled man to gain a measure of control over the environment. This is the distinction that made a difference for the future of the waste makers. We can safely ignore dentition.

A picturesque (though possibly erroneous) theory of how man's ancestors separated from the other primates, which headed the lines that led to the great apes, supposes that in late Miocene and early Pliocene (c. 10–20 million years ago), when a general drying up of the African climate caused the forests to shrink, man's ancestors (possibly genus *Ramapithecus*) lost out in a struggle with progenitors of the ape for the dwindling habitat. Man-to-be took to the savannas, having no choice, and in adapting to this initially uncongenial living space he improved upon two talents that were to be critical for his evolution: He became more generally omnivorous than his late brothers in the trees, who remained primarily vegetarian, and he learned to run on his hind feet, there being no trees to climb to escape predators. If one wished to find the essence of human nature in its beginnings — as has sometimes been done — according to this theory we were not programmed as carnivores and creatures of violence but as born losers who made it into history by running away. The survival value of running was simply to escape predators, but the evolutionary value turned out to be that it left the front paws free to develop into hands. And so they had by the time the definitely man-like creature, *Australopithecus*, emerged perhaps two million years ago.

Though one may endlessly debate how it came about and in what order the steps were taken, the evolution of man is inextricably and centrally associated with skill in using tools. However it began, in the particular circumstances in which *Australopithecus* found himself the skill evidently conferred immediate and progressive advantages, presumably because it answered a pressing survival need. George B. Schaller and John T. Emlen have observed that the mountain gorilla is similarly adapted to the use of tools and has developed a way of life that leaves his hands free of locomotive responsibility much of the time. Yet the potential talent never developed. The reason is probably that the forests in which the animals live are so generous in satisfying their needs that no advantage would be gained by further manual skills. So the odd young gorilla that may now and then in history have knocked down a fruit with a stick did not get ahead or, more to the point, get the girl thereby.

On the other hand the use of tools is not in itself a specifically human characteristic. Chimpanzees not only use a stick to probe into termite hills but they select exactly the right length for their purpose and commonly trim it to serve. The remarkable Galápagos finch, which has also learned to pluck twigs and use them to dig grubs out of dead trees, is a warning against assuming that tool using is even the mark of higher, much less human, intelligence.

Man did not become man *because* he used tools. The critical fact seems to be that he was put in an environment in which there was decisive advantage in using tools *in a variety of different situations* rather than to solve one simple and recurring problem. The other critical fact, of course, was that *Australopithecus* was preadapted to meet that challenge. In any event his use of tools made special demand on his brain; those whose brains best met the demand tended to live and reproduce a disproportionate number of more intelligent children. Because it paid, the ancestral brain emerged rapidly until at something like human size it permitted man to graduate from the art of merely using tools to the art of manufacturing them. Across that threshold the advantages of being bright became ever more selective and the evolution of intelligence proceeded ever more rapidly. That point — when a creative momentum took hold that was to lead man increasingly into adaptation by control rather than by submission — is perhaps as good as any from our perspective to pick as the moment of human metamorphosis.

For most of his career man has been a food gatherer and hunter. Archeological evidence presently in hand suggests the emergence of genus *Homo* sometime between one million and two million years ago. When he settled down to tilling the earth and developing the culture and social organization that modern man accepts as the very essence of the human condition is a matter of dispute. The traditional dating of the invention of agriculture at the beginning of the Neolithic, 10,000 years ago, may be too late by ten or twenty thousand years. But despite all the wide uncertainties in chronology, there is no doubt that at least 90 per cent and probably nearer 99 per cent of our generic history has been spent on the prowl in the wilderness, a predator-scavenger hardly distinguishable from other wild animals in our relations to the natural system.

Yet there were some early differences whose implications might have alarmed conservationists among the more conservative of our cousin apes, had there been any. Our simian relations might have noted, for instance, that when their own populations scattered in search of food and fresh living space the emigrants tended to change biologically to adapt to new conditions: Populations lost touch with one another, and in isolation so changed forms and habit that they became separate species. They could no longer interbreed and often became physically so altered as to hardly seem like the same animal. But man was different. Like almost every mobile organism he could avoid or respond to local crowding by searching out new habitat. He dispersed probably in family hunting bands that were probably not nomadic but territorial — that is, they settled in an area big enough to supply them with game and forage and presumably defended it (or tried to) against invaders. This was normal. The unusual circumstance was that man by the middle of the Pleistocene had wandered into and settled in three continents without important biological change. He remained a single interbreeding species from arctic to tropics, from mountain slopes to valleys, on islands large and small. Geographical isolation that submits organisms to differential environmental selection normally leads to the evolution of a new species, as Darwin was one of the first to observe in the Galápagos. That did not happen to man, for one thing because he was omnivorous. With a digestive system able to handle almost anything any animal could eat except cellulose, and being clever in killing and plucking, he could make a living in almost any environment that had enough fresh water. Man moreover competed with his brain, which proved an instrument with unparalleled flexibility of response. Man could adapt to a new environmental challenge by concerting rational action to deal with it. He did not have to wait to learn genetically, permitting the new challenge to defeat those whose genetic make-up could not handle it and leave the field clear to those who could. So he could, as it were, remain himself in all manner of conditions that, but for his brain, would have forced a splintering into perhaps dozens or even hundreds of species.

Among the early agencies of human adaptation, one of the most important was man's control of fire. The critical importance of that discovery is recognized in the Prometheus myth, which makes Prometheus (the forethinker who stole the brand from the forge of Hephaestus) representative of the creative nature of man, which recognizes the first source of fire from lightning (the thunderbolts of Zeus) and finally poetically observes that control over fire is a perilous bid by humanity for divine power, the means potentially for great evil as well as great good. It is difficult to be sure when the gift of Prometheus was given. Probably it happened at different times in different places. Some men certainly have had this secret for two or more hundred thousand years. And they used it as a primitive but often exceedingly effective instrument with which to alter the environment for their own convenience and advantage.

Controlled fire enabled men to emigrate into much colder climates than they could otherwise have survived. Campfires probably helped protect man against predators, especially those that hunt at night, and perhaps they also served, then as now, as candle flames to draw social groups together. Most importantly fire aided the hunter. By setting woods or fields afire he could flush or drive animals into ambush. This he did often on grand scale with splendid early indifference to the economy of nature.

A by-product of this hunting technique — eventually recognized and deliberately practiced — was to clear forests, which divert a large amount of energy into woody growth that neither man nor the animals man feeds on can use. On the plains of Africa, if the trees are suppressed grass will grow to nourish those grazing animals that have probably always been man's preferred diet. By periodic reburnings, the regeneration of the forest can be prevented and an ecosystem steadily maintained that from man's point of view is highly productive. It is interesting to note that such "cultivation" by fire, while not equivalent to agriculture, creates for man's use systems that have something in common with farms: Both are artificially maintained intermediate stages in succession, with substantially fewer species than the forest climax they preempt. Both in short are systems deliberately simplified to channel energy into the relatively few plants and animals that man can eat or wishes to eat.

Since man knew how to control fire long before he learned how to light one, early man (like some primitives in historic times) was always more concerned with keeping the camp-fires burning than looking out for Smokey the Bear. In all likelihood deliberate fires were abundantly supplemented by accidental ones; Paleolithic man, despite small numbers, was already therefore an agent of environmental change to be reckoned with.

As grazer and predator, man like any other animal can continuously crop only the excess progeny of other populations: He is free to take for his nourishment day after day and year after year only those plants and animals that in his absence would die from other causes or not be born. If man as a newcomer into — an invader of — old environments already in equilibrium (his historically typical role) adds his kills to the deaths already occurring, and if no additional births result, he must deplete the population of whatever animal he preys on and throw the system into those feast and famine oscillations that signify instability and threaten collapse. If, on the other hand, he competes with other predators so that he shares their prey or forces them to exploit other food sources or drives them out altogether, or if by reducing the number of prey he trips the density-dependent switch that tells the prey to produce more offspring, then he will merely establish a new equilibrium state with different numbers, perhaps, and different actors.

Harvesting the wild may thus be regarded as a process by which man replaces other "natural" causes of death. (That is true, of course, only when man is living within the system and depending on it for prolonged sustenance. It is not true of market exploitation as, for instance, in the modern slaughter of whales, which treats a population of animals as a gold mine to be exhausted as quickly as possible for a one-time profit.) Human predation, however, like most things human, tends to depart from the nonhuman norm.

Wolves hunting caribou are most likely to catch the young, the halt and the blind — those least able to cope with wolves. These are also the individuals of least value to the caribou. Hence natural predation tends both to control prey populations and select the fittest for survival.

By contrast man as predator tends to be undiscriminating. Since he depends less on agility than cunning for success, he is not physically matched against his prey. The physically competent animal enjoys a smaller relative advantage over the less competent. When man hunts by ambush or fishes with a net he takes all the animals who by chance come into his trap. As a result the population he leaves alive has roughly the same mix of the fit and unfit as before and is therefore subject to the same rates of mortality from other causes. The take of human hunters that is consistent with maintaining the prey population is thus less than it would be if man were selective.

More seriously, the use of fire and the discovery that herd animals could be stampeded over cliffs to their death gave man techniques of mass slaughter that he seems never to have been reluctant to use. Some paleontologists have even suggested that man became so efficient on the hunt that he brought about the extinction of many species of animal, including the great tusked mammoths and mastodons that roamed the plains of the southwestern United States as elephants now roam in Africa. Though unlikely, the theory is at least tenable. Paleolithic man had already achieved the status of an environmental force, even though still limited and local.

There is a fashion among some biologizing observers of human history to resurrect original sin in the guise of a species birthmark (once a killer always a killer). The more pertinent observation, discussed in the last chapter, is that man, like other organisms, tends to continue patterns of response long after the environmental conditions to which the patterns were first appropriate have changed. Paleolithic man faced what was in fact from his point of view a limitless bounty. Being able to hunt and eat almost anything that moved, he could not be concerned (even if he could foresee) that a particular species might die out. If he killed a hundred horses in order to feed on two, what did it matter? The herds remained sufficient for his needs; if they got too thin to be hunted efficiently he could catch other game. As for waste, the excess carcasses left to be eaten by others were after all returned to the closed alimentary loop that is life.

So on the North American continent almost to the present people have been few and resources seemingly unlimited. To harvest wholesale in excess of need paid because it saved labor, the scarce commodity, at the expense of resources so abundant as to seem almost free. Waste had no persuasive meaning so long as supplies were obviously greater than anyone could use. Some Alaskans continue in this view and find it inconceivable that exploitation could ever so deplete their bounty of land, timber, minerals, air and water as to make a difference. "Hell," said a member of the governor's staff recently, "this country's so goddam big that even if industry ran wild, we could never wreck it. We can have our cake and eat it too."

The Paleolithic view, even if it may possibly have helped the mammoth to leave the scene too soon, was not wicked.

Nor did it threaten the human habitat. In a world of relatively scarce resources and rapidly increasing demand it has become highly inappropriate even for Alaska, which looks like a huge reserve of space and nature only if you forget the rate at which people with demands upon it increase.

# CHAPTER 11

# The Agricultural Revolution

HUNTING, SCAVENGING, grazing, browsing, collecting — taking, in short, whatever one can find in the environment — can provide man and beast with a life of relative ease and leisure. Monkeys may spend only a small part of each day foraging and eating. Lions who are good at their work need not hunt every night. In tribes of primitive men not everyone has to hunt or pick, and those who do may have more time off than a worker on an assembly line. Yet their leisure appears from the point of view of cultural development to be largely wasted. Among hunters and gatherers cultural evolution universally holds at a plateau well below the demonstrated human potential. Throughout the million or so years of the Paleolithic Age the same chipped-stone artifacts were repeated wherever man went. Commenting on this prolonged dullness, Carl Sauer wrote: "It was not his brain that held ancient man back; it was the little he had to think about for so long." To break that repetitive cycle something had to change to develop fresh environmental challenge to force man to use his leisure and talent creatively and to permit denser settlement. The first change was probably imperceptible; at least it left no record. But the new direction clearly marked at last was toward agriculture and a settled village life.

The indispensable foundation for civilization is agriculture, including the domestication of animals as well as plants. Yet the invention of agriculture, the single most revolutionary event in human history, occurred so unobtrusively with the modesty of the inevitable that no one knows where or when or how it happened and probably never will. The classic hypothesis of origin, developed most carefully by one of the greatest students of prehistory, V. Gordon Childe, set the place in the Middle East, the time as late as about 9000 B.C., and the cause essentially the inventiveness of men pressed to increase their food supply in the face of a gradual drying out of the climate.

Professor Childe supposed that a slow decrease in rainfall in North Africa in millennia preceding the first evidence of agriculture squeezed early hunting and food-gathering peoples into oases of compact settlements along streams. There, hemmed in but continuing to multiply in the usual fashion, men might have begun to exploit deliberately their first accidental or casual sowing of seed from wild cereal plants, chiefly wheat and barley. As they shared limited water supplies with other animals, the enforced close associations "might promote that sort of symbiosis between man and beast best implied in the word 'domestication.' "

An attractive and relatively simple theory, it has alas been knocked down by later scholarship. Karl Butzer and Carl Sauer, for instance, have noted that archeological evidence does not support the thesis, and both anthropology and ecology argue strongly against it. Both the facts recently established and the hypotheses they tend to support are particularly interesting for our purposes because they suggest that the most profound transformations of history may be effected by a wholly unplanned series of almost imperceptible "improvements" undertaken more often to preserve the custom-

ary ways than to change them. Man on the threshold of civilization appears not as a visionary but as a fixer whose little
repairs of convenience became irreversible and by compelling
others established a sequential pattern that looks purposeful
in retrospect but in fact was not ever designed.

Agriculture probably arose independently in several places
at different times (China, Southeast Asia, the Indus Valley,
Mesopotamia, Mesoamerica and Peru) and none of these can
be correlated with climatic change. Indications are that agriculture was introduced into North Africa from southwestern
Asia. The near certainty is that it developed in Asia among
peoples who were not pressed to sustain themselves but on the
contrary had both a surplus of food and an unusual variety.
Similar conditions prevailed in Mesoamerica when cultivation of maize and other staples arose independently there.
Professor Sauer has speculated about a much earlier agricultural beginning in Southeast Asia, also in societies of relative
ease and abundance. Nowhere does it appear that necessity
was the mother of invention. There were rather the usual
complicated processes of evolution churning up haphazard
experiments to be culled in accord with unplanned but revealed advantages or disadvantages of each.

The causes of agriculture remain elusive. (Indeed causality itself in history is an elusive concept.) What can be described are the conditions permitting and facilitating it.
There are several that are indispensable: First, people do not
plant crops unless they intend to stay around until harvest
time; agriculture can only develop among peoples who are
*already* sedentary. They must therefore have found natural
food in abundance sufficient to allow them to gather it continuously in one relatively small area. In Sauer's speculation
the rivers of Southeast Asia, teeming with fish, would have
provided an ideal situation permitting substantial numbers of

people to settle down and assuring them some leisure to try gardening.

Leisure is the second precondition, for early man could not have regarded the first transplantation of tubers or wild wheat, much less the first taming of wild cattle, as a practical way of increasing his food supply. They simply were not. Sauer thinks both may well have been done first by women bored by a life in which men monopolized the fishing and hunting. Charles Reed believes domestication began in a gradual drawing together of social species (man and dog, man and goat) who found mutual advantages in the relationship and that it was already far along before men saw the significance and took a deliberate part in the process.

The banks of a stream are by no means the only kind of habitat that would allow food-gathering man to settle down. The evidence from both Mesoamerica and Mesopotamia is that wild cereal grasses grew in sufficient abundance to provide a staple food for settled tribes. In 1963–64 archeologists in Turkey had a stone sickle made on the ancient model and set an untrained man to harvesting wild einkorn wheat. He gathered two pounds of clean grain in an hour. On that basis they estimated that a family living some 10,000 years ago where the einkorn grows might have accumulated a ton of clean grain during three weeks of harvest within easy range of its home. That would have provided basic nourishment for five people for about a year. Supplemented by hunting and other gathered foods, it is clearly more than enough to permit permanent and relatively dense settlement. Indeed one ancient city, Jericho, seems to have been supported without agriculture entirely by wild harvests of grain and fish.

Besides a settled way of life and some leisure, the evolution of agriculture required a diversity of native plants and — to look at the other side of the same requirement — a diversity of environment. This for very interesting ecological reasons. It is easy to see how tribes might pass from food gathering — rather like a daily browsing for the daily meals — to a more intensive, purposeful food collecting. The latter stage would be encouraged by uncertain climate and seasonal growth patterns that would reward intensive harvesting and storage, with the by-product, as we have seen, of at least occasional food surpluses. But what led man to the next step, cultivation? No doubt the environmental or cultural nudging differed in different climes among different peoples. Robert J. Braidwood finds that in Mesopotamia throughout the late glacial and earliest postglacial periods ending about 10,000 years ago there was a steady trend to an ever more intensive food collecting from "ever more localized environments," along with lessening dependence on big game animals and development of more specialized and composite tools. In short, settling down, localism and specialization were mutually reinforcing changes in the human exploitative system. The Mesopotamian environment rewarded these developments because in a wide variety of ecological niches it grew a wide variety of edibles, including alfalfa, wheat, barley, oats, wild capers, lentils, vetch, chickpeas, dates, almonds, pistachios, acorns, even — in the northern mountains — grapes, apples, and pears. Sheep and goats as well as gazelles and various game abounded. The range of each of these, however, was narrowly restricted by light and uneven rainfall patterns in the valleys and highlands. As human populations grew, the tribes would tend to get locked into more or less one-crop territories where perhaps they had more wheat than they needed but fewer sheep than they would like. At the same time, as they got more numerous, contacts among them would become more frequent. Kent Flannery believes primitive trade thus developed.

Man the food gatherer had known for thousands of years before he became farmer that seeds falling to the ground in late summer would sprout new plants in the spring. He did not need instruction in basic biology; he needed only a situation in which such knowledge could be useful. Now that situation arose. With seed in hand from parts more or less distant from his settled home, gathered by himself perhaps, or received in trade, why not grow it at home and save himself the trouble of a journey or the cost of barter? Braidwood believes some "manipulation" of plants and animals — preliminary domestication — actually preceded such transfers in their natural habitats. In any case it seems agreed that the critical step was transplanting. Mesoamerica with similar geographical diversity appears to have undergone a similar pattern of development.

Transplanting a seed must have seemed like a simple, natural, and not very important rearrangement of the familiar order. In the very act of transfer, however, man began, at first unconsciously, to reshape the wild plant to his use and then consciously to design a system to support it. In the wild, the most successful wheat plants are those best able to scatter their seed, and these are the plants whose rachises (the stems to which the seeds are attached) become brittle at maturity so that a gust of wind can shatter them and let the seeds separate and spread out. A man harvesting wild wheat with a stone scythe would lose a high proportion of such seed and collect mostly the grain of plants whose rachises were comparatively tough. This is the seed he would carry off to a new, more convenient ground for planting. Thus over generations selection by scythe would assure that the naturally disadvantaged genes for a tough rachis would become dominant in the artificial ecosystem. Other changes over time, adaptive to the cultivated field, also occurred naturally and were selected by man until new plants were born suited to the farmer's need and dependent on him for survival.

In the flattened perspective of the distant past, agriculture appears like a vast self-improvement project by early man — in the jargon of this day, a technological breakthrough. Man found a better way to live than by hunting or browsing; he embraced it and prospered, realizing his perennial dream. But to look more closely at the steps of the process as they probably occurred is to see that man never had any intention of changing his way of life or even his means of subsistence. Like so many changes that turn out in retrospect to have been revolutionary, domestication was at first a conservative adaptation. Tribes having specialized to exploit a particular environment struggled only to maintain themselves in that environment; it was to avoid any obviously disruptive change, like emigrating, that they found it useful to bring home some goods from abroad. They did not thereby become farmers; they continued to live primarily by hunting and collecting, as it must have seemed to them they always had.

A long way down the road was village agriculture, from which civilization took off and in a few thousand years remade the world. But the road was open. Man, who had become relatively adaptable to a wide range of habitats through his ability to eat anything and his command of fire, had now taken the next giant step: He had discovered how to adapt the environment to himself. That is the change that justifies the term "revolution," even though the actual development of systematic farming took another several millennia — about 3000 years in Mesopotamia, 5500 years in Mesoamerica. Once established in southwest Asia, village farming spread to Europe, but that needed almost another 3000 years. In North America 2000 years elapsed between the first introduction of maize from the south and the first farm communities.

These long adaptive periods to accept what in retrospect seems like such a striking and obvious boon are a reminder of the profound alterations in both natural and human systems that acceptance required. Settled village agriculture, Braidwood has said, "is probably the point in all human history at which man commences to manipulate seriously and to control the environment." But manipulation involving plant selection, experimentation with irrigation, fallowing, and manuring was a game played among the generations. At the same time, changes in the natural economy had gradually to be matched by cultural changes, so that the increasingly dense society managing the environment could learn how to manage itself. These mutual accommodations clearly must have evolved together, rapidly in evolutionary time scales, very slowly in historical ones.

Use of fire by Paleolithic hunters was a kind of environmental management. But it was only a negative intervention in the natural system, checking development short of the stage where from man's point of view it became relatively unusable, like a cabbage patch gone to seed. The farmer not only eliminates (or does his best to discourage) the forms of life he does not want because they are not tasty in themselves or because they eat what he would eat; he also introduces and defends against natural adversity those he does want. Once the farmer is on this course, the logic of the new, managed system suggests more and more deliberate manipulation to concentrate all available energy on producing edible goods and speeding it through the system as rapidly as possible. By selective breeding and other techniques the sophisticated manager can also channel artificially high proportions of the available chemical nutrients into those portions of the animal or plant that are intended for the table.

A modern hen house is a kind of parody of domestication.

Here life forms once thought of as chickens, with interesting idiosyncrasies like impulsively crossing the road, are converted as nearly as possible into mere production lines. Energy and food are force-fed through all but inert bodies to manufacture eggs, and every channel that might needlessly divert the intake to other uses is blocked off. No doubt battery laying will come to seem primitive shortly, as compared to food factories yet to be invented. But it is squarely in the evolutionary line and at this time nicely makes the point of what man as manipulator of natural systems has been up to.

Just as in cropping the wild, man can take from a domesticated system only that part of the production which is in excess of the need for replacement. Biologically he continues to function in reference to his managed systems as a substitute for other causes of death. But now he can reduce the toll from those other causes. He can, for instance, cut down the competition by weeding his fields, by fencing his herds or tending them and periodically shifting their pasturage. He can breed selectively for the most productive and hardiest stocks. He can see to it that they do not lack for food and water. He can protect them from disease and nature's other hungry creatures, whether wolves among the sheep or chinch bugs among the sorghum. By comparison with a natural system, the domesticated one has a much higher proportion of individuals that can be cropped without impairing reproductive capacity *because it has a much lower death rate from nonhuman causes.*

Domestication multiplies the death eligibles. It does so essentially by creating what in a natural system would be a gross surplus of one species. In nature that bulge would be removed in one or more of several ways — by dispersal, by predation, by disease, or by density controls internal to the population. In man's system, death is by harvest. Until the moment of harvest the farmer or herdsman must wall off his standing crop (which in nature's terms represents an arrested stage of development) against the natural forces that seek to mature it and restore the equilibrium of populations.

Man as domesticator thus has not improved the natural order; he has taken arms against it. Evolution on the geologic time scale and succession on the historic one both move, as we have seen, in the direction of multiplying species in order to occupy every viable niche in the environment. At climax, when every niche is for the time being occupied, the system is just maintaining itself. It is making good the ravages of death and emigration, but it is not producing any net growth. As a matter of fact, the bulk of the energy that flows through a mature system is used in the decomposition of dead matter. What man wants is just the opposite: a system in which the bulk of the energy flows into the production of edible material. To achieve that "unnatural" result he has to frustrate the natural processes that would otherwise frustrate him. He must check diversification, halt succession, preserve simplicity.

Farmers, who work so hard, may be forgiven an impatience with bugs or rats that come along at eating time to steal the fruits. But from nature's view the pest belongs in the system; it is man who is the alien, disturbing element. Pests are doing what the whole natural order is driven to do: fill the empty spaces of the world. Man does routinely what only natural catastrophes like flood and fire do otherwise: empty the environmental niches so that instead of sharing the bounty as one creature integrated in the community he can appropriate the whole community to his own use. From that capacity vastly to increase the food supply for people and to store it in granaries or in herds of domestic cattle have arisen the whole of civilization and many of its discontents.

# CHAPTER 12

# Country Ecology

NOWHERE DID EARLY MAN find agriculture the key to survival. He tried it only where he could afford to experiment and accepted it only as it proved to have marginal utility in his hunting-collecting economy. Man did not need agriculture when he discovered it, but the discovery soon developed a need. This is the perennial irony of human progress: the richer the achievement, the larger the dependence on it, and the more importunate the demand it engenders for more of the same. Domestication made man's environment more productive. It does not matter that at first the gain may have been so small as to have left his way of life seemingly unchanged. Man, like all other organisms, took advantage of even the smallest environmental increment by increasing his numbers. More food in a tribe's home territory meant that more people could grow up and live there; the population would be thinned a little less by death and emigration.

The net effect was thus to maintain roughly the same environmental pressure on the larger tribe that the smaller had always coped with. The same thing must have happened often throughout man's history as tribal numbers fluctuated in response to climatic change, local abundance of game, fertility of the collecting grounds, and so on. But now there was a momentous difference: Man for the first time could react to hunger by trying to increase food.

Cultivation first took place in alluvial or light wind-blown soils easily worked with sticks or stone hoes. Such soils ordinarily are wooded, and the primitive farmer's first task was to cut and burn the trees. Universally he grew his plants on the cleared ground for as many seasons as the accumulated fertility of the soil would support them. Then he moved on, cleared a new plot, and let the old ground renew itself under the ministrations of a natural community of weeds, bush, animals, and soil organisms. This method of cultivation persisted throughout history as the first step in opening new lands, and it is still widely practiced in many parts of the world today. It wears scores of local names, even in English, such as bush-fallow, slash-and-burn, shifting cultivation; the most generally accepted technical term is "swiddening," after the Old English for "a burned clearing."

Swiddening has most importantly survived in the wet tropics, where its virtues and drawbacks as an exploitative method can best be observed. Despite the lushness of nature where temperatures are high and rainfall abundant, cultivated plants do not necessarily flourish. Tropical forests often grow on very thin soils and the cycling of minerals through roots and leaves takes place at or very near the surface. With lots of energy (heat and light) the forest leaf-fall does not stay on the ground as it does in temperate-zone woods to be slowly decayed and leached into the soil. Bacteria and detritus feeders are so numerous and industrious in the heat that they break down the organic compounds in the dead matter almost as it falls, and the resulting inorganics can be taken up again at once by the trees before sinking deep into the ground. Clearly, if the trees are removed from such an environment the cycle is broken, and since the soil has virtually no stored nutrients other plants cannot live in it long.

Deeper forest soils in the tropics are better candidates for farming — but not much better. Where the soil is deep, heavy rains tend to leach out the essential minerals, leaving the top soils acid and relatively infertile. In the mature forest the leaching problem is dealt with by the presence of many leguminous trees, which can partially fix atmospheric nitrogen to replace that lost through leaching, and by trees with very deep roots capable of trapping the minerals washed many feet below the surface. In such a forest trees may be cut and other plants grown, but only for a while. Since without the trees there is a net loss of essential minerals, the system must run down. If allowed to deteriorate beyond a certain point, the soil will no longer support plant growth at all, and then, being deprived itself of organic matter (humus), it becomes ever more heavily leached until only clay remains that bakes in the sun and washes away in the rain.

Swiddening nicely adapts man's special need for vegetable crops to these natural constraints. The burning of the cleared trees was perhaps meant at first merely to dispose of the slash. But it also importantly provides potash for the soil and has been shown to enhance fertility substantially. Oddly, crops grow better when the burning is done in place than when equivalent ashes are brought in and spread on the ground.

Once the swidden is cleared, the farmer with stick or hoe plants directly, without trying to turn or harrow the soil. Ordinarily he plants a variety of edibles intermingled to make maximum use of the incident sunlight and to provide a continual supply of food from plants maturing at different dates. On Mindoro Island, the contemporary Hanunóo people, who have been studied by the anthropologist, Harold C. Conklin, cultivate more than 400 different plants, some from seeds and some from cuttings. The swiddening culture of tropical America that is known as conuco typically intersperses maze, beans, and squash. The corn grows tall, reaching up for energy by its storied leaves, while beans climb the cornstalks to share the sun, and squash plants overspread the ground. Sometimes farmers mix with these basic plantings shrub plants like cotton and manioc. The layered system makes efficient use of energy and moisture. Moreover, since the combined produce is only partially harvested at any one time, the soil always has a vegetable cover to protect it against the leaching and erosion of heavy rain. The possibility of pest infestations is much smaller than in one-crop field farming, since nowhere is there a massive or continuous stand of any one kind of pest food.

In one to four years the food crops will ordinarily have mined out the fertility of the swidden, and it must be abandoned again to the bush. Depending on conditions, it may take ten to thirty years for the forest to rebuild a store of nutrients sufficient to support another couple of years of farming. That rotation pattern means that a community of swidden farmers might require up to thirty times as much land as a community of plow farmers, even assuming an equal productivity per acre. In fact the per-acre yields from swiddens are typically far lower than from even moderately efficient permanent tillage.

It has been estimated that swidden agriculture on the average comfortably supports only about fifteen people to a square mile, though considerably higher densities may be locally or temporarily possible. That is sparse settlement, but it is significantly denser than typical hunting populations — ten times as dense or more. Thus the Neolithic dawn of agriculture marked the first of mankind's population explosions, recorded for posterity as an exuberance of death in the graves where archeologists find most of the clues to ancient life.

As the new environmental niches, greatly enlarged by agriculture, began to fill, and population once again pressed against the limits of environment, people sought various ways out, depending in part upon the state of their culture but in larger part upon where they lived. The swiddeners in the wet tropics could, and often did, try to spin the hoe-and-fallow cycle faster. That temptation has been almost unavoidable where tribes have settled adjacent territories and hemmed each other in. With migration and land annexation effectively closed, the tribes tend to come back to the old burned-over districts a few years sooner than is traditional and before their full fertility has been restored. The consequence has often been to break the system; the overused land no longer has minerals enough to support a regrowth of forest. Instead it goes irreversibly into coarse grass that has no capacity to renew the soil, or it grows no cover at all and the denuded earth washes away. In recent times considerable areas of Southeast Asia, especially in the Philippines and Indonesia, have gone probably forever out of production into Imperata grass.

The same situation, in which neighboring tribes are locked into territories insufficient to support increasing numbers, may also lead to more or less continual intertribal wars. Indeed, it has often happened that a tribe has found it easier to fight for its neighbor's swiddened land than to reclaim more from the virgin forest, even when there was plenty of virgin forest around. Whatever the morality of such behavior, biologically it can sometimes be shown to be a rational choice conserving tribal energy.

The one great civilization known to have been dependent on swidden agriculture — the Mayan — at last succumbed to overpopulation. It is not certain whether the mortal failing was exhaustion of the soils, or enforced migration from the hills into the unhealthy lowland forests of the Yucatan, or these plus other causes. The civilization's decline was marked by a period of heavy human sacrifice, ritual machinery by which it tried in vain to eliminate the suffocating human surplus and save itself.

In dry climates there were other ways out of the swidden sack swollen by too many people. Mesopotamia, the Indus Valley, Egypt, and the highlands of Mesoamerica all contained immensely fertile soils whose natural productivity was limited by lack of water. After periodic flooding they could be intensively sown to cereals. Over the millennia of their settlement the people in these regions learned to divert river water to their fields by canal and at last to construct elaborate irrigation works. This again was a slow evolutionary process, in which changes in the agricultural systems were reflected in changes in social organization and vice versa, until in watered and manured cereal plots the great pristine civilizations of the world bloomed.

Evolution, whether biological or cultural, has normally the appearance of an illusory triumph of irresistible forces over immovable objects. Creatures and societies most often seemed to be dragged backward into the future: they welcomed only those changes that seemed to assure that there would be no change. People did not give up extensive cultivation after they found how much more productive intensive, irrigated farming could be. The evidence from Mesopotamia is that throughout antiquity down to the early dynastic period, intensive agriculture remained exceptional. In Mesoamerica swiddening yielded only partially to an infield-outfield system with watering and manuring, and only in reluctant response to heavy population pressure. Similar reluctance has been observed among contemporary primitive peoples. Pierre Gourou tells of West African tribes who in flight from slavers left their native lowlands to find refuge in the mountains. There, in order to survive on limited tillable land, they had to terrace and fertilize. But once the danger passed and they went home, they returned to swiddening. Similarly, official efforts to compel peasants in Indochina before 1940 to plow and till rice paddies failed. When the pressure relaxed the people went back to their old ways.

For this conservatism there are two main reasons: In certain soil and climatic conditions swiddening may produce more per unit of labor than any other economy while doing less damage to the natural systems; secondly, intensive agriculture is always a lot more work and peasants sensibly avoid it if they can. They begin to have to take on the job only when their numbers increase. But thereafter, though they may try to hold back, they often find themselves driven on by another of those self-stoking fires in natural and social systems: If conditions permit, the response to more people is more intensive food production, and the response to more intensive food production is more people.

So it happened in what Karl Wittfogel has called the "hydraulic civilizations" to mark their central dependence on irrigated agriculture. Clearly it is no accident that the great centers of ancient civilizations were river valleys (Indus, Tigris-Euphrates and Nile) in semiarid regions. Low rainfall and abundant river water suggested artificial watering of plantations, and irrigated agriculture established preeminently the reflexive conditions necessary to induce dense population: It was extraordinarily productive per acre of ground and it correspondingly demanded (and rewarded) intensive labor.

In addition to all the chores of the rainfall farmer, the cultivator of irrigated ground must ditch and plant in furrows and keep these constantly in repair. He must terrace if the ground is not level. He must regulate the flow of water and often must lift it onto his fields by his own or animal labor from a lower source. Twentieth-century Chinese farmers, studied in one province, spent three fifths of their time on water management chores. Where the state builds and operates the irrigation works, peasants have normally been conscripted for those jobs during any part of the year they can be spared from cultivation, planting, and harvesting.

As the producers, who were also consumers, multiplied to meet the need and exploit the opportunity, density facilitated and demanded ever more intensive cultivation. More people and animals in closer confines produced more fertilizer to increase the yields to feed more people. As the irrigation systems grew in size and complexity they represented a very large investment of labor and social capital. Wherever possible it paid a farmer to increase the yield from his existing lands rather than to bring more under cultivation. So every interacting part of the system conspired toward greater density, and the whole obeyed the universal rule of the maximum, tending to cycle materials just as rapidly as the available energy would permit. No wonder there came the second of mankind's periodic population explosions. Compared to the average of 15 persons to a square mile (and maximum of 60) that can be supported year in and year out by tropical swiddening, Egypt 2000 years ago, watered by the Nile, had at least 500 and perhaps 750 inhabitants to the square mile. Contemporary densities in India and China have similarly risen on the foundation of rice paddies, for which meticulously sculptured watering systems have been created over the centuries.

Density, as we are well aware today, has profound implications for social organization and control. Wittfogel has argued that the demands of irrigated agriculture and accompanying dense populations led directly to the political system he calls oriental despotism. Only despotic rule could mobilize the labor needed for public works — impoundments and canals — and assure a productive distribution and use of water. That seems true of the end result but probably does not truly mirror the process. The evidence from Mesopotamia, for instance, is that the Sumerian civilization was well launched at a time when irrigation appears at most to have been peripheral and small scale. The truth seems to be that civilization was just as much a cause of dense population as a result and that social organization interacted with agricultural organization continuously both as the mover and the moved. In similar fashion writing and mathematics were invented to keep accounts in the state granaries, and so can be called a product of social organization; but in developing in the hands of the priestly rulers they also became a primary source and guardian of class structure, and so a cause of social organization. So, too, with astronomy, which assisted in managing the agricultural cycle and tightened the dominion of the priests. So, too, with the great works of art, which are the popular measure of great civilizations; they were both cause and effect, achievement and burden.

Civilization was no more than the tip of vast pyramids of human drudgery. As Wittfogel observed, the characteristic of hydraulic agriculture in ancient Mesopotamia, as in modern China, is that it utterly consumes the time and energies of its people in repetitious chores that permit no scope for cultural invention. The more successful the process, the greater its productivity, and the more people survive to work that much harder on dwindling acreage to feed themselves.

Where hydraulic civilizations have depended on large-scale irrigation projects there has been another trap: Because all natural water contains dissolved minerals, irrigated soils must be drained and enough water put through to flush the excess salts. If all the water applied is used up by the irrigated plants, then the burden of minerals will remain in the soil and increase with each watering until the earth is more saline than the plants can tolerate. The temptation to just this fatal parsimony has in fact proved irresistible. With the hungry competing for water to make their crops grow, managers of irrigation works have seldom been able to provide the extra needed to preserve fertility. In consquence all the great irrigation projects have ended in disaster. We have apparently not learned the lesson even now. The irrigation of the Indus plain of Pakistan in the 1950s turned hundreds of square miles into saline desert. A Harvard University team of experts recently estimated it would take 20 years and $2 billion to bring the ruined acreage back into production, a sum greater than the total spent on the irrigation project itself.

The rise and fall of the ancient hydraulic civilizations is a paradigm of man-managed systems (both biological and social) created with great ingenuity and brought to dazzling complexity but never stabilized. They played out an unclosed circuit, like Greek tragedy, from the careless beginning of a transplanted einkorn to the final catastrophic collapse of the productivity of nature that supported the whole structure. It was not, of course, inevitable in any predestined sense, nor was the end related in any simple way to the beginning. Folk wisdom notwithstanding, history offers no examples of a chain of inevitabilities hitched to the want of a nail. The point is a quite different one: The first intervention — the removal of a wheat plant to an alien habitat — disturbed a natural system that had been stabilized by a long period of evolution and adaptation. That disturbance carried with it a requirement to artificially reestablish comparably stable relationships in the revamped system. Just as adaptation takes place over time, so the management responsibility, once assumed, continues forever in time, as every compensatory adjustment requires other readjustments literally ad infinitum.

That is the critical point: The job is not done once, like throwing a bridge across a river, there to let it stand until age or accident removes it. As environmental manager, man has to stay with the new system he has launched, sensing each adaptive change and responding. Civilizations were not born doomed. They failed through our misunderstanding the essential processes at work and through consequent inattention to the compensating mechanisms needed to restrain their own excesses. It is only those excesses that, if unchecked, *inevitably* upset and destroy us.

While the most primitive farmer is aware that a plantation requires special care if it is to continue to yield food, the concept of managing the environment and the principles involved are still struggling for acceptance in sophisticated societies. Agricultural experts, as one of them recently observed, generally consider themselves good "country ecologists." They are aware, of course, that no plant is an island, that the interrelations between the plant and its environment can encourage or inhibit growth. Nevertheless it is a fact that throughout the world the development of agriculture, so crucial to man's survival, under the aegis of the best agricultural scientists is treated as a problem of biological production, not of environmental management. There *is* a difference.

Ecologist Kenneth Watt, studying the formal properties of natural systems, was among the first to point out that in managing them the best is not the same as the most. One might manage a population of fish to assure the largest possible catch, or a population of boll worms to make them scarce — the management problem is formally the same. Indeed, in the real world, managing the environment in the best interests of man usually involves simultaneous attempts to suppress populations of the undesirable while encouraging populations of the useful. The single problem is to find the tactic in any given situation that over a period of years will produce the highest yield consistent with stability of the system as a whole. How can one get the most rice out of the paddies of Southeast Asia without so multiplying the pests and pathogens as to risk disastrous crop failures?

The trick is not easy. Pursuing stability (avoidance of disaster) and productivity (the biggest possible harvest), one faces at once in opposite directions. A densely sown field of a single kind of plant generally is most efficient; a wide diversity of plants more widely scattered generally provides the greatest insurance against plaguing pests. Now it is common sense that with conflicting goals one cannot hope to reach both.

While the winning tactic may well be found in some middle ground, it is not necessarily so, and seldom can one hope to discover the best management policy by simple weighing of the advantages or disadvantages from partly or wholly conflicting alternatives. Suppose, for instance, that one could substantially reduce the incidence of bacterial blight on rice by wider spacing of plants in the paddy; then one could compare losses from disease under dense planting with losses in production from fewer plants and find a figure representing the economic difference between the alternative practices. But this would not in itself be helpful. There may be other methods of controlling disease — a different water regimen, for instance, application of chemicals, selective breeding for genetic resistance, crop rotation, and so on. Each of these choices also carries costs. Some are immediate; some are to be reckoned actuarially as long-run risks; many are difficult to define with precision or confidence. Assuming they can be defined, the gains and losses of each maneuver can be compared against the gains and losses of another. But to complicate the problem further, it is obvious that many alternative tactics can in fact be used in combination. The tremendous number of possible combinations, the complexly ramifying consequences of each, and the time lags in the system, which require that one look at it over a period of years to weigh present and prospective costs and benefits against each other — these are among the real complications of environmental management that put it effectively beyond the reach of country ecologists.

The search for techniques of environmental management goes on among ecologists, economists, and a few (regrettably few) engineers and agriculturists. They are seeking principles common to the management of living systems and trying to formulate mathematical languages capable of describing the real complexity of nature. They are looking for keys to stability, so that instead of just warning that intervention in a mature, adapted natural system is dangerous, they may be able to say precisely where the dangers lie and how they might be reduced. What applies to agriculture, applies also to dams and irrigation works, highways and subdivisions, fish and game conservation — to all those points of contact between man and other life where he is engaged in the unique and typical human activity of rearranging the world for his own profit and convenience.

# CHAPTER 13

# Home Is the City

MAN'S FIRST BID, through agriculture, to direct the course of his life instead of merely submitting to it, led directly (though by no means inevitably) to a second, still bolder step, creation of the city. The first step modified nature to make it yield more food for people; the second superimposed on nature an artificial habitat shaped by the cultural institutions it was to develop so brilliantly. Domestication asserted for the first time in the world external, deliberate control over systems that hitherto had been wholly self-regulating. The object was to drive natural processes with greater efficiency for man's purposes. The city (as an idea, if not quite as a fact) invented a new artificial system, wholly dependent on man for its continued working and wholly subservient to his needs. Though it could never exist independently, it was itself outside nature; that is to say, it was a niche man did not find but developed. As such it is the ultimate (so far) expression of man's nonconformity as a biological species and the supreme test of man's capacity to manage his environment successfully.

So different in kind was the city from any habitat known before and so momentous were its consequences that V. Gordon Childe speaks of the "urban revolution," though the coming of cities had none of the suddenness of revolution, nor did it mark in any immediate sense a rejection of or turning aside from the cultural stages that preceded it. How did it happen? As with most of man's earthshaking steps, as heedlessly as he began to walk by successively putting one foot in front of the other.

Lewis Mumford has insisted that before there could be any physical city there had to be a disposition toward the kind of life that cities support and develop. He speculates that such a disposition may be found in early and primitive man's communal burial grounds; even while the living were forced continually to be on the move in pursuit of food, the dead could enjoy the permanence and spectral sociability of necropolis. Moreover, communities of the dead could serve as periodic ceremonial meeting places for the living. Mumford calls these nodes of pilgrimage the "first germ of the city," and sees their significance as concentrating "certain 'spiritual' or supernatural powers of the family or clan."

There can be no hard archeological evidence for or against that hypothesis. That the first cities depended on — could not have existed without — a sense of spiritual community and faith in spiritual powers is abundantly testified. That they also had certain cultural and economic preconditions is also clear. Indeed, as the most primitive city imaginable is already a highly complex organization of people and resources, it cannot be thought to have come into existence by the operations of a single cause or even a single predominating influence. What must have happened is what happens of necessity in the evolution of all systems, whether biological or cultural: Accidental or locally adaptive changes (often quite small) set up reverberations in the system, causing other changes that in turn require further adjustments as the disturbed system probes for a new equilibrium. Because cities have had revolutionary consequences, it seems reasonable to imagine that a revolution really occurred and to ask how and when. In fact they probably came to be and to evolve as innocent of their own significance or directions as are natural systems.

As with all products of evolution, it is impossible to define a city in such a way that the definition will embrace all phenomena everyone agrees are clearly urban and neatly exclude all others. But cities do have certain characteristics that most share and that most nonurban settlements lack. Childe named ten that could be verified archeologically: (1) a dense and extensive population; (2) specialization of labor; (3) concentration of wealth; (4) public buildings; (5) a definable class structure; (6) writing; (7) science (normally astronomical and mathematical); (8) great art styles (as distinct from style viewed merely as a way of doing things, which of course characterizes all cultures); (9) long-distance trade; and (10) political structure of a state. These are strikingly the qualities as well as preconditions of civilization, and equally strikingly, they are found not at all or only in most rudimentary form in the primitive village.

If one were to try to bring these ten qualities into being by an orderly evolutionary process, where would one begin? That is the question that sets off a search for prime causes. What seems like the most plausible first cause is Professor Childe's point number one. Cities are impossible without a dense and extensive population (dense because there must be people enough to aggregate within a small area, and extensive because the resulting concentration requires food from a wide region); population moreover can grow seemingly spontaneously, that is, without an external impulse. In fact, however, the evidence of history is that the development of dense and extensive populations in the early centers of civilization

(Mesopotamia, China, India, the Middle East, Mesoamerica) followed — it did not precede — the establishment of cities. There seems to have been no gradual population increase putting unbearable pressure on the village economy and literally squeezing people into larger agglomerations that in time became cities. On the contrary, in Mesopotamia, for instance, village agriculture lasted in stable form for at least 2500 years before the first city, with no evidence of crowding.

The other urban traits listed could emerge only after the city existed. All, moreover, are so interdependent that one could hardly exist without the others. A concentration of wealth, which is dependent on class structure, is meaningless without specialization of labor, for which it is a precondition, and specialization of labor is in turn a precondition of class structure. And so the interweavings of urban institutions can be traced out in baffling permutations, until at the end of analysis looms the paradox that a city could only have been invented after it existed, or that the causes of urbanism are the results of urbanism. That paradox is real: What it says is that while we must talk about one aspect of urban development at a time, that is not how development occurred. The mix of causal and feedback relations among all the changes leading to the mature city are so complex that it makes no sense to try to disentangle priorities.

More rewarding is the examination of the city fully emergent to see in what ways it prepared a new life and new problems for people, as compared with settled village agriculture, which preceded it. Villages typically are clusterings of houses, each with supporting arable land variously plotted to make tight or loose aggregations. In all villages each household has its own food industry in field or flock. By contrast, the houses of a city themselves cover the productive land to a density in the center that precludes productive use. People obviously would not elect to live so close together if it meant that they had to go far afield each day to get their food. Even a very small city is viable only if its inhabitants are being fed by others who live outside. In fact the very form of preindustrial cities reflects the decreasing self-sufficiency of its people as one moves in from the periphery to the core.

At the center, culturally if not always geographically, was the temple. (No evidence has yet been found of religious structures in the great cities of Harappa and Mohenjo-Daro in the Indus Valley. But if in fact these cities had no temples, they appear the only significant exception to the rule.) Its function was nuclear — to hold the urban system together spiritually, politically, and economically, and it in turn subsisted entirely on tribute. Encircling the temple were the dwellings of the priests, princes and bureaucrats, nonproducers all. Then concentrically the homes and shops of the poor, the artisans and, in the outermost ring, the partly urbanized peasantry who continued themselves to subsist on agriculture and to trade or yield to the tax collector some of the surplus needed to support the citizens. This is of course a generalized picture of the ancient city, to which none exactly conformed. Yet the pattern, represented in Sumer and Mesoamerica, worlds and eons apart, is sufficiently common to suggest it inheres in the nature of cities.

To ask perhaps the simplest of all questions of the urban system (how and why do the nonproducers get fed?) is to come again upon one of those complexes of interacting factors in which causes are effects and vice versa. People who do not get their own food can exist only when those who do produce food collect more than they use. But while a food surplus is indispensable to urbanization, it is not enough in itself. The individual surpluses have to be aggregated as deployable wealth and systematically distributed to the nonproducers. Already that implies a central power — a rudimentary state. From the fact that cities appear to have grown out of ceremonial centers one may infer (as Lewis Mumford does) a primordial aspiration toward civic life reflecting a vision of "a better life, more meaningful as well as esthetically enchanting." The more immediate significance is the need for a power to organize and operate the urban system. The first temples, which were also granaries, markets and municipal headquarters, were operated by priests deputizing for a god-king, in all likelihood because religious feelings of awe and terror were indispensable sanctions to make the revolutionary new institutions of a city work.

Each of the early Sumerian cities was ruled by a king who was also god and priest. The local god-king owned land on which his subjects were forced to work a part of the time. The temple could also levy taxes or tribute further to squeeze the peasantry down to a subsistence level in order to monopolize their surplus. The process of course also normally increased net production and accrued social capital not merely at the expense of the peasant but by making him work harder. (People who can neither store food in large quantity nor exchange it for other goods will rationally choose to labor only long enough to feed themselves and that — as may be seen in many a tropical paradise today — may be a day's work well below what an efficiency expert or a New Englander would recommend.)

The god-king provided a central granary in which to store the social capital. He could expend this not only to feed himself and his attendant priests but to sustain the city's specialized laborers who made pots and jewels, swords and crowns, temples and mausoleums for the glory of the god and the profit of the king. To maintain his granary and assure that revenues due him were collected and expenditures were constrained within the limits of prudence, the god-king needed to keep records. So was writing invented and so is writing properly listed as among the marks of a true city. Without it the temple administration would break down, and without administration the city itself must disintegrate.

The city's nonproducers of food got fed by organizing and controlling power. But why should the producers have put up with a system that made them work harder, robbed them of the fruits of that extra toil, and seriously limited their personal freedom? Because essentially, as Robert Adams among others has observed, they got a measure of security in return. Archeologists have found in both Mesopotamia and Mesoamerica evidence of frequent climatic extremes, particularly droughts and floods. Many of the early gods were identified with generative powers in nature: grain, sheep, flocks, asses, and rain. Worship of these gods could have supplied early man with the illusion of control over nature. Perhaps more importantly, propitiatory offerings to the gods in good times could accumulate food that in times of disaster might be partially distributed to keep the city alive until another harvest.

The god-king's power to preserve in this case was of course also the power to destroy. His control over the agricultural surplus was literally a power of life and death. The power, moreover, tended to be despotic, if only because the surpluses initially could support only a very small ruling class, which for survival had to act in concert as agents of a single tutelary spirit. Mumford speaks of the ruler's exactions as an "artificial creation of scarcity in the midst of abundance," and calls it "one of the first characteristic triumphs . . . of civilized exploitation." More interesting is the fact that expropriation and redistribution were instruments of environmental management. They served to maintain stability in the new artificial urban system, which could no longer look for stability to biological controls. From the point of view of the human community (though not necessarily of every member) the new controls were much to be preferred to the old. Instead of responding to ups and downs in the food supply by corresponding changes in their own numbers (chiefly in practice by selective death or migration), city dwellers had found a way of managing supply. It was not of course perfect. For one thing, the control mechanism was operated by people who did not think of themselves as ecological flywheels serving the collective interest of the community. They behaved more as if their power existed to reward their cleverness and gratify their greed. In so acting they exacted considerable injustice and hardship as a price of stability.

As cities prospered, the rich normally grew disproportionately richer. When they were conspicuously rich, the city's concentrated wealth became a suitable object of war, tempting alien god-kings to conquest. In fact, cities were not long in being before they began to be agglomerated by force into larger states. One may regard that process too as a search for a new equilibrium at a higher level of accumulation, requiring a higher level of political organization, permitting an increase in the size of the ruling class, and providing opportunities for increased production and exploitation.

No human society has been found in which there is not some usual and traditional division of labor, even if only between men and women. But in most primitive societies the differences between the cultural functioning of their members are small and generally nonessential. Every man can kill an animal, skin and roast it, build a shelter, scoop out a canoe, chip a stone, manufacture a fishhook, plant a taro, cultivate a paddy, grind the grain. Some members may at times or even by custom do more of one job than of another, but all are omnicompetent. Each can do for himself all that is needed for survival.

That is not to say that each is wholly self-sufficient. Even without specialization, each may greatly depend on his family and neighbors and on the coherence of the group. Man has always prospered in the bosom of a certain cooperating social mass that compensated for the vulnerable nakedness of one. Social mass, moreover, has not been just a physical multiplier of force against adversity, associating soldiers in a company; it has been the vessel for the development and transmission of culture. Nevertheless, in a relatively unspecialized society the ties binding the whole together can be relatively unspecific: a sense of kinship, a willingness to suspend hostilities within the group, an overall perception of advantage in numbers. No elaborate structure is needed to federate jacks-of-all-trades.

To exploit special skills systematically, people had to live settled lives in communities dense enough to offer a market for those skills. On the continuum of human settlement from hunting camp to metropolis, it is impossible to pick any point where it can be said that here the revolutionary change involved in division of labor occurred. In full-blown and institutionalized form, however, specialization of labor is the mark of the city and exists nowhere else. A city does not make specialization possible; it makes nonspecialization impossible. A peasant village may support a blacksmith whose skills are special and not universally shared, but the blacksmith is normally also a peasant and has his own land that he works or helps to work; were he to lose his trade, he could still support himself; were he to depart, the villagers could somehow shoe their own horses.

Cities support exclusive specialists because they are larger than villages; they are larger than villages in part because they support specialists. Indeed a city can best be defined by its function in establishing cooperative relationships among people of different occupations in such way that all can share each other's production. The most rudimentary kind of division of labor implies exchange; a city is an arrangement physically and culturally to facilitate exchange.

If residents of the city are to get shoes, and the shoemakers are to get food and other necessaries in return, all must be close enough together for the transactions to be made as often as needed by whatever means of travel are available. The size of a city is thus set in tension between the push for increasing specialization — capable of exploiting to the utmost the skills, resources and energies at hand — and the pull on physical communication required to keep the system functioning as a system. Through most of history travel within cities has been by foot, and the limits on city growth have been severe and absolute. Medieval towns extended no more than half a mile in any direction from the center. The historic mile in Edinburgh, Lewis Mumford has observed, measures the ancient city, connecting the extremes of Edinburgh Castle and Holyrood Abbey. Like the skin of a body, the great medieval walls held the city together and kept it intact within the generally anarchic space of the country. But the wall only confessed the fact that the city could be just so big while subsisting on the available supplies of food and water and permitting its citizens to deal daily with each other. Since each urban cell had thus innate constraints on growth, urbanizing before the industrial age was generally a process of multiplying cells. These might be assembled then by a larger imperium, or alternately (as in the case of Rome) they might be sown by the central power.

# CHAPTER 14

# The City Means Business

THE SIZE OF CITIES, though it has "organic" significance, has been imposed by technology. With wheels instead of feet, with more efficient production of food and better means of supplying water and handling wastes, the ancient and medieval city, dependent on personal contacts among all citizens, could, and did, burst its bounds. This happened in different ways in different cities over many centuries, but incomparably the most important and drastic change came with industrialization. The full-blown industrial city has radically different dimensions, a different shape and a different ethos.

From the beginning, cities were systems that greatly increased the net wealth available for human use. From that point of view they could always have been seen as essentially economic systems. But, in fact, they were not so viewed in ancient times. With the temple or the medieval church at their center they appeared as aggregations of buffeted mortals under the protection of god, however defined or exploited. In walled entities they materialized as nodes not only of comparative security but of comparative order. As political capitals they focused society and its aspirations, expressing these in often splendid public buildings and public displays. The economic base was the essential support for the life cities made possible rather than their perceived reason for being. By the seventeenth century in Europe that scale of values was shifting, perhaps because of the increasing dominance of the merchant classes.

Industrialization completed the shift. Cities in the nineteenth century were delivered over to the exploitive passions of the age and they began to be reshaped as places of business in what Jean Gottman has called a "transactional civilization." The fact that people lived in cities came to seem incidental to the fact that they worked there, and it was not long before the city itself was a kind of sweatshop for millions of its inhabitants. The functioning of the city could be described almost wholly in terms of problems. A city, I have said earlier, is an arrangement that can physically and culturally facilitate exchanges of all kinds among people, not least the exchanges of friendship among like spirits who, but for the magnetic focus of cities, would be widely scattered. Once the exchange of goods and services and production of wealth took precedence over all other kinds of human relationships, the physical and social patterns of the city rearranged themselves to reflect and promote the new priorities.

For the city the fact that industry moved work out of the home had far-ranging consequences. Industry collected the economic portions of men's lives, sorted and shaped those pieces to fit specialized niches, and concentrated them geographically. One momentous consequence was that people had to move about to reassemble their dispersed lives. Cities came to be divided for the first time into work districts and residential districts. While the work districts drew to themselves satellite economic services, they preempted living quarters and made living conditions ever less attractive. Those who could afford to moved away, and those who could afford most moved farthest away. The city was remade in a wholly new shape to new functions.

The core of the preindustrial city had been the temple and its associated public buildings and public gathering places, including the market, all related to the governance of the city and its tutelary spirit. That was replaced by the central business district, so ubiquitous and gray that planners know it by its initials, CBD. It does not house the city's government, now in America often isolated in a civic center that is not at the center of anything — like a piety whose ancient purpose has been forgotten. CBD contains instead the headquarters of the largest businesses, whose central importance is in no doubt: department stores and specialty shops, hotels, banks, wherein reside the tutelary spirits of finance, and the principal entertainments — theaters, museums, and specialty restaurants. In the preindustrial city priests and bureaucrats lived in or near the city center because their role was not just to do city business but to preside over it. The CBD normally offers few places to live and spreads blight around it. An inner ring of wholesalers is enclosed by a ring of slums that shades outward into middle-income housing. At the farthest circumference are the upper-income uptowns and suburbs.

So the industrial city has turned its predecessor inside out, just as it upended earlier priorities. First cities were essentially evolved systems of culture based upon the material wealth that they made it possible to amass. Their nuclei were therefore the highest concentrations of that wealth in the most splendid possible forms, whether pyramids or Gothic cathedrals or royal palaces. Tradesmen and artisans serving this central splendor and the enslaved or semi-enslaved peasantry whose labor and stomachs were squeezed to support it occupied the tributary positions on the peripheries. But when the game was changed, when the amassing of material wealth limited by the capacity of the ruling classes for conspicuous consumption gave way to the pursuit of money (called by Aquinas "artificial wealth" because he saw it as having no natural limits), the city tended to evolve into a transactional convenience. Its core no longer expressed its achievement but only its daily preoccupations. Its traditional shell, moreover — the ring of services and productive land that described the limits of viability — was smashed forever. For the industrial city the only apparent constraint on expansion so far has been the efficiency of commuting between shop or office and home.

In America the street railway in the middle of the nineteenth century began an accelerating series of improvements in transport. Cities responded by growing concentrically out from their older neighborhoods commonly blighted by industrial and commercial use and by overcrowding of the rural immigrants drawn to jobs there. Because people generally stayed in these decaying inner-city quarters only if they had to and moved as far away as incomes or job ties permitted, the industrial city in expanding tended to curdle in economically segregated clumps. Typically the white-collar workers pushed just over the peripheries of the inner slums, but the well-to-do, seeking exclusiveness as well as amenity, have successively leaped over the straggling growing edges of the city to plant new colonies. In time these have often been swallowed in the urban advance. Thereafter they have sometimes endured as precarious elitist enclaves; more often they have declined, changing hands down the economic scale like used cars.

If one extends the typical lines of urban development, most appear to predict a future not far off in which most people will live in cities, but most cities will not be cities at all in the traditional sense. Demographer Kingsley Davis figures that already 38 per cent of the people of the world live in urban places, more than one fifth in cities of over 100,000 population. At present rates of change it will take only 16 years, he estimates, before half the world is urbanized, and only 55 years theoretically before we all are. No doubt long before that threatens, the rates of urbanization will slow. At some not-too-distant time, migration into the city from the country — the principal source of urban growth in the past — must cease. Since urban birthrates are typically lower than rural, cities may at some point decline relatively. For the moment, however, the city exerts an apparently irresistible attraction worldwide, as notable in Africa as in the United States. For the U.S., the projected city population by the end of the century is 255 million out of a total of 310 million.

Urbanization used to be broadly describable as a process of concentrating more and more people in increasingly dense clusters. Today it is more complicated and more ambiguous. While metropolises expand, core cities shrink; but while core cities shrink, densities in certain districts within those cities sometimes increase.

In the United States the central business districts and the inner slum areas generally have been thinning out. Manhattan's CBD has only one half or less the population now that it had at the beginning of the century; people have moved out and business has engrossed the available land. In addition, slums have here and there been losing people by an interesting aging process. Manhattan's Lower East Side, for instance, in the years around the turn of the century was a prime reception area for young immigrants with big and growing families. The East Side grew from 339,000 in 1890 to 532,000 in 1910. Then in the course of a generation, as is biologically fitting, the children grew up and mostly moved away. The parents, with the conservatism of the once uprooted, mostly stayed, occupying with two the same quarters that may once have housed a dozen. Between 1910 and 1930 the East Side's population fell to 250,000.

Flight to the suburbs is not new; it has long been an option of the wealthy. But as with so many modern phenomena, the sheer mass of the contemporary movement has made it a new force. The greatly extended range of commuting, moreover, has new implications for the hitherto safely rural lands that are being invaded.

In the first thirty years of this century the American city's growing points were at its edges, not its center — already a process of suburbanization. Since 1930 the automobile and improved highways have pushed the process dramatically outward, creating the newly recognized phenomenon of urban sprawl. Mass-built bedroom towns, beginning with the first Levittown in 1947, have speeded the process.

"New sprawl" is not just "old suburb" writ sloppy. For instance, the new urbanizing, unlike the old, is engrossing prime farm lands. California, one of our greatest agricultural states, is losing crop land to subdivisions so fast it will soon become a net importer of food. The expanding city, typically reaching thinly out along interurban highways, now regularly meets and merges with neighboring cities and then with neighboring metropolises in the specifically modern phenomenon that planners call conurbation (or, following Jean Gottman, "megalopolis"). Esthetically and socially formless, these urban streams flow around and through older settlements, evolving in time political and cultural overlays that most observers characterize bluntly as chaos, though some see as shaping new patterns. These new conurbations at least now lack the organic unity of functioning communities and are even less able than central cities to associate people in humanly productive relationships.

Most urban prophets see the future as belonging to the metropolis: the city as a well-defined cultural nucleus, they think, is already on the way out. And yet there are strong centrifugal forces also at work. If a city, as noted, is essentially a system that facilitates personal contacts, it will continue to exercise attractions so long as those contacts remain important.

One significant sign of life is the continuing plantation of skyscrapers in central business districts. Jean Gottman has argued that the skyscraper retains its popularity, continues its push skyward and its spread worldwide, even to cities that have no barriers to horizontal growth, because it admirably serves the needs of economic bureaucracies. He observes that insurance companies, "whose business is entirely bureaucratic," were among the first to build high. The vertical housing of bureaucracy fits its internal layering and its needs for rapid intercommunications (elevators get you there a lot faster than taxis). Business bureaucracy is growing at least apace with public bureaucracy and probably faster, since it is relatively better financed. Galbraith among others has described the multiple processes of agglomeration in the modern economy that result in increasingly large and complex management structures. Great economic polities require their private city halls to aggregate large numbers of people in relatively intimate contact. Some business headquarters, it is true, have found it expedient to escape the congestion of central cities and follow their executives into the suburbs. More stay put and the construction of new office space in Manhattan, for instance, shows no sign of slackening. One reason, suggested by Edgar Hoover and Raymond Vernon in their study of New York, is that the managerial elite, having multiple and free-ranging responsibilities, never know from one day to the next what their problems are going to be; they are therefore better off in close proximity to the widest possible variety of political, legal, financial, and technical services. In that light the established city has insuperable advantages over any new center.

It is true, as Gottman observed, that the concentration of offices in skyscrapers may mean centripetal dispersion of residences, since the tall buildings so increase the square-foot value of the land and so overbear its amenities for living that few can or want to live in their presence. Yet in recent years a number of one building live-and-work centers have arisen: the John Hancock Tower and Marina City in Chicago, both of which contain offices, parking spaces, and apartments. The Fox Plaza Building in San Francisco combines apartments, offices, and a shopping center. The Prudential Center in Boston adds to these a hotel.

Besides the arguments of economic convenience, there is reason to think the central city has retained its unique cultural significance and will continue to do so despite its currently staggering disabilities. The mass of a city is needed to support its variety, to provide a sufficient market for theater, music, art, crafted goods, and special services. So long as people value that variety — which is to say so long as they are interested in exploring the full range of human experience — they will not abandon the city, if it continues to be possible to live there.

CHAPTER 15

# Are Slums Necessary?

BECAUSE A CITY associates specialists who literally cannot get along without each other, cities are not just places to live and work; they themselves have to live and work and evolve in response to changing purpose. In this regard cities have had rare and transient success. They have been as distinguished in history for horrendous (and remarkably repetitive) human problems as for cultural triumphs. Traffic, water supply, waste disposal, slums, crime, epidemic disease — these are the perennials on urban sick lists, and except for the last they seem today about as resistant to rational treatment as ever.

Since the city consumes in part what it does not produce and produces in part what it does not consume, it must import, circulate, and export to exist. Nature knows no such system geographically separating production and consumption, and cannot. Though these facts are elementary and obvious, some implications are less so: Because the urban system is artificial, it can work only under constant management, and whenever that management falters the city tends to revert to nature. In ecological terms the multiplication of disease organisms in filth or of rats in garbage is a step toward putting together the divided production-consumption cycle. A second implication of the city's artificiality is that it must not only be managed to work at all; it must be deliberately controlled to work within limits of stability.

In natural communities, plants and animals evolve sensitivities to their own requirements for space and to the competitive and cooperative relationships with other members of the community that will enable as many as possible to survive. Communities that have achieved such adaptations tend to be stable: they resist automatically take-over bids by, say, rabbits or eagles, mulberries or silk worms, provided, of course, that environment itself does not dramatically change. The city, not being a "natural" system, has no such natural controls.

Automobiles, for instance, might be regarded as competitively preying on the city's streets. As every city man knows, motorists have no innate sense of space needs nor any competitive forbearance. Cars pour onto the streets until the streets can no longer hold them. That is analogous to the multiplication of predators to the point where they have exterminated their prey. The ideal is an equilibrium between numbers of cars and space to move, at the point where as many motorists as possible share the benefits of mobility. Growth beyond that point consumes the benefit, and what is shared is frustration.

This result is not at all surprising, though it seems often to be wondered at. There is a mind set that cannot escape the delusion of the balance sheet, that regards traffic management (or city management for that matter) as a search for enduring equivalences between demand and supply: so many cars, so much road space; so much garbage, so many dumps. The trouble with that approach is that there are in fact no givens; demand changes with supply and vice versa.

One of Julius Caesar's first decrees on taking power in Rome was to require that goods be brought into the city only at night, in order to reduce congestion in the narrow streets by day. Today the streets of the world's great cities are almost equally impassable, whether jammed with ox carts and pedestrians as in Delhi, or taxis, buses, and automobiles in London or New York. Rush-hour traffic was described as the number-one problem of big American cities as far back as 1905. It has made no difference whether streets were narrow or broad, straight or crooked, mud or paved; their two-thousand-year lot has been to suffer more traffic than they could bear: This will continue until artificially we can impose that natural kind of control that holds demand below the limits of supply, instead of pressing supply ever upward.

Wastes — another of the urban problems that arise because the city is an artificial and open-ended system — have not been handled any more expeditiously. It is one of the remarkable facts of human history and a puzzling commentary on human nature that people in cities have normally lived amid their own excrement and literally buried their civilizations beneath it. In site after site archeologists have shown that the ancient method of disposing of garbage in a city was to throw it into the streets. Excavations of Ur show continually rising street levels and houses remodeled with raised front entrances as the old got buried. An accepted measure of urban development in Mesoamerica is the amount of refuse on site. In some cases man's dirty habits — which, so far as we know, we share with no other animal — had one partial corrective built in: the putrefying mess together with generally inadequate and contaminated water supplies led to frequent epidemics and fires; the former reduced the population of garbage makers temporarily, while the latter cleaned up the nuisance also, alas, temporarily.

Sewering and trash collection have reduced fires, improved health, enabled cities to grow larger and possibly last longer. But litter and filth remain a condition of cities, especially where the poor live, a disgraceful stigma on our civilization and one more reminder that the management of urban systems is an exacting job and we don't stick with it. In fact it is only in the past few years that science and officialdom have agreed that the generation and disposal of waste is a problem in systems management and will remain intractable until we can make the system work. In Boston recently, social scientists, designers, engineers, and community leaders took the first systematic look ever — so far as I know — at how people, both householders and sanitation men, actually handle wastes, how they perceive them in the environment, how cleanliness can be affected by the spaces within which people try to manage their lives and by the equipment that may assist or handicap them. The revolutionary assumption behind the study was that people are not necessarily careless or swinish; they may just be ill served by the forms in which their lives are set.

Congestion, dirt, dilapidation, human deprivation and misery — these are at the heart of every contemporary city. It is the fashion among the liberal middle classes to point with shame and to call periodically for drastic public action which, however, must always be postponed until the "government" can reorder its priorities, get out of war, and divert tax revenues to the domestic front. The sense of shame is possibly genuine; it is certainly called for. But it is too easy. The society appears to accuse itself of negligence; the more serious indictment is of malfunction, supported by the fortunate majority who benefit from the inequities and are protected relatively against the consequences. Slums are that part of every city where the city's failure as a viable system is most obvious and where the consequences of that failure concentrate as a charge on the poor.

To the extent that the city continues to be regarded as essentially an economic mechanism — a large firm whose primary function is to produce and distribute goods and services — and so long as this firm is left to respond to the requirements of the market, slums are not only inevitable but necessary. Regarding the city historically as concentrating people through time, its core is both the strongest attractive force and the oldest; the city both draws in and grows out. Congestion at the core makes space increasingly rare and valuable (and this is true, incidentally, irrespective of the economic system, whether the land is being traded for money or managed for use of the elite). But being valuable does not automatically insure it against decay; capital must be deliberately and continually invested to maintain it. That will normally be done when the core is occupied by the elite, as in the preindustrial city; it will not normally be done when business takes over, because at some point the land is too high priced and the congestion too severe in relation to the economic benefits. Capital then will yield higher returns in new construction outside the core than in rehabilitating the aging buildings within. And so the old places come to be successively occupied by users whose demands are less exacting and whose incentive or capacity to maintain them is almost nil.

So far America's only serious answer has been to reach for the wrecking ball. We have regarded slums as a nuisance to be literally wiped out so that a new beginning could be made. The new beginning has been old folly repeated and even improved upon: nice new public housing, esthetically antiseptic, designed with no concern for the way people want to live and set aside like plots in a cemetery for the perpetually deprived. Since the basic economic forces that made the slum in the first place remain in full sway, the processes of decay begin again at once. This time around, moreover, there are not even any human attachments or traditions or community

spirit to resist them. It is as though society had set for itself
the problem of getting rid of eyesores rather than the real
problem of making the city work. Slum clearance is not addressed to correcting the system, but only to sweeping up now
and then its accumulated blunders. Even if done on a scale
and pace to match deterioration, urban renewal would remain irrelevant.

Here and there, run-down neighborhoods have been reha-
bilitated, sometimes by the wealthy on their own in search of
something solid, old and different, sometimes with government subsidies under various urban improvement programs.
The net social effect of the rehabilitation has been to remove
old housing from the reach of the poor, and the total physical
effect on the face of cities has been so spotty and small as to be
negligible. The truth is that the economic forces resisting the
channeling of capital into urban cores are so powerful that
only determined and massive efforts at reversal could make a
difference. If you look at national, state, and municipal
budgets you know that such efforts are not going to come soon
(or probably ever) in the form of multi-billion-dollar public
expenditures. So far the record of public housing programs
parallels the record of all public maintenance: It stays consistently below the level needed even to keep up with current
deterioration, much less begin improvement.

Will nothing therefore happen? On the contrary. The
deadliest of laissez-faire delusions is that society may elect at
its fiscal convenience to repair or ignore its ailing systems. If
free-market forces tend rather to enlarge slums than to reha-
bilitate them, and if the public purse will not stretch to do
the job at taxpayers' expense, then we must somehow think of
other ways to turn the tide, for no society can long endure
processes that produce inevitable physical rot with accompanying social disorganization and human misery.

Lewis Mumford pointed out that "the city from the beginning of the nineteenth century on, was treated not as a public institution, but a private commercial venture to be carved up in any fashion that might increase the turnover and further the rise in land values." It has paid certain inner-city businesses to neglect their property and at some breaking point sell out and move. It pays slum landlords to promote congestion and forgo maintenance. It pays certain landlords to allow buildings to decay and be deserted while people cannot find places to live. It pays others to move people ruthlessly out if the land can yield a higher return in other use. It pays new industry that draws an increasing proportion of its labor from the white-collar classes to locate in the suburbs away from congestion and high-cost land and give another kick to the inner-city spiral of joblessness and decay.

The important fact to note is that slums are not created by poverty but by affluence; they grow in response to profit calculations on a number of rich men's ledgers. To say that is not to raise a red flag or deplore the profit system. It is simply to observe that the private real-estate market geared to making money out of property does not automatically produce communities that best serve the needs of the people who live in them. So far we have tried to medicate the slum as a disease of poverty. As a spawn of wealth and the quest for wealth, it has a quite different look and suggests quite different lines of attack.

The most promising of Great Society programs aimed at improving the lot of the urban underprivileged have been grounded in community organization and action. The underlying principle is that individuals may improve themselves as they improve their environment, and as they improve their environment they improve themselves. Product of private greed, the slum is a social environment and has

to be dealt with by social action. The physical setting —
the crumbling, crowded, dirty, rat-infested buildings; the
dirty and dangerous streets; the garbage-covered back yards
— these shape and are shaped by those who live in them.
It is logically absurd and tragically inhuman to deliver the
physical basis of people's lives to the mercy of the market,
manipulated by people who don't even live there and care
nothing at all about the values of those who do. I will perhaps be accused of being soft-headed in challenging rational
operations of the market in the name of sentiment. But I am
not at all sure that this particular hard-headed emperor has
any clothes on.

Consider the reversal of rational human values implied in
the following conclusion to a distinguished economist's analysis of the "urban problem." "The final concern must be with
the health and safety of the city's residents. In arguing for an
optimum degree of congestion and intensive use of streets as
well as the rest of the urban land, with the optimum measured in terms of efficient performance of the city's economic
function, we must not neglect the noise, noxious exhaust
fumes and dangers to pedestrians posed by the motor vehicle.
Any measure of the most efficient economic use of land for
streets must take into account human resources and the desire
for pleasant, safe, and healthy living conditions." The health
and happiness of people are "finally" to be reckoned, but only
after "efficient performance of the city's economic function"
is assured.

Various efforts by inner-city communities to assert communal interests in the management of their lives, including their
homes and places of work, have struck some sparks of life in
the generally dreary patterns of public assistance. But community action opposes the prevailing patterns of urban life as
well as the dominant economic philosophy. We are quite
willing that people should get together to deal with common

problems. Indeed groupism is nearly as much a touchstone of success now as personal ambition used to be in our fathers' day. But typically the kind admired is the committee form by which individual interests are temporarily pooled in order to buttress them all with consensus. A committee is in search of that consonance found where individual interests overlap; its product is a least common denominator distilled out of variety. But community is something else. It is the perception of common interests different from the separate interests of persons — interests arising out of the facts of association. Our society, dedicated economically to the proposition that the welfare of all is but the sum of the welfare of each, traditionally resists that notion of community, indeed finds it subversive. Nowhere is the resistance stronger than in the city, which tends to break down even the kinship groups through which man anciently has found his basic social expression. And so community action and community control must somehow associate in a common cause people who for the most part do not feel they have a common cause, except sporadically in defense against a hostile outside world.

What are needed, therefore, are measures to define the common cause, make it visible, tangible, substantial. For instance, inner-city property might well be owned and managed by community corporations financed by publicly guaranteed bonds and assisted by the powers of taxation and eminent domain. Surely if there is a physical basis for community — and to assert that is the whole point of the environmental movement — then the community must somehow control it. If that principle were accepted, scores of workable mechanisms might emerge from the currently visionary scrap heap.

Slums are where the malfunctioning urban system most tragically precipitates its evil consequences on those least able to bear them. But slums are not the city, as sometimes our obsession with the city as problem has made them appear. The city in the Western world is preeminently the human habitat today; if the graphmakers are right, cities will soon be the environment of most human beings everywhere. It is already late in the day to be questioning the outmoded model of the city as essentially a business firm and to be asserting the obvious: that it is a place for people to live and the choice before us is simply whether it shall be a good or bad place to live. Nor can we escape that determination by wishing it were not so and dreaming of new towns or garden cities whose problems by exquisite tailoring are solved in advance.

Whether the future belongs to urban scatter, in which the CBD dissolves and vast conurbations overspread the land knotted here and there by a shopping center and a theater; or to revived and further-compacted business and cultural centers surrounded by hierarchies of suburbs, in which all can find a home made miraculously accessible by new kinds of transportation; or finally to a patchwork of green-belted new towns, small, self-sufficient, traversed from home to job by foot close to a well-groomed nature — whatever the shape of tomorrow's urbanity (and it is safe to bet that it will be many-shaped), it will require hard and unconventional attention as the environment of man. It gets little attention today.

An interesting fact about our rapidly urbanizing society has been the proliferation of plans and planners and the tiny and often equivocal role these have played in guiding growth. Plans and planners have proliferated largely because government requires a plan as precondition to virtually any kind of financial assistance. Government in so doing responds to an unexamined piety that planning is a good thing (unless, of course, it interferes with business). Planning of the sort that does not interfere with business has become a profession of great prestige and far-flung presence. We have, indeed, become a nation of planners, as Rome under Constantine became a nation of Christians; we have not become a planned nation. Far from it. The trouble is often said to be that the politicians and businessmen who have the power to make decisions on the ground are not forced to follow the plans, or alternatively that the planners are not given the authority they need to make rational development prevail. Either interpretation marks a gulf between the ideal and the real and defines the problem as one of bringing the two together. That may not be the problem.

Planning can be a technique to make things happen that would otherwise not happen. So it is used by the governments of the Soviet Union and India, for instance, in setting production goals, in order to create and operate the systems capable of achieving those goals. But in America planning has rather a negative or disciplinary role: it is called upon to confront systems in full and exuberant operation and trim off some of their disorderly vitality so that they may yield a more rational orderly product. The urban planner is not asked to make the city grow (it will grow all too fast), but rather to create constraints so that the new houses may not lack sewers and playgrounds or satellite schools, or so that they may be related to each other in esthetically pleasing or economically advantageous ways. Underlying this planning mission is the assumption (abundantly confirmed by experience) that the systems operating "naturally" will not produce the "desired" results.

But planning, though called in because the systems are sick, does not try in any way to cure them, does not even diagnose the illness. Perhaps the most telling of Jane Jacobs's counts against planners is her observation that they seldom concern themselves with how a city works. Some planners heartily agree. Those who do not, produce a series of sterile civic centers, cultural centers, trade centers, zoned ghettos, unused parks, high-speed transportation links between prison blocks, as in the name of esthetic order they butcher human functions in marketable fragments and package them in architecture. Such plans do not, in fact, represent anyone's ideal city — not even the planner's — and they are irrelevant to the problem that brought planners on the scene in the first place. The problem is not to create an ideal city (no such thing could possibly be defined, much less exist) but rather to adjust the forces governing growth to produce a kind of growth more conducive to human welfare. The typical impotence of planning does not come from the fact that the good guys lack power and the bad guys lack good sense; it comes from an almost total misconception of the need.

Consider, for instance, the problem of locating and planning a shopping center for a new community. At present that problem is solved entirely in economic terms — the center is built wherever the entrepreneur in charge thinks it will profit him most, and it is designed to do the most business at the highest net yield to the owner and the participating merchants. The resulting form and place may indeed also serve the community best. But not necessarily so. The community may also wish to preserve the character of a residential area that the center proposes to invade, or the integrity of a fishing stream that the center will dam and divert, or the quiet of a neighborhood that the cars of the shoppers will shatter. It may indeed not wish a single massive center at all but prefer, for various reasons of amenity and even convenience, a decentralized system of small shops. It is possible for a planner to examine all requirements, poll the residents, model the whole problem and arrive at an optimum solution that in theory would yield the greatest benefits to the greatest number. Clearly to do so is preferable to trusting market forces alone and more likely to give people what they think they want. It is, however, inherently a procedure so clumsy, costly, and demanding of special talents that no community is likely to call for its exercise more than now and then. Meanwhile, the old systems continue in their old way to generate development of the chaotic and antisocial kind that we say, at least, that we don't want.

By carefully analyzing the real processes that shape a city's development, one might be able to alter these to take more complete account of all society's requirements, not just the economic, *in the process itself.* If that were done we could then trust evolution to evolve arrangements suited to the whole man. We would not have to project in advance precisely what these should be — a hopeless task in any event that discounts the creativity of the future and instead of guiding growth in fact tends to frustrate it. Planning would focus not on blueprints of desired end products but on the healthy, productive functioning of systems. Come to think of it, that is almost precisely the way human settlements evolved in the past before technology so speeded the pace and greed so preempted the purpose that we rushed hell-bent to turn everything into a money machine.

# CHAPTER 16

# A Passion to Consume

MAN'S EXPLOITATIVE WAY of life is essential to his survival; the more he can squeeze out of nature, even at the cost of profoundly disturbing other living systems, the more he can enrich his culture, whether with gadgetry or poetry. One cannot quarrel either with the process or with the drive to push it as far as possible. The only question is: How far is possible? At what point does exploitation become a losing game? Where is the elastic limit of the systems exploited? Today's troubles seem to warn that limits are at hand. But we are not sure. Many who profess concern for the "environment" in fact worry only about pollution, and they talk and act as if they would clean up pollution in order to continue running the exploitative game as before. The message is not getting through. What warning signal would be so clear that everyone would heed it? Is there any? Is our economic-political-social system tuned to sense the limits to which we can go in pursuit of prosperity here and now?

C. S. Holling believes that the signal of limits from the environment is necessarily weak for man because as man expands his numbers he also expands the capacity of his environment to accommodate more. The limits therefore recede and he approaches them rather as a speeding car catches up with another that is going only a little more slowly. Not only is the signal weak, but our civilization is shaped to muffle it and our way of life to ignore it.

In contrast to traditional, preindustrial societies, Western man's sensitivities to his environment are blunted not only by his own works that interpose themselves between him and nature but by an ethic that tends to make of exploitation an absolute rather than contingent good. Industrial capitalism partly discovered, partly invented the free-market system, which was held to be able to work without social or political controls so long as every individual pursued his own self-interest in conditions of perfect competition. The same proposition turned around asserted that social or political controls over economic activity could only disrupt the automatic (and assumedly beneficent) operations of the market. A remarkable consequence was that for the first time in human history the business of getting a living took precedence over all other human activities. No less remarkable, covetousness, a human trait that used to be regarded as a sin, became a duty. The economic system detached from the social would no longer be constrained to serve social purposes; it had its own purpose, to produce and consume. That purpose has no inherent limits because it includes no external values: production of what? consumption for what? The most obvious trait of our production-consumption economy is that it is wholly absorbed in process and cares little about what it produces, much less about the impact on people. Without built-in controls, it is like a Sunday motorboater substituting for the tug of a goal the sheer exhilaration of speed.

For primitive man individual satisfactions tend necessarily to be found wholly within a social group that is small enough to let everybody intimately know everybody else. Within such a group no one could hope to win social approval by actions that tended to weaken or disrupt the social ties or put the whole group in jeopardy by, for instance, killing off a herd of pigs on which all depended. Since by and large none can hope or wish to escape (bearing his expropriated salt pork and hides to sell in another land), each is bound by the body of custom that evolves to assist the society to survive. Individual economic goals must be consonant with social goals or they cannot be reached.

Economic institutions, moreover, are necessarily shaped to support society. The method of exchanging goods is one. We tend to regard buying and selling — basic to our economy — as basic to all, indeed as a natural and unavoidable human activity. Yet in some societies giving, not selling, is the chief means of circulating economic goods.

Melville J. Herskovits, one of the few anthropologists to study comparative economics, describes an extraordinarily elaborate system relating the Kota tribe of India to its three neighbors, the Toda, the Kurumba and the Badaga. Each tribe is a specialist. The Kota are musicians and artists; the Toda keep cattle; the Kurumba live meagerly from the produce of the forest; the Badaga grow crops. In a material way the Kota are chiefly dependent on the Badaga, from whom they receive annual gifts of grain as well as sacrificial animals when needed. In return the Kota make ritual gifts of pottery and iron tools. But though on both sides the exchanges involve essentials of life, no bargaining takes place over equivalent quantities; the transactions are conducted between Kota and Badaga households that have lifelong mutual obligations, well understood by each. As for the Kurumba, because they live in the forest, they are believed in league with dark spirits. The Kota need their magic and woo it with gifts. But in these exchanges there is little of the spirit of altruism. The sorcerers normally press their advantage and regularly come out materially far ahead.  Even so there is no notion of a market in magic or a price for a charm or a pot.

With the Toda the Kota's ritual exchanges have little material significance on either side.  The Kota play for Toda ceremonies and in return are feasted.  But reward for the musician is chiefly the pleasure of playing; for the audience it is the assurance that their dead receive appropriate services in the other world.  "From the point of view of the Kota, the ledger may be balanced somewhat as follows: They benefited materially from their contacts with the Badaga, since these were principally concerned with the exchange of commodities under social and legal sanctions.  They suffered material loss in their dealings with the forest-dwelling Kurumba, since here the return was non-material, the services of a magician.  As far as their relationships with the Toda were concerned, neither people enjoyed any appreciable material gain.  Yet because of the sanction of tradition and the pleasure the Kota derived in rendering their services to the Toda, they never slighted their part of the exchange, the performance of which was marked by a feeling tone which contrasted to that which pervaded the other types of contact."

In societies practicing ceremonial exchange of goods, those who receive are under the strongest social and psychological pressure not just to repay but to excel in generosity.  The drive to give away all one has, therefore, can be at least as powerful an incentive to work hard and get more as the drive to accumulate.  In both systems a man's prestige — his standing with his fellows — is at stake.  This, more than material wants, is demonstrably what makes him hustle and what in success brings commensurate satisfaction.

From the point of view of society, however, the systems have different effects: The intertwining obligations of compulsive altruists tend to hold society together, for success is to be found only at home and only at the hands of the people one knows. Acquisitiveness, turning each individual against his fellow and offering success in a kind of common currency independent of friends and neighbors, tends to disintegrate the social fabric.

Anthropologist Raymond W. Firth wrote: "In a primitive society there is no relationship which is of a purely economic character . . . [The] economic relationship [of members] is strengthened through their reciprocal duties and common interests in other fields. Therein lies the strength of primitive society in that it enlists the binding forces from one aspect of life to support those of another." The strength *and* the limitation — for the primitive is also the prisoner of his group. The wholeness and harmony of his life can persist only so long as society remains closed and nothing changes much from year to year.

The industrial age discovered that economic activity liberated from social constraints could — in the exuberant language of development — "take off." In taking off it left behind traditional social obligations and satisfactions. It had, therefore, to invent purely personal satisfactions, not dependent on the welfare of any particular society, which the economically successful could take with them. The system run by self-interest became also the system that gratified self-interest in a rational symmetry that discouraged questions as to whether the net result was good or not; it worked. The common currency of human satisfaction became common currency, universal and transportable. It could be gained at the expense of one's neighbors; it could be expropriated from resources needed for the common support; it could be amassed even by directly antisocial activities such as the near starvation of workers, the destruction of the health of women and children, the deceiving of buyers, the ruin of competitors. In classic formulations of laissez-faire, society had no right to protect itself against even the most blatant of the assaults of private greed, lest interventions on behalf of justice disturb the system. Social Darwinists extolled those who ground down their fellow man for weeding out weaklings and so improving the human race. Western society to be sure has come out of that dark passage to recognize wide-ranging social regulation as necessary and desirable. Nevertheless the economic system retains its separate rationale, particularly its dependence on self-interest and its devotion to growth, neither of which has clear relevance to human welfare.

Contemporary economics texts are firm in asserting that self-interest freely pursued is the indispensable motive power of the system. The system so run is rational, internally consistent, and predictable, but it is not necessarily ethically good. Economics texts are also firm in eschewing value judgments. One of the most widely used and highly regarded texts by Nobel Prize winner Paul Samuelson observes that a system in which everyone "seeks his own advantage" will in conditions of near-perfect competition result in "a pattern of order . . . not, mind you, any proven condition of utopia."

But for most of us caught in the system, judgments are obligatory. We insist on values because without them we cannot tell how to act. Self-interest in competition, Samuelson warns, produces only a kind of order, not necessarily a utopian kind. But those to whom the market has been good have been saying for a couple of hundred years that the result *is* utopian (or at least the best imaginable), and those to whom the market has been not so good have waited for its turn and theirs.

For one thing, the economy has been an economic success — at least in its primary objective to spin the production-consumption spiral ever faster. Success always establishes a presumption of merit, despite evidence to the contrary. It is nearly inevitable that the free-market economy and its limited and largely functional goals should have imposed themselves on the whole society as if both were absolute rather than at best relative goods. John Kenneth Galbraith has eloquently described how unlimited consumption, being essential to keep the economy functioning and growing, has taken over other human values. No theme in advertising is more pervasive or insistent than that all desires for sex, beauty, health, prestige, and happiness can be satisfied by consumption, thus assuring that "the level of consumption is the proper measure of social merit."

I attended some time ago a conference of power company executives, government officials, assorted academic experts, and conservationists. We were asked to discuss how the conflict between the society's demand for more power and its concern over destruction of the natural environment might be reconciled. On the premise that more power plants would inevitably be built, were there not more reasonable ways of deciding where and how than by industry edict, challenged after the fact by community protest and confrontations in court? It turned out that was not the question most of the conferees wanted to discuss at all. They insisted rather on challenging the premise. Did more power plants really have to be built? If some were inevitable, how many? Who was making plans eventually to cut back? When would the industry — when would the society — begin to treat ever-escalating demands with denial, and instead of trying to sate the consumer say to him, you've had enough? When would we stop growing? That undoubtedly is the question of the day — the *cri de coeur* on every environmentalist's banner, particularly those waved by young radicals — for growth, once considered the one unquestionable social good, is now on the way to becoming the goat for all social ills.

Since the product of the nation is assumed to be the composite of the products of all its economic units, national economic growth is reckoned as the net of all the increases and decreases in goods and services produced and consumed by all the beavers in the nation. The technical deficiencies of the gross national product as a measure of economic reality have been repeatedly pointed out by economists. The GNP, for instance, takes account of services only if marketed: So, if a man marries his housekeeper, her labor is subtracted from GNP and the nation, though unchanged, will appear poorer. The training of an apprentice welder enters the GNP if he goes to school, but not if he learns on the job. More seriously, GNP, which can only add quantities, pays little attention to the real value of what is added. The output of a paper mill goes into GNP, but its wastes are never subtracted; on the contrary, if someone cleans them up the worth of that activity is counted just as though it were new wealth. It makes no difference, as one economics text blandly observed, whether the system turns out food or cigarettes; both get equally counted as part of the nation's wealth, which is then taken as a measure also of its welfare. Indeed cigarettes are apt to weigh disproportionately in GNP, for so far as they help make people sick they lead to increased demand for hospital and medical services, and the more medicine dispensed and the more doctors employed, the greater the GNP. Since, indeed, GNP assumes that economic activity produces only goods, not bads, it is more like a fever thermometer than a report card: The more economically active we are, whether in peace or war, making homes or destroying habitat, harvesting wheat or extinguishing whales, the more gets counted on the growth side.

The recent debate over whether or not to continue government subsidies of the supersonic transport plane showed
starkly what we are about. Every qualified and independent
scientist who looked at this machine warned of its power to
change the environment and make life on earth less comfort-
able (to say the least) for man and beast. Besides the noise in
flight, which has been experienced and found intolerable, engine exhausts could create cloud cover at high altitudes that
could materially alter world climate. No responsible critic
said that the climatic change would certainly come about;
none said that people might not accustom themselves in time
to the takeoff and landing racket or even to the sonic booms.
They observed only that the SST posed a threat to the quality of human life, that this was, or might be, a major threat,
and that therefore one had to be sure that the benefits alleged
justified taking the risk.

What benefits did the proponents offer? The plane was
needed to maintain America's supremacy in the international
aircraft market. (The need for America to be supreme in
everything is of course beyond argument.) We had to have a
homemade plane to forestall the drain of dollars to buy foreign craft. (What about the drain of increased tourism?)
We had to keep Boeing employees at work in Seattle. (Boeing said 5000 were involved; the President raised this without
explanation to 150,000.) We had to continue the subsidy or
lose the millions of tax dollars already invested. (This neatly
paralleled the argument that we had to send more Americans
to die in Vietnam in order to be true to those who had died
already.)

Each proposition was arguable, but even if all were sound
they left out the most important consideration of all: What
good is the plane for people? How does it promise to make life
or even travel better? Is it something we need or just a plane

for the traveler who has everything? Strikingly, these questions were scarcely passed in review. Yet if the SST will not itself contribute to human welfare, then making it cannot be a sensible use of our resources. Since environmental degradation is one of the possible costs that would be borne by everyone, not just users of the SST, what compensating benefits would inure to all, not just to those whose trip to Paris might be shortened by a couple of hours?

Silence. Either there were no answers or we have become so bemused by the importunities of the military-industrial system that we no longer recognize that it too is supposed to serve people. The jobs argument is an absurdity; it supposes that if men and women don't work on the SST they won't work at all. Once it was self-evident that people worked only to make the things they needed. Now we seriously argue through the looking glass that men have to accept things they don't need, which will probably shorten their lives and lengthen their miseries, in order to be able to work. It used to be believed that trade was instituted among men to facilitate the exchange of goods that each party to the exchange wanted. Defenders of the SST alleged that the market is a battlefield to test national prestige and that if we are in danger of having a foreign-made super pig-in-a-poke foisted on us we must embrace one of our own so that we will not be fatally tempted. We have come a long, mad way.

Even if a proper calculus of GNP were made that subtracted from goods and services the costs of their adverse social effects, the measure would remain essentially quantitative. In increasing, it would tell us only that in some sense we enlarged or in decreasing that we lessened. For fiscal management that is important, and GNP has proved a valuable tool in achieving some economic stability. But as a measure of progress or welfare, size is inadequate and may be seriously misleading. A man at seven feet may be unusually valuable on the basketball court; he has no advantage in playing the piano. At eight feet or more he will bump his head against ceilings that signal normal limits on growth. Size clearly is relative and may have relative advantage or disadvantage in different circumstances. But there is no rational basis whatever on which one can assert that to enlarge is in itself to improve.

Most of those who defend adding an economic inch to the national girth each year contend that the addition is needed for other purposes: to elevate the standard of living of the people, to wipe out poverty, to remain secure in a dangerous world, to demonstrate to the Communists that our system is better than theirs. By letting growth stand as the surrogate ideal for all these the hawkers of growth avoid what might clearly be embarrassing arguments on behalf of particular objectives.

The goals of any society are of course multiple, overlapping, changing, conflicting. It is never in practice or theory possible to prefer any one goal absolutely to another; we cannot forgo security to clean up the slums, nor vice versa. Very complex compromises and adjustments are essential and no enthusiast for any particular cause is going to find the mix to his taste. Nevertheless the proponent of growth who defends it as the way to wipe out poverty may properly be asked why then are antipoverty programs so low in national priority that they await adequate funding until after the current war, hot or cold, is paid for, after the requisite number of antiballistic missiles are bought and the aerospace industry guaranteed a sufficient subsidy. Why does so much growth go to make the rich richer? The champion of growth who argues that growth provides the indispensable wherewithal to raise everyone's standard of living must then address himself to the real meaning of the standards he extols, the real human values of more cars and more roads, more consumption and more waste.

The reiterated and largely unexamined assertion that we must grow economically as prerequisite to social choice is a serious obstacle to reexamining values. It is therefore time for the experts to either demonstrate the truth of that proposition beyond reasonable dispute or else prove it false. Growth has lost the status of a self-evident virtue and is in danger of becoming a bone of angry, futile contention among conservationists and industrialists, neither of whom have done the analysis to support a judgment.

Ever since Adam Smith discovered the "invisible hand" of self-interest guiding free economies, laissez-faire economics has assumed a reciprocal relation between means and ends: Self-interest freely pursued assures the welfare of society, defined as the largest possible sum of the satisfied self-interest of its members. Unarguable as that circular proposition sounds, Kenneth Arrow, among others, has observed that it is really meaningless. Individual satisfactions cannot be added together, because they have no conceivable common denominator. One man's happiness is his alone, and remains distinct no matter whose may be joined to it. Any pair, moreover, may be mutually exclusive. If one man's joy is to sleep late and his neighbor's is to blow reveille, their joint welfare will not be formed by simple addition. Arrow concludes that the concept of social welfare requires that there be consensus on the ends of society. Such consensus will embody an ideal, which must be general and altruistic. It must have precisely the qualities the market ignores, indeed boasts of ignoring. The market, therefore, cannot provide for the social welfare.

Under laissez-faire the state has accepted by default some of the rationale that drives the economic system. In particular the modern corporation, as Galbraith observed, has imposed its ethic on society, not least in making it appear self-evident that its own needs are equally national needs. In part, the ideal of national economic growth is the business ideal compounded.

Business operates for profit. In common usage "profit" may mean no more than gain, but properly it means the excess of the selling price of goods over their marginal costs. After you have reckoned all expenses including not merely labor and materials but rent, overhead, reimbursement for managerial skill, and all other direct and indirect costs, you tack on a little extra for "profit." Profits are not needed as work incentives. Without any profit at all it could pay a man handsomely to do business, provided he got full return for his labor, capital and land. Moreover, if the free market worked the way classical theory described it, competition should extinguish profits by assuring that the price of all goods exactly equaled their marginal costs.

What, then, are profits? Joseph A. Schumpeter suggested they are an inducement for innovation. In a perfectly operating mature market, goods would be produced and sold at marginal costs exactly equaling their marginal utility; all demands would be met; buyers and sellers would prosper; and nothing much would change, because there would be no incentive to change. The reason that change in fact does take place, that new products come on the market and new processes are devised to make old products more cheaply, is that the entrepreneur by suddenly disturbing the system can seize a temporary advantage and hold prices temporarily above costs. The differential achieved by temporarily upsetting the price-cost equilibrium is profit, and its lure induces business to try out new technology and open new markets. It is also an incentive to instability. By their nature profits can inure only temporarily in the early states of change. To maintain profits, therefore, businesses (so far as they remain competitive) must continually innovate. That is another way of saying they must grow.

Classic discussions of profit assumed the economic model of free competition. Modern reality among the giant corporations is something else. Where prices are set by various kinds of countervailing powers, as Galbraith has shown, the amount by which they exceed costs (the profit margin) can more or less be controlled by arrangement of a relatively few firms. And it is. Galbraith has observed that in practice, however, corporations do not try to make this excess as large as possible. Rather, they seem to aim at prices that will assure maximum consumption and a return sufficient to capitalize expanded production. Growth rather than profits thus appears to be the main incentive for corporate management. Yet profit manipulated in this way has a generic resemblance to profit in classic garb; both seem inextricably entwined with growth. The drive for profits, whether found or contrived, upsets market equilibrium, forcing the system to grow; profits can be sustained only so long as the system does grow.

The command to grow is the first law of survival for corporations. They might, of course, grow at the expense of each other, and sometimes do. There are, however, good reasons why the larger slices each craves will be accommodated for the most part by an ever larger pie. The government since Keynes has managed both its monetary and fiscal policies to promote real (noninflationary) growth as an article of faith. Industry is served by an increasingly pervasive and dominant advertising machine engaged without scruple in enlarging demand for any and all products. Corporate (i.e., bureaucratic) instincts for survival generally prevail over competitive aggressiveness, well short of the kill. So, as the parts have to grow for the good of each, the whole enlarges with an inevitability that leaves little room to question independently whether more and more goods and services, admirably testifying the success of their producers, equally answer the aspirations of the country.

An easy way to end the argument over growth is to admit an economic need for expanding production and consumption but add the proviso that society must care equally about what is produced and consumed. Growth then becomes a prescription for more of the "good" goods ("healthy" consumer goods, "useful" services, education, symphony concerts, hospital care and the like) and all as a net gain over the "bad" goods (smog, waste, noise, etc.). To move in that direction would probably generally be thought to move toward a better life, provided that the system was at the same time better adjusted to distribute both goods and bads more equitably.

Still the difficult questions remain: How can one seriously propose to live in a finite world as though it had no limits? How can one species, man, hope for itself an exception to the rule that at some point in time and space every organism must come into a stable relationship with all others and with its physical environment, or not survive? In fact the philosophic answer to those philosophic questions is that we are not exceptions, and the finite has us in its grip quite as firmly as it has any other creature. Growth unlimited is a delusion of a very young species that is now carrying the fixations of its youth into early maturity. The practical answer is that our choice is only where and when to stop growing. Like all other organisms, we can expand our dominion over the planet only at the expense of others. That we are doing just that in our infatuation with growth is clear from every report out of the vanishing wilderness. Biologically, the drive to indulge the power to extinguish others and possess their habitat is strong.

Culturally, it could be resisted to preserve the possibility of richer, more satisfying experiences than are in prospect from a technological victory over a world of suburbs occupied wholly by our own kind.

Because the limits of environment are relatively elastic for man, we have time to slow down growth and begin the search for livable conditions of stability. There is little time to delay the search. Too few of the experts in economics, politics, sociology, and psychology are now trying to determine what stability would mean. The only models we have are traditional preindustrial societies. They will not do; cultural backtracking is never a real option. For technological man to exist within a cyclical no-growth economy will require profound new adaptations, to say the least. And it will require in America above all, profound modifications of the traditional wisdom.

# CHAPTER 17

# American Dreams

THE IDEA OF progress took hold in the Western world not very long ago. Though implicit in the Jewish-Christian concept of history moving from innocence lost in Eden to innocence regained in heaven, progress was only set up as the guide for life after the various democratic revolutions of the eighteenth and nineteenth centuries had broken castes and set individuals free to make their own way. Individuals so liberated found new constraints substituted for the old. They were not free to do as they pleased but only free to succeed or fail. Progress, in such nineteenth-century formulations as Spencer's, was held to be inevitable for the world; it was therefore mandatory for individuals, who could either tune in or drop out. In America progress scarcely needed to be discovered in philosophy; it so manifestly beckoned from all those unoccupied homesites.

The American dream of the subjugation of a continent accompanied by an extravagance of greed and idealism had two essential themes: the unlimited bounty of nature, and the unlimited power of free men. Space in the sense of fresh habitat and fresh opportunity open for losers had profound consequences in shaping the nation. Just as America served as a haven for dissenters from Europe — all those who did not wish to conform to their own society and were too weak to change it — so the west received America's own dissenters. Secession has been a typical American process of growth. When Roger Williams quarreled with the church authorities of Massachusetts Bay he did not try to overthrow them or adjust to them; he gathered his flock and moved to Rhode Island. When Horace Greeley urged young men to take the way west he was consciously promoting migration as a way out for the discontented. American space thus made room for multiple differences; at the same time it tended to relieve established communities from the pressures of dissent. Geography thus preempted the role played by toleration in more settled countries. In this view the vaunted rugged individualism of Americans may mark a perennial failure of adaptation rather than a triumph of character.

Space also nourished the typically American brand of extravagant optimism. Through most of our history no one was really sure how much space there might be out there. Not only was the continent in fact huge and for a long time incompletely explored, but a series of expansive wars and diplomatic maneuvers continually pushed out even its nominal constraints, suggesting that America had indeed an unlimited career to subdue and populate the west, defined hardly more precisely than yonder where the sun sets. Daniel J. Boorstin believes that vagueness has been historically a great American resource. He writes that in the years between the Revolution and the Civil War, "Americans were being united by a common vagueness and a common effervescence . . . Their America was still little more than a point of departure. The nation would long profit from having been born without ever having been conceived."

Anything was possible. American history is full of get-rich-quick schemes, attempts at instant empire, undertakings to transplant heaven to earth. There were probably few times and places that have provided men with such a powerful sense of total control over both environment and destiny as did nineteenth-century America. The reality was, of course, always much less than the dream, and the dream did not equally affect all Americans. But throughout the nineteenth century, and at least through the First World War, the conventional wisdom had no patience with Americans who kicked against fate; fate was of a man's own making. The opportunities were open; all that was needed was energy and determination to exploit them.

The myth that America began and continued as the only nation in the world entirely peopled by truly free men has survived the facts of Puritan theocracy, indentured service, slavery, sweatshops, corporate oligarchies, yellow and black racism, Prohibition, the FBI, conscription, militarism, Joe McCarthy, the silent majority, and the all-pervasive dominion of public and private bureaucracy. It survived because there was — and still is — some truth in it. The truth, however, is more complicated than the myth.

If there was a bias in the sample of Europeans self-selected to become Americans, it was in the direction of people with more than average confidence in their ability to make it on their own. And among them was probably an unusual proportion of idealists. In the early emigrant propaganda the appeal to self-interest almost never stood alone. America was held up as a challenge to men who aspired to build a new society, convert the Indians, enlarge England's empire and exercise the heroic virtues. The New World was a pristine stage on which one might do good as well as get rich, and that vision never quite faded from the immigrant view. Carl Bridenbaugh has suggested that the most influential of the promotional tracts in the seventeenth century may have been

the Bible, filled with stories of migration and texts command-
ing the children of God to leave inhospitable lands and seek
others where the Lord promised to prosper them. Contemporary propagandists regularly emphasized that the great trek
would serve a higher cause and should be seen as a kind of
crusade, not a running away. So great were the wrench
of leaving home and the perils of the voyage that the hope of
making it could seldom have been motivation enough; it
needed at least a pinch of spiritual zeal besides.

By the same token, those who responded to such appeals
tended not to be simply the displaced and the malcontent,
but rather the more intelligent, courageous, resourceful, and
ambitious of these. But while they were not on the whole
escapees, they *were* generally shuffling out of various political,
social, economic, and religious constraints. Exceptional were
the Puritans, who migrated in groups to reconstruct on this
side societies rather more rigid than those they left. Outside
New England and after the first waves of settlement, colonists
came normally as individuals. Squeezed out of more or less
rigidly organized societies, and on their own, they were disposed to social mobility and even on occasion to near anarchy.
For all comers the New World was to be made not in the
image of the old but as a lesson to it.

So selected, America's first immigrants found that the wilderness, by and large, rewarded just those self-reliant qualities
that the best of them had. The frontier as it moved west continued to select and stamp with success similar qualities.
From the beginning, effete eastern observers, both native and
visiting, complained of the obstreperous, lawless, bumptious
behavior of American provincials. Life on the frontier encouraged such behavior or, more precisely, it discouraged the
conforming routines familiar to the civilized observers and
appropriate to their own settled society. It is almost a redun-

dancy to point out that in conditions where a man must primarily rely on his own talents to survive, without recourse to the support of an established order, he must behave as if such an order did not exist. Having nothing to conform to, he could hardly conform. Not surprisingly, men able to prosper in those conditions found evidence both of their own independent strength and of the superfluousness of the more or less remote customs and institutions they had left behind.

Early in this century, Frederick Jackson Turner, seeing this frontier independence as a uniquely American trait and finding that it had permeated American institutions, developed his famous frontier thesis of American history. What Turner essentially contended, though with great sophistication and considerable poetic insight, was that American democracy came out of the forest. Subsequent generations of historians have recognized the Turner thesis as one of those brilliant intuitions that change forever the way people view reality; but as explanation of American democracy it was flawed. For present purposes the most important reservation is to be entered against the implied equivalences of individualism, freedom, and democracy, and against the color that the Turner thesis seems to give to the popular notion that the frontier was the golden age of an unfettered personal liberty that made strong men great.

In fact the dominant lesson of the frontier, from the time it lay on the eastern seaboard, was that it took well-organized social cooperation to tame a wilderness. Despite the real and legendary Daniel Boones, who were little more than advance scouts of a settlement they themselves never made or wanted, the westward movement was not a series of individual combats between man and nature but rather a succession of social experiments pushed out in waves from a civilizing base. The peopling of the continent was by groups, cooperative and interdependent, whose survival hinged at least as much on their ability to organize for mutual protection and welfare as on the skills and courage of individual members.

The kind of individual enterprise that won the west was that which organized and led the communities that were the primary units of survival. Westerns which act out the frontier fantasy turn on personal combat that provides heroic alter egos for small boys and others. But more often than not, what is at stake is the social structure of a town threatened by lawless, individualist exploiters. All those guns are symbols of aggressive ego, but the good guns are on the side of the law. When the sheriff or the itinerant cowboy pinch-hitting for Messiah has plugged the villain, the fade-out implies that another raw town has had its law and order respectably restored and has thereby been set on the track of civilization.

Frontier communities were, of course, on-the-spot creations, partly improvised, whether from army manuals or memories of home. In that sense they were achievements of private enterprise. Boorstin has observed that the transient companies formed to move settlers into new lands were in effect communities created to serve private interests, and so tended to blur distinctions between realms of private and public welfare. Permanent communities established on the ground had a similar autonomy and self-sufficiency that made government a private business and thereby bred local jealousies. It is these local jealousies that throughout our history have been more obviously characteristic of Americans than any unusual predilections for personal freedom. Westerners, from the time the west lay only a few miles from Boston, have always been suspicious of government, other than their own, because it was remote, seemed irrelevant, and acted more often as a meddler on behalf of outsiders than as protector of the home folk. The more distant it was, the more they distrusted it. The settlers' own society owed nothing to the government that subsequently asserted jurisdiction. Many squatters were persuaded that they resisted in the name of rugged individualism government intervention that would have evicted them; in fact they championed perforce the cause of a primary society that was their support against the claims of a quasi-colonial power that threatened to displace them. Politically and economically localism, not individualism, is to be reckoned as the effective opposition to central government in America.

Since America began as a scion of Europe and its development largely coincided with the dominance of the free-market economy in Europe, laissez-faire dogmas acquired here almost the status of first principles. As an economic rationale for personal freedom and minimum government, they nicely complemented the separatism that flourished on the frontier to create a single and dangerously persuasive myth of American democracy as a loose association of self-reliant men and women, imbued with a healthy suspicion of government, an admirable distaste for class distinctions, a go-getter spirit, and free energy, all dedicated to the proposition that every man could make a million — and should. Free enterprise equated with democracy and each with an ideal absence of social constraint became in the myth the twin sources of American success unblushingly identified with material prosperity.

The facts, as usual, were somewhat different. The state in America until mid–nineteenth century always "claimed and exercised the right to regulate the economic activity of its citizens to any extent considered socially useful." During that time conservatives often questioned the wisdom of state economic interventions, including John Marshall, who thought state regulation dangerous and unwise; but none asserted the sovereign right of business to be let alone. That right could not be discovered so long as business needed state help in form of subsidies, tariff protection, road, railroad, and banking services. In time the need lessened. In the era of the Civil War the private corporation was becoming strong and prevalent; democratic government, lacking expertise and continuity of administration and riddled by corruption, was proving clumsy in the management of economic enterprises. Only then did business philosophers reveal it to be against both reason and nature for the state to engage in or regulate business or take any part in it except of course to protect and encourage. Ironically, the new and absolutist formulation of economic individualism applied to fictional, not real persons. The reason, of course, was that only corporate "persons" could be strong enough to stand alone.

In its most uncompromising form, laissez-faire flourished as social Darwinism in America between the Civil and First World Wars. Herbert Spencer, its English creator, even opposed measures of public health on grounds that anyone too stupid to take care of himself ought to die for the good of the race. Spencer enjoyed a phenomenal popularity in this country, and in the 40 years following the Civil War his books sold more than 350,000 copies. For Spencer and his American disciple, William Graham Sumner, the command to be fit and prove it by defeating your competitors was the first of all commands that launched life on its career. So the industrialists working little children 14 hours a day in Manchester appeared as nature's gentlemen, doing what they could not help doing and what in the long run served not only their own interests but the advancement of the human race.

Among the social Darwinists, none bothered to examine the actual processes of natural selection; none perceived that the "fittest" in nature were not necessarily the strong nor necessarily anything at all but by definition those who survived; none looked into the reality of the so-called "struggle" for existence to see whether it was ever, in fact, the chronic state of war within one species that economic competition implied. Social Darwinists, while pretending to find justification for human behavior in nature, were in fact looking at the incredible conditions of inhumanity in the mill towns of the Industrial Revolution and interpreting Darwin's struggle for existence by that image. Spencer learned biology in Manchester and taught the world that there could be no appeal from the brutal system of economic repression because it was "natural."

The enthusiasm with which American wealthy and literate classes embraced a doctrine that enthroned selfishness as the supreme natural virtue, condemned humanitarianism (except as a purely voluntary moral exercise), confused material success with human fulfillment, and equated ruthlessness in the service of power with the fitness of survival testifies to the extraordinary fever of greed that gripped this country in the nineteenth century and even today does not easily let go. The most durable intellectual scar is that the social Darwinists in their infatuation with the fitness of individuals overlooked entirely the fitness of groups. Yet the plain evolutionary fact is that man survived in groups and only in groups. The capital key to human evolutionary success has, therefore, been collective cooperative adaptation to the challenge of environment. The disciples of Spencer made nonsense out of both Darwin and human experience by regarding competition as the sole principle of selection and ignoring all the devices of cooperation and mutual forbearance that in nature and culture permit creatures to coexist to the advantage of all.

This was not only bad biology but bad sociology. The social Darwinists wrote like tough-minded realists, but they observed nothing. At the moment that they were glorifying free competition as the law of nature, businessmen, perceiving how destructive competition could be, were suppressing it wherever they could. At the moment when Darwinists were passionately denying the state a legitimate role in the economy, all around them state legislatures were grinding out laws that, according to one unfriendly contemporary, were consistent in their "utter disregard of the *laissez-faire* principle." Another observer figured that of 13,000 bills enacted by states and territories in the single year 1889–90, about 29 per cent were "socialistic." Throughout the flourishing of extreme laissez-faire doctrine the states were unusually busy promoting internal improvements, subsidizing agriculture, regulating railroad rates, supervising banks and insurance companies, not to mention opening the door for utilities commissions, wage and hour legislation, safety laws, boards of health, housing regulations, and state park, forestry, fish and game commissions. The fact is that without these interventions to repair the worst consequences of economic assaults on the structure of society, selfishness and individualism might indeed have won out.

Social practice in America, whether on the frontier or in the business world, never conformed to the doctrines of unfettered individualism. That the doctrines became more uncompromising the more widely the practice diverged may underline what is psychologically an important fact about the American experience: Settlement began anarchically in a state of nature and moved toward organization and order. In a sense, that was the democratic revolution turned inside out. As a British observer once put it: "Liberty in England has been wrung from power — power in America has arisen out of liberty. In the one case, power has been fettered that freedom might expand; in the other freedom has been restricted

that power might exist." In such a regression from innocence, it is natural for fantasies of the pristine self-sufficiency
of the individual to masquerade as memories of a golden age.
Each new constraint on a person's powers to do what he
pleases with his own could seem a slip from virtue, a retreat
along the road leading to the loss of all freedom. Perhaps that
is why we shrink from "socialistic" experiments that European democracies take to readily, and why they have less difficulty than we in perceiving the nature of the commons for
collective care.

PART III

# Earthkeeping

CHAPTER 18

# A Price on Everything

SOME FORTY YEARS AGO a creative student of human affairs,
R. H. Tawney, described economic fundamentalism: "It regards the institutions and habits of thought of its own age and
civilisation as in some peculiar sense natural to man, dignifies
with the majestic name of economic laws the generalisations
which describe the conduct of those who conform to its prejudices, and dismisses as contrary to human nature the sugges-
tion that such conduct might be other than it is." The great
value of comparative anthropological studies has been to
show that all human institutions are specific and temporal
adaptations to the particular set of facts and experiences they
organize. They all of course conform to "human nature,"
and none is more inherently fitting to the human condition
than another or, in an ethical or teleological sense, more advanced. It is as "natural" for men to vie with each other in
generosity as in acquisitiveness, to cooperate for the welfare of
the group as to compete for the supremacy of self. On the
other hand, to argue from admiration of the past or the primitive, as some romantics do, that our industrial present should
turn back from paths that have led to human unhappiness
and seek to recover Eden is not merely impractical; it is a
view that wholly mistakes the nature of life, time and the
world. We move in only one direction.

The view of the primitive world reveals something of the evolutionary range of possibilities for mankind. The view of one's own history sets the real limits of change in the historic scale. The two views are complementary and both are required for reform: The reformer must be released from delusions of permanence and inevitability on the one hand, but disciplined on the other to the constraints of a building process that can only use the materials given and must use nearly all of them.

To the extent that our economic system does not sufficiently answer human needs, the first try for a remedy is to improve the system. A number of economists, especially in the past decade, have been working to develop new economic models and practical economic measures. Recognizing social needs that are not just aggregated private needs and private needs that are not satisfied in the market, they have been trying essentially to deal with both by enlarging the market.

Most of the deferred costs of environmental maintenance described earlier could be reckoned as actual costs of doing business that business has never been made to pay. The manufacturer of paper dumps the afterbirths of his product into a nearby river without charge and generally up to now without thinking, as though rivers were public sewers. The motorist permits his automobile engine to discharge unburned hydrocarbons, carbon monoxide, nitrogen oxides and other more or less noxious substances into the air, as though again the air were a public dump for gaseous waste. At low ratios of people, industries, and cars to space, air, and water, such dumping in fact imposed little real cost. The air was able to dilute the wastes and no one was the worse for it; the streams were able to degrade the sewage and, since many creatures were thereby fed, perhaps their collective welfare compensated for an occasional bad smell. Our economic system grew up under these uncrowded conditions. If sometimes in cities or mill towns the environment was significantly befouled, it was only the poor on the whole who paid. That could be considered not a flaw in the system but just another of the penalties it exacted of losers. In any event, economists continued to reckon that water and air were free goods, and dumping therefore incurred no costs since it preempted no scarce resources.

In the past few decades these "free" goods have acquired ever higher negative values, which can be reckoned in several ways: The cost of dirtying a river can be set as equivalent to the cost of cleaning it up (if society decides that it must have clean rivers). Or it may be only the cost imposed on the next user of removing impurities damaging for his purposes or of accepting lower efficiencies in his use of the water. Finally, it may be figured as equivalent to the value of forgone opportunities — the worth of swimming, boating, fishing, for instance, that have been damaged or preempted.

By any reckoning, the costs soar as competition for the water resource mounts. Precisely the same analysis can be applied to air pollution, solid waste disposal, or pesticide residues, even to power plants and wilderness values or subdivisions and urban sprawl. In each case an economic process imposes costs on society that are external to the market. The paper plant's free dumping has been subsidized exactly to the amount that others suffer damage from the polluted stream. Logically, the cost of dumping is part of the cost of manufacture, and many economists believe that it should be paid by the manufacturer, who would pass it along to the consumer. In that way the market price of paper would more accurately reflect the real cost of producing it. One might then go one step further and ask whether the cost of disposing of the paper after use should not also properly be charged to the consumer. Some economists would again answer that it should be.

There are several ways of internalizing external costs so

that consumers will pay the full price for their privilege to consume. Allen Kneese has long and eloquently argued the virtues of effluent charges for industries dumping wastes into watercourses. Worked out with some success in the Ruhr Valley of Germany, the effluent charge is a tax on dumping that is graded to reflect the cost of cleaning up. The manufacturer may elect to pay if the market for his goods can bear the extra charge, or under competition he may be induced to change his processes in order to reduce or even eliminate the effluent altogether. Selective taxes on commodities could be used similarly to pay for the costs of their ultimate disposal. Again, if graded to reflect actual costs they might tend to discourage such environmental nuisances as disposable bottles and encourage the design of things that either degrade easily or can be readily salvaged.

The tactic of effluent charges has the great virtue of seeking to correct the system rather than merely clean up the consequences of its ill-functioning. It confronts the fact that we are now paying less for the privilege of consuming the things we buy than it actually costs us as a society to produce them, and in the most direct way possible it proposes to make up the disparity. Moreover, despite the obvious difficulties of fixing appropriate charges that will accomplish the purpose and be fairly applicable to competing industries, this is probably an easier job administratively than writing and enforcing other similarly effective and fair regulations.

There are also disadvantages. Conservationists have objected that the effluent charge is a "license to pollute." Feeling that the end is to protect noneconomic values of a clean environment, they are uncomfortable with a plan that leaves the question of whether to pollute or not to the determination of the market. To which an economist, paraphrasing a current advertising slogan, might retort, "Which do you want, good principles or good environment?" A more fundamental objection is that the effluent charge passed along in the price of goods puts the cost of environmental protection on all consumers regardless of ability to pay and regardless of the distribution of the benefits. Is it fair that the user of a school composition book in P.S. 180 should pay in part for restoring salmon runs to the Penobscot? One would like to know at least just how effluent charges might affect the distribution of costs as compared to alternative methods of control — such as subsidies, or tax incentives, or direct regulation — whose burden might fall differently. Special charges on packaging, for instance, could easily have the impact of regressive sales taxes.

Leaving aside the question of distribution, an affluent society has shown itself willing to pay for noneconomic goods, such as the amenities of cleanliness and beauty, but no one really knows how imperious that demand may be. When a highway threatens to fill and destroy a marsh that is the habitat of rare wildfowl or merely someone's favorite nature haunt, highway departments are often rocked by citizen protest and even forced now and then to put the road, at greater expense, somewhere else. Is that extra cost a fair measure of what the nature haunt or those wildfowl are worth? Americans are spending an increasing proportion of their increasing wealth on outdoor recreation; does that aggregated sum reasonably represent the human values of recreation?

Traditionally, benefit-cost analysis holds that if you get more out of an enterprise than you put in, it is worth doing. Costs and benefits traditionally have been figured in dollars because dollars are comparable (or seem so), whereas it is no easier to weigh a view against five minutes saved in getting to work than to add the proverbial apples and oranges. Where cash flows in market transactions, costs and benefits are not hard to specify in common dollars. But how much social cost in dollars should be attributed to the destruction of a marsh?

How much social benefit in dollars is accrued by creating another artificial lake for swimmers and boaters?

Some economists have been trying to invent a plausible scheme to translate nonmaterial values into material equivalents. In brief, their idea is to simulate a market that if it existed would be capable of establishing prices for the things that in fact have no price. By a number of ingenious devices they ask themselves what people might be willing to pay if, for instance, views and ducks on the wing were for sale. Thus Marion Clawson and Jack Knetsch developed methods to relate the quality of recreation resources to the distances people travel to enjoy them. Ronald G. Ridker made elaborate estimates of the costs of air pollution, including simulated costs for psychic damage. In reverse, presumably, these (or some of them) could be added up as the benefits of clean air.

Such efforts stem from the admission that there is more to life than money. Yet, paradoxically, they come right back to assert that what more there is can also be measured in money, that those human aspirations thought of as priceless can in fact be priced, and that though they are not bought and sold they might rationally be if the market could be subtly expanded to include them. To assert an equivalence between a sum of money and a day on the lake is to contradict the premise from which the whole exercise took off. Ultimately all benefits, up to and including breathing, are achieved at some cost. For almost everything except breathing, each person has some limit on what he will pay for the good he covets. But to harden those generalizations into an equation with dollar signs on both sides is a quite different statement, to which grave theoretical and practical objections may be raised.

The hardening, in fact, asserts not just that all benefits have a cost, but that the rational way of deciding whether or not to seek the benefit is to determine and weigh the cost. That is a true proposition only if the notions of benefits and of costs are extended to include the whole range of human satisfactions on the one hand and the range of human expenditures in energy, psychic sacrifices, accepted discomforts and so on, on the other. It is not true of an equation in dollar equivalents. The danger of using such equations lies in promoting delusions that quality can at last be translated into quantities, along with the corollary delusion that only a reckoning to which numbers can be put is entirely rational. That no market exists for trees and birdsongs and a sense of justice suggests that market mechanisms are not appropriate to their production and distribution. Rather than simulating a market to deal with them, we might better accept the reminder that some things, among them the most precious of human aspirations, are neither marketable nor countable — an observation as old as the moral sense.

All this is not to say that the economists' efforts to tune the market economy more precisely to human need are wrong or useless. Effluent charges *are* capable of making the environment cleaner; simulated values applied to nonmaterial enjoyments *can* restrain some of the worst excesses of the earth movers and concrete mixers. Clearly, that much is gain (provided always that we pay due attention to the distribution of the costs). But if we are concerned, as we should be, with evolutionary direction, there is an equally clear danger that refinements of the economic analysis may encourage undue dependence on it as a complete guide for public policy. No economist would argue that proposition; the danger is rather an uncritical acceptance of another neat methodology that makes convincing use of equations, graphs and computer programs.

The ecological awakening has helped to point up flaws in

the economic system. This, however, is minor compared with the dawning recognition that the ethic of the exploitative, industrialized society does not answer the range of human need and does threaten to impoverish human life. Helpful as refined methods of economic analysis and improved economic incentives to cleanliness will be, it would be tragic if the ecological insight into man's part in nature — disclosing the opportunities as well as constraints of that interdependence — bequeaths only a better system of figuring benefits and costs.

# CHAPTER 19

# All There Is

ENVIRONMENT, now on everyone's lips, was first on America's not because American sensitivities have been greater, nor even because unusual affluence brought the problems more urgently to the fore. Rather, it is because America, having begun in visions of unlimited bounty and having pursued them with such zest, came most poignantly on the revelation of the finite. By accidents of geography and timing America played out the drama of economic development under laissez-faire most nearly according to the nineteenth-century script. Growth was its mission and became its obsession: to fill out the vast shell of opportunity that was the undeveloped continent.

The first American to warn of the approach to limits was George Perkins Marsh, whose publication in 1864 of *Man and Nature* anticipated by a hundred years the contemporary discovery of ecology. Marsh's special insight (all but lost from view until now) was that man stood in opposition to nature, that his greatness depended on his power to manipulate nature, but that manipulation was inevitably disturbing. Man must therefore watch what he did and work to replace with managed harmonies the natural ones he had to destroy.

Marsh, a Vermonter, was minister to Italy when he wrote

his book. His early life, he says, was spent "almost literally in the woods." From that background, viewing Europe and comparing the landscape of the nineteenth century to that described by classical authors, he was most impressed by the destruction of the ancient forests. He could see the same destruction beginning in America. This broad and prophetic perspective, however, was all but unique to Marsh. His compatriots generally had another view; they were about to close out the Civil War and open the Great Barbecue. Although Marsh's book was surprisingly widely read, his concerns did not enter politics until the end of the century.

It has seemed to many social and intellectual historians that the year 1890, in which the frontier was officially proclaimed to be closed, not only marked a watershed in American development but was so perceived at the time. The country was far from full in 1890, its energies far from exhausted. Boosterism and an uncouth exuberance remained sufficiently national characteristics to be satirized in the 1920s by Sinclair Lewis, among others, as the very essence of Middle America. Yet to have reached the ends of our particular piece of earth was already recognized at the turn of the century, however dimly, as a kind of conclusion. The prairie schooners were beached; if the journey was to continue, it would be in a different way, to other destinations. These were neither so simple nor so certain. Rampant optimism gave way here and there to uneasiness. Imbued with the greatness of America's accomplishments, the pessimists saw greatness past; the sturdier optimists cast about for ways to continue onward within the new constraints. It was essentially those sturdy optimists who fathered the first conservation movement under President Theodore Roosevelt, who indeed gave conservation its name in 1907 and shaped it as a peculiarly American form of an American dream.

At the turn of the century the darkest thought generally prevailing seems to have been that the United States might not be able to go on indefinitely using resources as it had. Alarm was sounded by graphs that showed a timber famine within a few years, and imminent exhaustion of such minerals as iron. The reaction essentially was a shocked determination to halt the visible waste and discipline private exploitation more nearly to the needs of the whole nation. To vow to halt sat well with the Puritan tradition of thrift that had somehow managed to coexist with greed in the heart of the locust for the hundred reckless years. The revulsion against private exploiters — Roosevelt's "malefactors of great wealth" — was in the Progressive air. Conservation in the hands of efficiency experts who were also the sort of men who could be friends with Teddy Roosevelt nicely merged the two to offer the country the possibility of an extended postfrontier future, to keep it yet awhile, as Roderick Nash put it, "young, vigorous, prosperous, democratic, replete with opportunity for the individual."

But the end of the century saw not only the closing of the frontier. Coincidentally came crises of industrial combination, labor conflict, urban squalor and corruption — all of which induced a malaise of the middle classes that was expressed politically in the Progressive movement. Across the wilderness dream of innocence fell the shadow of the wicked city, which Americans have agreed in detesting throughout most of our history. The disillusion was almost the classic syndrome of adolescence, complete with brooding thoughts. Wallace Stegner, who was born on the prairie and in spirit has never quite left it, recently wrote: "It seems to me significant that the distinct downturn in our literature from hope to bitterness took place almost at the precise time when the frontier officially came to an end, in 1890, and when the

American way of life had begun to turn strongly urban and industrial." It *is* significant, but probably not as evidence that urbanization is cause for literary despair or wilderness for hope. Among the voices of earlier American optimism, Walt Whitman was the child of Brooklyn, William Dean Howells of Boston and New York. Emerson in a suburb of Boston was as far in body and spirit as one could get from the frontier. And those such as Frank Norris and Theodore Dreiser, who sounded the new notes of bitterness, surely did not protest a loss of wildness, with which none was concerned, but rather the repellent commercialism, social injustice, and raw ugliness epitomized in the form and function of the new industrial cities. They and many others were saying at century's end that these stigmata of industrialism now were the American reality, no longer mere growing pains; the way west was closed; we were complete and now had to reckon with what we were. Awakenings are always rude, especially those of growing up. The first conservation movement, integral in spirit with Progressivism, embodied significantly a hope that the dawn might yet be put off.

In its first American incandescence, conservation did little immediately to check the exploitative course it protested. The protest seemed, rather, to cushion the shock of too-sudden maturity, enable the nation to adapt to the idea that indeed there was no more frontier, and then proceed with its affairs almost as before.

Wilson's first administration was marked by conservation failures; the second was dominated by war. Then came Harding and the extraordinary decade of the twenties, when the nation dipped back into the Gilded Age for one last fling. (In keeping with its pose of youth all through the fling, it had to sneak its drinks.)

In the twelve Republican postwar years (1921–1933), laissez-faire was enthroned again in Washington, as by return of an ancien régime that had learned nothing from its Progressive exile. Harding and Coolidge let the reins go slack on high principle backed by incompetence. Until 1929 the country was run by business and after 1929 by no one. The last three Republican years put to the test the old optimistic conviction (or hope?) that a nation so gifted by nature with abundant resources and an energetic citizenry could indefinitely thrive without plan or direction, simply by letting the citizenry freely have at the resources. We failed the test — and fairly, for Herbert Hoover was certainly the ablest exponent of the purist doctrine ever to occupy the White House, and he struggled with indomitable courage and consistency to make it work. That failure is the principal significance of the Great Depression in history.

To the new, traumatic awakening of the crash the nation responded much as before: essentially by trying minimal adjustments to repair the system and reopen the vision of the old future, temporarily blocked by the cave-in. The New Deal, exuberantly experimental in method, remained staunchly conservative in objective. It wished to make the old system work. Its conservation programs — typically miscellaneous and pragmatic — sought some discipline and control over private resource use, but clearly for the sake of encouraging individual enterprise and helping it to prosper: The Tennessee Valley Authority, though damned as government usurpation of the vested rights of private utilities, actually aimed at and brilliantly achieved an economic base for an entire region, on which private enterprise could and did flourish. The Soil Erosion Service established in 1933 and rechristened the Soil Conservation Service in 1935 provided direct aid to farmers suffering the exhaustion of their lands. The Agricultural Adjustment Administration, aimed primarily at bolstering farm incomes, had conservation implications in the notion of an ever-normal granary and in the unexpected assist it gave to diversifying agriculture by taking thousands of acres out of one-crop staples. The Civilian Conservation Corps, launched shortly after the inauguration, was essentially a scheme to give work to young men; but in the process it replanted forests and saved marginal lands from flood and erosion.

No popular conservation crusade in the 1930s echoed that launched in 1908, but curiously, in view of the general necessitous preoccupation with economic recovery, there was considerable public interest in recreation and wilderness, to which the government responded in calling the first Federal Wildlife Conference in 1936, instituting national wildlife refuges, and more than tripling the acreage in national parks. It was in this era that Aldo Leopold, who wrote so eloquently of the land ethic, founded the Wilderness Society with Robert Marshall.

After the Second World War, America perhaps would have liked another return to normalcy. It moved that way in the first rush to demobilize, end rationing, and convert the factories back to producing consumer goods. But this war resolved one set of international rivalries only to expose another that seemed at least as irreconcilable. While the cold war, adventures in Asia, and the space race all kept the economy hot and so contributed in one sense to the kind of boom for which normalcy has become the classic label, they checked whatever inclination there might have been to try for another withdrawal into the nineteenth-century dream. Moreover, the continuing huge military demands, added to those of a rapidly expanding population, resurrected the old fears of running out of resources. In the late forties a handful of books, such as Fairfield Osborne's *Our Plundered Planet* and William Vogt's *Road to Survival*, prophesied doom to a nation that continued to overexploit and overreproduce; many thousands appear to have listened.

Nevertheless there was no rush to the barricades. Even the loudest of the conservationist cries of alarm must have seemed to the dedicated to reverberate discouragingly among the deaf. Grant McConnell, writing in 1954, looked back at the Teddy Roosevelt crusade and called it a "phenomenon the like of which we shall not see again"; by contrast the contemporary movement seemed to him "small, divided, and frequently uncertain." Established conservation organizations hung on, but mostly to serve the special interests of their nature-loving membership. A few new ones, such as the Nature Conservancy, started up, brave but almost invisible in a nation most of whose leaders were not remotely interested.

At mid-century President Truman appointed a Materials Policy Commission headed by William Paley, which was directed to answer the question: "Has the United States of America the material means to sustain its civilization?" It was a question that necessarily summoned what optimism one could command or invent. The Paley Commission found that we had indeed the necessary means to survive. But in the year of its report (1952) a national conference met to discuss substantially the same question. That conference was managed by a new organization, Resources for the Future, established by the Ford Foundation. In the following decade Resources for the Future looked exhaustively into all the ramifications and implications its resident and grant-supported scholars could imagine arising from the Paley Commission charge. The finding at last was not so much a reiterated "yes, we do have the material means," as a carefully documented rejection of the question itself and of the point of view from which it obtruded.

Since resources are not dissipated in use (with a few minor exceptions) but simply transformed, the resource issue cannot be properly defined as scarcity or abundance. The critical considerations have rather to do with the nature of the transformations (whether they are more or less socially beneficial), the costs entailed reckoned both in dollars and energy, and the social and environmental consequences of production and use. By the 1960s it had become all too obvious that we were more likely to suffocate from the residues of rampant production and consumption than to find production and consumption crimped by a shortage of materials. With that perception, both sensual and intellectual, conservation took a new turn, or rather it turned back to its deeper spiritual roots in a value system that questions not the adequacy of earth to man's purposes, but the appropriateness of man's own systems to the realization of his purposes.

# CHAPTER 20

# The Meek Take Heart

THE PROGRESSIVE MOVEMENT in the age of the first Roosevelt, the New Deal in the age of the second, and now in our time the ecological revolt have all been efforts to readjust the gross imbalance between economics and all other human concerns. Though each correction has had a different primary focus, set by particular historical circumstance, each has been in turn an awakening to suddenly perceived limits. Progressives faced the closing of the literal frontier and the end of the dream of growth unlimited; the New Deal awoke with a terrible headache from an orgy of avarice. The ecological dawn draws wisdom from both earlier awakenings and is more complex than either. It recognizes not just the limits of earth, not just the inadequacy of greed as the social helmsman, but the nature of man as a partly dominant and partly dependent creature whose greatness is to be realized not in showing off his power to rearrange the world but in disciplining that power to serve his own real needs.

That sounds grand and it is grand. But lest we cheer prematurely, congratulating ourselves that being at last awake we are in possession of our destiny, it is well to remember the alarming alacrity with which we went back to the old delusions after the two world wars had ended the earlier bursts of reform. The odds favor another relapse.

Already there are signs of weariness. Everybody has heard of our bad, dirty troubles and everybody smiles a little as if at an in joke. We have had our Earth Day and duly thundered in unison against sin. Since then no one has told us what else to do. Moreover, things have not got noticeably worse, and the old messages of alarm have been worn smooth by repetition, like pastilles for a minor throat ailment. If the ecological awakening was ever touched with the spirit of revolution, that has been plucked from it in this age of instant communication and universal salesmanship by the enemy or the old guard — the polluters themselves. Worried about clean air? Burn only Sir Galahad gas in your car. Want to keep the rivers sparkling pure? Wash your dishes with St. George's detergent. It is hard to shout from the barricades slogans that appear daily on television commercials. It is hard even to remember what they mean.

But we will be reminded. The problems we have just begun to address will not go away; they are points of friction among highly complex systems bound to heat up more and more unless basic changes are made. In fact the systems themselves have to be changed. They might be changed by revolution — a literal and violent overthrow, for instance, of capitalism (and communism too, since as concerns man and nature it accepts the same values), or a moral and ethical revolt that subverts the production-consumption economy by refusing to play by its rules. Or they could be better and more surely changed by actions well short of revolutionary but different in kind from and more radical than the measures of repair and minor adjustment that government has endorsed in principle.

Effective action must be radical in the sense of challenging the conventional wisdom. But it is a mistake to think that it must, therefore, be grand in scale to count. On the contrary, the entire record of man's relations with nature reveals that the significant changes have been set in motion by almost imperceptible shifts in direction. That is the method of evolution. It can also be a deliberate tactic of change. It is the tactic of current citizen action; what is important is to recognize how effective such action can be and not give up before the immensity of the task.

In 1965 some citizens of the mid–Hudson River Valley decided to contest the plans of the Consolidated Edison Company to build a pump-storage power plant at the base of Storm King Mountain. They joined forces in the Scenic Hudson Preservation Conference. The plant they opposed was designed to take care of peak demands for electricity in New York City. During periods of slack demand it would pump river water into a holding reservoir on top of the mountain; when needed, the water would flow down again to turn generators at the river's edge. The Federal Power Commission, finding the power was needed, granted a license; Scenic Hudson joined by the Sierra Club sued, and the Court of Appeals in a classic ruling reversed the grant on grounds that the FPC, in failing to consider the environmental impact of the plant, had not done its job. The Commission, the court said, was not created to act "as an umpire blandly calling balls and strikes for adversaries appearing before it; the right of the public must receive active and affirmative protection . . ." Moreover, the court continued, "in our affluent society, the cost of a project is only one of several factors to be considered." The court required the FPC to reconsider. The FPC did so and four years later again recommended the license be granted. Scenic Hudson and its friends promptly asked the court to set aside the new ruling. At this writing the impasse continues.

The interest of the Storm King case lies less in its outcome than in its myriad ambiguities and apparent inconclusiveness, which are just what one should expect where age-old processes and still older assumptions are suddenly called to question. First, opposition to the plant attacked the transmission lines that were to span the beautiful river gorge at Storm King, then the plant itself, typically square and ugly, on the bank of the river. From that beginning opponents discovered scores of other objections: Fish might die in the heated effluent; polluted, brackish water might seep from the reservoir through fissures in the underlying rock to contaminate water supplies; the plant's presence would attract industry, set precedent for further deterioration of the river. By redesign Con Edison met many of the objections: The plant was to be dug back into the mountain and merged with the landscape; the power lines would cross under the river; the reservoir would be made practically invisible from almost any point on the river at any season; and so on. The remaining objections, such as possible damage to fish life, could have been considered relatively trivial compared to the advantages the power might bring to the people of New York. But that was not the point.

Objectors to Storm King, some moved at first to protect their property, many possessed only of a hardly defined love of the countryside together with hostility to a highhanded power company, came stumblingly to a position that pitted one clear set of values against another. The worth of the Hudson Highlands was that they were natural, that they spoke to the human spirit from the world that was not man-made. Once man moved in his power plant, no matter how he decorated or concealed it, the "integrity of the mountain" was lost forever and this was what counted, not some fine calculation as to how visible concrete abutments might be when painted green. "Painting concrete green," David Sive, counsel for the plaintiffs, argued, "cannot deceive its beholders into believing that it is the handkerchief of the Lord, or, if it can, the Commission [the FPC] should not, in the absence of some overwhelming economic necessity, direct such deception." One was not weighing fish against air conditioners or even beauty against convenience. To figure that way would be to admit a possibility that air conditioners might be in such demand that fish would have to be exterminated or that convenience at some price might banish beauty altogether from rational consideration. In fact, no matter what the price of either beauty or convenience, man absolutely requires both.

For industries and regulatory agencies used to thinking of their job as to supply a single wanted good at the least possible price, the assertion that there are other not subsidiary but at least coequal requirements comes as a radically new directive, to which it is not easy for them to adjust. The Federal Power Commissioners' predictable reaction was to reassert their old position. After duly considering the environment, they could not see what business that was of theirs; on balance the production of power seemed more important. Of course, no other result could have been imagined now, but others are in the making. This case and others like it have marshaled strong social and economic forces behind a point of view that has not traditionally commanded Establishment support. Even though the court was willing only to return the case to the Federal Power Commission for review, and not to find more broadly that there are public rights in the preservation of the environment that public agencies may not rule away, the judicial lecture at least set the FPC (and by political carom all other regulatory agencies) on notice that the old ways of figuring costs and benefits no longer suffice. Even though the FPC resisted the invitation to take a broader look both at the real costs of power and at its own regulatory role, its narrower views have been put on the defensive. That is the first step toward their abandonment. And the nudging continues.

Late in 1970 the governor of New Jersey signed a bill that gave the state authority to restrict or prevent the development of its remaining marshlands. The governor had been under very heavy pressure not to sign from developers and their political allies, particularly in South Jersey, where the marshes along the Atlantic are very valuable real estate. Since the bill was carelessly drawn, there were reasonable grounds for a veto that would not have directly challenged the conservationists. Many of them therefore felt the bill had little chance to become law. In these circumstances the governor's signing not only did him credit but flagged new directions that thousands of fighters in scores of small fights here and there have established over the past decade. It is now well known to politicians and people generally that salt marshes are indispensable in the food chain that yields fish for the table; that freshwater marshes support wildfowl and store water to check floods. Such knowledge has been drilled into the public consciousness by repeated pitched battles: the fight to save the Great Swamp in New Jersey, for instance; the long campaign that eventuated in a wetlands protection law in Massachusetts; the continuing missionary work of conservation organizations, such as the Izaac Walton League, Ducks Unlimited, the Nature Conservancy, the Audubon societies. Transcending the recognition of particular practical values in the marshes is the growing sense that man needs the wild world even if, like an expanse of tidal flats covered with spartina grass and infested with mosquitoes, it does not seem like one of nature's handsomer gifts.

In the sixty years or so since San Francisco flooded the priceless Hetch-Hetchy Valley to get a water supply it might have gotten elsewhere, the careless dam builders have been stung and buffeted hundreds of times by the earthkeepers. More often than not, disputed dams have been built anyway, but after every battle the Philistines have been more on the defensive. It took heavy guns, chiefly the Sierra Club's, beginning in 1966, to kill proposed dams that would have flooded part of the Grand Canyon of the Colorado. In March of 1969 the Army Corps of Engineers agreed to relocate an already authorized dam in order to spare the Red River Gorge of Kentucky under hardly more pressure than public reminders of the beauty threatened. The engineers, incidentally, have their own ecological advisors now and complain with some justice that today it is they who are cooperative and conciliatory, their opponents who have become obstinate and unreasonable.

Over the whole range of environmental concerns people possessed of the new consciousness and the courage to assert it have already begun changing the system in ways that would have been inconceivable twenty — even ten — years ago. Many individual battles have been lost; none in itself can surely be called decisive; most have achieved only tentative victories. (This year the airport was not built, the bay was not filled, the marsh was not dredged; but bulldozers are in the shed with motors idling.)

Changes in the system are of course not permanent, nor necessarily pervasive. (Signs that highway builders have got the environmental message, even the fragmentary ones acknowledged by the dam builders, are scant and unconvincing.) The search for new values and new ways entails battle and surrounds itself with the rhetoric of battle. But change when won is not in any military or moral sense a victory; it is only a fresh opportunity. Saving the swamp holds open options for the community to make rational use of its land and natural resources; such options, however, lapse quickly unless they are exercised. If the game is not war but evolution, then one has to think not of battles but of directions. Freedom from smog is not something that is going to be achieved by one heroic effort, after which we can forget about *that* problem. Much less can even major readjustments in the way we live assure forever a harmonious relationship between men and the land and its other life. That is why the cry should not be for revolution but for pointing the snout of civilization upwind to sense out better, safer paths to human fulfillment.

In what quarter do those better paths lie? Some seem clear and relatively easy, such as the good earthkeeping paths leading to clean, nontoxic air and to efficiently managed water supplies assuring us enough for all the manifold purposes of an industrial nation. In one sense these *are* simple tasks. Provided people maintain and articulate their insistence on such minimal care of the common resources, there are only relatively minor obstacles to eventual success — chiefly money and the shaping of federal and state laws efficiently to express the majority will against the few who would thwart it. The job of cleaning up pollution may be done badly, expensively and late but, if we insist, it will be done — unless, of course, some swifter catastrophe overtakes us.

But this is not ground for complacency. If the ecological revolt exhausts itself in a giant pick-up–clean-up, if indeed the new awakening to man's dependence on his environment is diverted into a passion for cleanliness, and we pursue that Doppelgänger without precisely counting the costs, we will have failed the challenge, and may end up with a cleaner but otherwise worse world. If, for instance, the charge for cleanliness is added to everybody's cost of living, the poor will pay disproportionately. If taking care of the environment is embraced in lieu of more difficult causes, and resources are diverted to sewage treatment plants or parks that might otherwise have gone to housing, health, welfare, and schools, most of us would think this a perversion, not a reordering, of values. Finally, if the economy purges itself of the burden of pollution only in order to be free to run even faster after endlessly elaborated consumer goods, then we will have profited no more from our sober interlude than the junkie who kicks the habit in order to go on to cheaper highs.

In a world where everything is connected, tinkering with one problem at a time is a sure way of multiplying problems. That lesson sounds as clear a warning to the antipollution enthusiasts as to the dam builders. So you would have the rivers clean because that is the "right" thing to do. But at what sacrifice? Who will make it? If the rivers are not merely to be made clean now but kept clean, the way we use them will have to be radically changed. It may be, for instance, that a paper mill unable to modernize economically may have to close up and put a lot of people out of work; who will find jobs for them, and how, and where? Or if government is to subsidize renovation and pollution control equipment, what are the implications of that for competition, for taxes? Questions of this kind are asked only at the threshold of change. In New York City day after day the air is reported to be "unsatisfactory." If "unsatisfactory" proves to kill or even if it just proves intolerable to long-suffering city dwellers, the effective cure may entail such drastic measures as banning private automobiles, developing on a crash basis methods of disposing of greatly increased quantities of solid wastes to eliminate burning, or reducing and rationing power. Repercussions on the automobile industry and through it on the economy would be significant; the implications of tightened controls over individual liberties are grave indeed.

Or look at pollution control in the context of political power. No resident of a big city can be under any delusion as to how relative power in our society affects the care of the environment. Life is not only more pleasant but a lot safer for New Yorkers who live in the East Sixties than for those who live in Harlem. Spokesmen for the poor can hardly be sanguine about how resources are likely to be distributed in the clean-up on which we have ostensibly embarked. They want to know whose environment gets cleaned up first and best. They want to know if the new sewage treatment plant is necessary, if it is more important than new housing, if it will make a difference commensurate with its cost, and if that difference will be equally beneficial to all. They want to know who has reckoned the distribution of benefits and costs of current clean-up programs and how priorities have been set. These are fair questions. There are not, so far as I know, good answers on hand or even under study.

Widen the context still further to take in the world. Poor nations, like poor people in rich nations, are aware of pollution and have seen that unbridled exploitation of resources can lead to catastrophic collapse of the producing systems. Most cities in the developing countries put up with polluted water that is not only a nuisance but frequently a menace to health. Most countries have known massive agricultural failure from various kinds of soil abuse. They do not want more. But as they survey their meager resources and overwhelming needs, a little dirt and a few setbacks must seem acceptable risks as compared to diminishing or slowing the processes of production. Many of their leaders now look askance at the newly awakened environmental conscience of the developed world and wonder if it may not be exercised partly at *their* expense. A case in point is DDT. Its use anywhere in the world is a threat to life everywhere. But if it is to be banned universally, who will pay the added costs of insect control? Might not foreign aid programs, which have never been politically strong, succumb to the new discovery that industrialism is a mixed blessing that the underdeveloped could be spared? If antipollution measures add materially to the costs of production, might not some or all of the developed countries try to protect themselves with new restrictions on trade?

Cleaning up is indeed a simple job. What is hard is to ravel out the implications and go about the job in such a way as to make the world not just cleaner, but better overall. Above all that means concern for the social costs and very difficult decisions to apportion the costs fairly. We need therefore to be clear what the task is: *The task is not to get rid of pollution but to manage producing systems of all kinds so that they do not pollute.*

A few entomologists, agronomists and others have been working quietly for a number of years to develop the principles and practice of what they call integrated pest control. It is not just a substitute for DDT but a revolutionary way of looking at and managing natural systems. And it has worked, sometimes brilliantly. In the Cañete Valley of Peru the staple crop since the 1920s has been cotton. It is grown under irrigation in an area that gets almost no rain. For a generation cotton pests were controlled well enough by the old-fashioned poisons such as arsenic compounds. But in 1948 a severe outbreak coincided with the availability of DDT invented during the war. The farmers embraced DDT as the miraculous cure. And for a time it seemed to be. Under its lethal mantle cotton yields almost doubled. Entranced with their success, the farmers sprayed more and more. They even cut down trees to make spraying easier. With the fallen trees fell the nests of birds that had eaten insects. Meanwhile, the DDT had been killing not only pests but the insects and parasites that fed on the pests. Year after year, moreover, the target populations built up immunity as those more susceptible to DDT died off, leaving the cotton feast for the fit. Without enemies and adapted to their poisoned world, the bugs took over. Seven years after the DDT spraying had begun, cotton yields were only half to two thirds of what they had been before. In their desperation the farmers called for help. Half the answer was to stop using the persistent organic pesticides, like DDT, and return to the more selective poisons of a half century ago. But with this went changes in cultivation practices. Schedules of planting and watering, spacing and weeding were adjusted to help the enemies of the pests while reducing the feeding opportunities of the pest itself. By experimentation, regimens were tailored to the place and its native life. These so effectively brought the cotton-feeding insects under control that yields climbed steadily back and now stand at the highest in history.

Success at Cañete was no miracle; it came out of understanding that led to good management; it eschewed the kind of procrustean bullheadedness that thinks to lop off whatever in nature does not fit the convenience of man. The trouble with DDT as a method of control is that it is essentially the method of war. It regards the pest as an enemy and seeks to destroy him. The trouble with war as an instrument of reform is that it does not discriminate. Attacking pests with broadcast persistent and general poisons is like trying to get rid of Communists with napalm. The side effects in both cases are disastrous, and for similar reasons. In spreading death indiscriminately you disorder functioning systems. As they break down, opportunities for plunder open up exactly as riots bring looting in train. Once the structure of the community, whether of man or nature, has been destroyed, the lawless, like the pests, can no longer be controlled. So the exterminator emptying niches in nature creates pathologic conditions that parallel the social chaos in the wake of devastating war.

The answer, of course, is to work with the system, not against it. In pest control the winning tactic is to see the pest for what he is, a sign of an already disturbed system, and then set about closing out his opportunities by restoring stability. That can be done, as it was done at Cañete, by setting as the goal not the extermination of a pest but production of the largest harvestable crop that can be managed and sustained. The object is not a farm free of pests but one in which the resident pests are under control and by being there discourage strangers who may be less easy to manage. Bollworms, lygus bugs and the rest still eat cotton plants in Cañete but not enough to matter. Bugs get some; people get more. That is not necessarily equity; but it *is* good sense.

I have written at some length about pest control because worldwide it is an extremely important environmental problem in itself, but also because it illustrates the broader principle of applying management methods to our relations with nature instead of the methods of surgery, medication, and war. Now we kill wolves and eagles because wolves and eagles occasionally kill sheep. But the cost of a few lost sheep is miniscule compared to the cost of disrupting the adapted relationships of the wild by removing the predators that help keep communities healthy and on even keel. We could easily instead keep the predators' numbers down if necessary and live with the comparative few that nature needs. It is the special arrogance of man, and may be the death of him, to think that any living thing can be dismissed as merely a nuisance.

The kind of management I have described contains a measure of tolerance, a spirit of accommodation, even a humility. Indeed that humble ingredient characterizes the very concept of management as distinguished from quasi-military command. It hardly characterizes man's typical attitude toward the world and its resources. We assume, for instance, that water must always be brought to people for whatever they want wherever they are. Yet sometimes people might be constrained to settle elsewhere or change their ways, not to insist on farming in arid regions perhaps, or forgo the use of water for waste disposal where the supplies are limited or better used in other ways. Is that so outrageous?

A wilderness area, precious but fragile, ought to be enjoyed by as many people as possible; but at some density visitors destroy what they came to savor. To keep the experience of the wild we must agree to submit to discipline, to stand in line and wait our turn. That would need a double dose of humility: a respect for the wild so great that one does not wish to destroy it, and a willingness to let the other fellow go if one's own turn does not come. (Such willingness, needless to say, can only consort with a system of scrupulous fairness that does not reward wealth or special favor.)

The most ardent conservationist could not defend an immediate ban on further road building. He can observe that so long as the demand for roads responds to the supply of cars and the demand for cars responds to the supply of roads, we are logically condemned to paving the planet. In the United States the Highway Trust Fund, plowing gas taxes directly and exclusively into highways, has given the chain reaction frightening momentum already. It can be slowed immediately by abolishing the Trust Fund and making much larger public investment in mass transportation. In the longer run, human mobility is also a management problem in which the demand for satisfaction of one requirement must be modified to accommodate other needs. There is no inherent right to drive. There is no absolute need for people to live spread out as they have come to live in large part because of the automobile. Of all the instruments of civilization, automobiles most obviously threaten to establish the kind of human dominion over earth that would empty it of other inhabitants. The automobile in this sense is the symbol and servant of that kind of ecological arrogance that is more to be feared than the air pollution to which it contributes. We will begin to bring the automobile under control only as we begin to lessen our dependence on it, not merely by developing other ways to get around but by eliminating some of the requirement for travel: denser settlements; improved electronic communications; alternative stay-at-home recreation; ways of life that discipline restlessness.

Few metropolitan areas in the United States have not had one or more airport crises in the past decade. When airports get dangerously crowded the only way out anyone ever thinks of is to build more airports. The possibility of cutting down air travel is never discussed, for more and faster moving to and fro is one of the symbols of progress and the air industry is very powerful. But if the real reason we build more airports — sometimes at high cost, destroying priceless natural areas, increasing noise and air pollution, adding to ground congestion — if the real reason is to flatter the egos of technological man or make more money for the industry, we should know that and not talk as though airports responded to deep-felt, indeed inexorable, human need. I would guess that air traffic could be held well within the capacity of present airport facilities by a ruling of the Internal Revenue Service limiting the amount of travel that could be deducted as a business expense. I would guess, too, that there is no chance of such a ruling.

Where man goes ecologically astray he is usually looking rather to serve his convenience than to gratify his needs.

Convenience is a negotiable demand. Conservationists by and large seek to negotiate it. The ecological argument is not that man should do without things he needs in order to spare other living creatures. One might indeed ethically argue that position, but long before we get to the garden of St. Francis there are realms of common sense to be explored. And the first is the needs of man himself.

Man thrives on differences; culturally and biologically they have enabled us to progress. Yet man everywhere acts to assure uniformity. He is driven by a passion to reiterate a few successes and let go whatever cannot make it big. That is a characteristic of mass civilization, of a technology that can stamp out copies cheaply by the billion, and of an economic system that rewards numbers more obviously than quality. But it is also a biologically normal consequence of creature drives. Humanity bent on the take-over of the earth for its own exclusive habitat wipes out the variety of competing life forms. Within the human race the dominant majorities tend to overwhelm the dissident and nonconformist minorities for no other reason than that they can. Man in this regard is not special.

In nature the losers in the fight for peck order, the less well adapted, normally are driven out and their chance for survival lies chiefly in their ability to adapt to another environmental niche. Through migration and genetic change natural systems thus both accommodate variety and enrich it. As man is in total occupation of the human niche, and this is coincident with the planet, there is no place left for difference to go. If difference is to survive it must somehow coexist with dominance. That is to say, those who have the power must be persuaded or forced by irrepressible rebellion (see the history of totalitarian societies) to moderate its use in order, for their own ultimate benefit, to tolerate those whom they could destroy. That forbearance is required equally of all men in regard to other living things and of human majorities in regard to the oddballs among us.

When, as commonly happens, a rugged (or merely jealous) democrat attacks the preservation of a wilderness area on grounds that it can only serve a few people and therefore smells of elitism, he is not merely being crass and Philistine; he is running with the bulldozers which, if they ever carry through their threat to homogenize the world, will surely destroy it. In the grand tendency of the universe to run down, the process is a gradual blurring of difference until all parts are alike. Then the machine stops, never to go again, because nothing more can happen. A nation paved with highways, built up to subdivisions, and engineered to have identical climate and resources, approaches psychologically at least that ultimate warm death.

To conserve the variety of the world is to conserve life itself — our life. And because it is our life, conservation is a personal responsibility that cannot be delegated to government. Government acts through bureaucracies and bureaucracies respond like all organisms to their own drives. None are and none could conceivably be driven by a passion to conserve environment. The Corps of Engineers, for instance, does large-scale plumbing to correct the inconveniences of natural hydrology. That is their job. No matter how enlightened they might be, that would still be their job, and they could never discover disenchantment with the virtues of large-scale plumbing.

So with all the other agencies. Good or bad, by their nature they cannot see social needs whole; they can grasp only the fragments of need that come within their purview. Seen through the windows of bureaucracy, what society wants is what a particular agency is under pressure to deliver. To create super agencies — the perennial dream of the coordinators — is no answer. However designed or enlarged, they acquire their own specialties, their own expertness, their own prejudices, their own passion to survive and special constituencies who learn how to press the right reflex points to get what *they* want.

Only to individuals can come the saving insights into the range of human need and the complexities of the world community that is to be managed to meet those needs. Because that is so, we face a paradox that could justify despair or bright new hope: At the same time that people have come to depend on systems so complicated and remote that no one can claim to control them, society as never before needs the guidance of the individual. The ecological revolt recognizes that need and to some degree is meeting it. There lies the hope. But realization will take persistence and courage never before demanded of a citizens' movement.

As the system prodded here and there by a successful lawsuit against DDT or a political fight to save a wilderness or beat a congressman begins to shift just a little, very powerful interests will feel the ground tipping and take alarm. The next prod thereupon becomes more dangerous, meets more resistance. To keep on pushing after the interests dig in will take not just courage, but faith — faith that the loneliest dissent, if it is sturdy and just, will make a difference in the world. That faith can draw what sustenance it needs from the story of life itself and the story of man: Evolution has been driven by difference from the beginning.

# Notes

PART I — SITUATION REPORT

CHAPTER 1. THE ENVIRONMENTAL CRISIS

[*Page*]

8 Have gone down a little. See *Nature,* vol. 22 (June 14, 1969), pp. 1017–1018.

8 Be sure just what. See, for instance, Walter Orr Roberts, "Inadvertent Weather Modification," in J. E. Caskey, Jr., ed., *A Century of Weather Progress* (Boston: American Meteorological Society, December 1970).

11 Of total destruction. Luther J. Carter, "Galveston Bay: Test Case of an Estuary in Crisis," *Science,* vol. 167 (February 20, 1970), pp. 1102–1108.

CHAPTER 2. AN AGREEABLE REVOLUTION

16 Obstructing "progress." Edward Teller in *The New Scientist* (February 19, 1970).

18 Has now become real. Victor C. Ferkiss, *Technological Man: The Myth and the Reality* (New York: Braziller, 1969), p. 21.

18 Interglacial period. John R. Von Neumann, "Can We Survive Technology?" *Fortune,* vol. 51 (June 1955), p. 108.

19 Else has examined. The so-called NAWAPA (North American Water and Power Alliance) scheme worked out by the Parsons Engineering Company. See "NAWAPA: A Continental Water System," *Bulletin of the Atomic Scientists* (September 1967).

20 The physical world. Charles R. DeCarlo, "Perspectives on Technology," Eli Ginzburg, ed., in *Technology and Social Change* (New York: Columbia University Press, 1964), p. 12.

21 Sickly effete. See, for instance, the cover of *Time* magazine (February 2, 1970) on which the picture of ecologist Barry Commoner, the good guy, is projected on a pastoral scene from which man is otherwise absent; the contrasting panel shows Commoner's and our problems: a city with industry belching smoke and city people spewing out garbage. Robert E. Coughlin and Karen A. Goldstein have written an intersting pamphlet on *The Public's View of the Outdoor Environment as Interpreted by Magazine Ad-Makers,* Regional Science Research Institute Discussion Paper No. 25 (October 1968).

21 They had 40 million. Marion R. Clawson, R. Burnell Held, and Charles H. Stoddard, *Land for the Future* (Baltimore: Johns Hopkins Press, 1960), p. 168; *Science*, vol. 161 (August 23, 1968), p. 771.

21 "Prevalence of people." See his book by that title.

22 "Is good politics." *The New Yorker*, vol. 45 (January 17, 1970).

24 "Concerned with all along." *New York Times*, March 8, 1970.

CHAPTER 3. HOW TO GET LESS BY MULTIPLYING

28 The 50 he expected. Frank Notestein, former president of the Population Council, quoted in Paul R. and Anne H. Ehrlich, *Population, Resources, Environment: Issues in Human Ecology* (San Francisco: W. H. Freeman, 1970), p. 37.

28 May be too high. Ibid., p. 38.

28 The Industrial Revolution. See, for instance, Lewis Mumford, *The City in History: Its Transformations and Its Prospects* (New York: Harcourt, 1961), p. 259.

29 To replace deaths. Ehrlich and Ehrlich, p. 39.

30 Fatal chance encounters. This, however, is only one of several population controls among Tribolium. While the particular mechanism is simple, the system it helps stabilize is highly complex.

30 Stress of crowding. Edward S. Deevey, "The Hare and Haruspex: A Cautionary Tale," *The Yale Review* (Winter 1960).

30 Predatory males. D. H. Stott, "Cultural and Natural Checks on Population Growth," in Andrew P. Vayda, ed., *Environment and Cultural Behavior* (New York: Natural History Press, 1969), pp. 111–112.

31 Succeeding generations. G. Evelyn Hutchinson, *The Ecological Theater and the Evolutionary Play* (New Haven: Yale University Press, 1965), p. 88.

32 Maintenance rate of 2.1. Tomas Frejka, "Reflections on the Demographic Conditions Needed to Establish a U.S. Stationary Population Growth," *Population Studies*, vol. 22 (November 1968).

33 Of 15.7 per cent. Ibid.

34 The "green revolution." See, for instance, Lester Brown, *Seeds of Change: The Green Revolution and Development in the 1970's* (New York: Praeger, 1970).

35 European wheat production. Jean Mayer, "Toward a Non-Malthusian Population Policy," *Columbia Forum,* (Summer 1969).

35 Remained unsold. *Nature,* vol. 225 (January 3, 1970), p. 1.

35 Back were saying. See, for instance, William and Paul Paddock, *Famine 1975!* (Boston: Little, Brown, 1967).

CHAPTER 4. NUMBERS, SPACE, AND TIME

39 Fifth of its cotton. Paul R. Ehrlich and Anne H. Ehrlich, *Population, Resources, Environment: Issues in Human Ecology* (San Francisco: W. H. Freeman, 1970), p. 50.

40 Having 1.4 billion people. Cited in Ehrlich and Ehrlich, p. 40.

40 Exist to facilitate. See, for instance, Melvin Webber, "Order in Diversity; Community Without Propinquity," in Lowdon Wingo, Jr., ed., *Cities and Space: The Future Use of Urban Land* (Baltimore: Johns Hopkins Press, 1963); also Kenneth Boulding, cited in Christopher Tunnard, *The Modern American City* (New York: Van Nostrand, 1968), p. 98.

41 Jane Jacobs. *The Death and Life of Great American Cities* (New York: Vintage, 1961).

42 To relieve it. Charles Elton, *The Ecology of Animals*, 3d ed. (London: Methuen, 1950), p. 71.

42 Taking them along. Joseph R. Birdsell, "Some Predictions for the Pleistocene Based on Equilibrium Systems Among Recent Hunter-Gatherers," in Richard B. Lee and Irven De Vore, eds., *Man the Hunter* (Chicago: Aldine, 1969), p. 236.

42 Part of Guatemala. Oscar H. Horst, "The Specter of Death in a Guatemalan Highland Community," *The Geographical Review*, vol. 57 (April 1967), pp. 151–167.

46 And their meaning. See, for instance, Judith Blake, "Population Policy for Americans: Is the Government Being Misled?" *Science*, vol. 164 (May 2, 1969), pp. 522–529; and Oscar Harkavy, "Family Planning and Policy: Who Is Misleading Whom?" *Science*, vol. 165 (July 25, 1969), pp. 367–373.

46 40 or 45 years. U.S., Congress, House, Subcommittee of the Committee on Government Operations, *Effects of Population Growth on Natural Resources and the Environment: Hearing*, 91st Cong., 1st sess., September 15–16, 1969, p. 85.

46 "Of compound interest?" Thomas Eisner, Ari van Tienhoven

Frank Rosenblatt, editorial in *Science*, vol. 167 (January 23, 1970), p. 337.

46 Attack on the problem. See Bernard Berelson, "Beyond Family Planning," *Science*, vol. 163 (February 7, 1969), pp. 533–543.

47 Is in prospect. See, for instance, Garrett Hardin, "Parenthood: Right or Privilege?" *Science*, vol. 169 (July 31, 1970), p. 427; Edgar Berman, "We Must Limit Families by Law," *New York Times*, December 15, 1970.

### CHAPTER 5. DEFERRED MAINTENANCE

49 Deferred Maintenance. Portions of this chapter are adapted from a report to the Ford Foundation Board of Trustees. I am grateful to my colleagues William E. Felling, Edward A. Ames, Janet Koch, Theresa Lisniewski, and Florie Hayes, and to Richard Carpenter and Wallace Bowman of the Legislative Reference Service of the Library of Congress for their assistance in preparing that report.

49 "Natural resources." *New York Times*, October 19, 1968.

49 Put the problem). President's Science Advisory Committee, *Report of the Environmental Pollution Panel* (The White House, November 1965). John W. Tukey, professor of mathematics at Princeton University, was chairman of the panel.

50 More than exponential. "Exponential" refers to an increase that results from applying a constant rate to an enlarging base. The population explosion has been characterized by an increasing rate.

51 Bituminous coal. Since all energy can be converted into heat — and in fact all eventually is — heat equivalents are the common universal measure. Quantities may also be reckoned in British Thermal Units (Btu) or calories, but coal equivalents are just as satisfactory and more graphic.

51 1341 million tons. Sam H. Schurr and Bruce C. Netschert, *Energy in the American Economy, 1850–1975: An Economic*

*Study of Its History and Prospects.* (Baltimore: Johns Hopkins Press, 1960), p. 35.

51 6100 kilowatt hours. Lowell C. Harriss, *The American Economy: Principles, Practices and Policies,* 6th ed. (Homewood, Ill.: Richard D. Irwin, 1968), p. 59.

51 7 per cent a year. *Science,* vol. 162 (October 11, 1968), p. 221.

51 Maintain his body. Robert U. Ayres and Allen V. Kneese, "Environmental Pollution," in Joint Economic Committee, *Programs for the Development of Human Resources,* vol. 2 (Washington: U.S. Government Printing Office, 1968), p. 683.

51 As fast as population. Ibid.

51 The national rate. Philip A. Leighton, "Geographic Aspects of Air Pollution," *Geographical Review,* vol. 66 (April 1966), p. 168.

52 Since 1918. Blair T. Bower et al., *Waste Management: Generation and Disposal of Solid, Liquid and Gaseous Wastes in the New York Region* (New York: Regional Plan Association, 1968), p. 13.

52 64 million tons. U.S., Congress, House, Subcommittee on Science, Research and Development of the Committee on Science and Astronautics, *Environmental Quality: Hearings,* 90th Cong., 2d sess., January 17–19, 31; February 1–2; March 12–14, 1968, p. 303.

52 Plastic, nonreturnable. Ayres and Kneese, p. 670.

52 600 feet high. Bower et al., p. 51.

52 The same minute. Leighton, p. 152.

53 Than an aspiration. The Council on Environmental Quality has commissioned a study by the MITRE Corporation of what it would take to build a national environmental monitoring system, "Monitoring the Environment of the Nation — a Systems Design Concept," MITRE report MTR–4176 (October 1970).

53 Air, and water. For pollution control the basic laws are the Clean Air Act of 1963 (amended in 1965 and 1966); the Air Quality Act of 1967; the National Emission Standards Act of 1967; the Water Quality Act of 1965; the Clean Water

Restoration Act of 1966; the Water Quality Improvement Act of 1970; and the Solid Waste Disposal Act of 1965. For acquisition of land (parks and natural areas) for preservation or recreation, the most significant legislation is the Land and Water Conservation Fund Act of 1965 and Title VII of the Housing Act of 1961 (as amended in 1964) that sets up the open-space land purchase and development program under the Department of Housing and Urban Development. Potentially as important as any of these is the first piece of legislation to consider environmental deterioration as a single set of interrelated issues and earthkeeping as an overall government responsibility: The National Environmental Policy Act of 1969 that requires every federal agency to consider explicitly and implicitly the impact on the environment of each of its recommended actions. A Council on Environmental Quality is supposed to see that they do and report to the President if they do not. Additional staff and money for the Council came with a later law, the Environmental Quality Improvement Act of 1970.

54 Other level of government. The Bureau of Public Roads, whose decisions probably affect the settlement patterns of Americans more than do the decisions of any other single agency, has apparently determined that land-use planning is unrealistic and therefore cannot be considered in locating highways. See Thomas A. Morehouse, "The 1962 Highway Act: A Study in Artful Interpretation," *Journal of the American Institute of Planners,* vol. 35 (May 1969), p. 165.

54 Presidential councils. As of the end of 1969 air pollution control was the job of the Department of Health, Education, and Welfare, which also had the principal responsibility for solid waste management. Until mid-1969 HEW could do nothing about the solid waste problems arising out of extraction, processing, and use of minerals and fossil fuels, which were in the jurisdiction of the Bureau of Mines in the Department of the Interior. Interior in 1970 remained charged with water pollution control but significant research

and development was also being supported by the Atomic Energy Commission, the National Aeronautics and Space Administration, the U.S. Coast Guard, the Army Corps of Engineers, the Department of Commerce, the Tennessee Valley Authority, the Department of Health, Education and Welfare, the Appalachian Regional Commission, the Department of Agriculture, the National Science Foundation, and the Department of Housing and Urban Development. These other agencies in fact spent $240 million on water pollution control in fiscal 1968 as compared to $303 million spent through the lead agency, Interior's Federal Water Quality Administration (until 1970 called the Federal Water Pollution Control Administration).

## CHAPTER 6. THE HIGH COST OF WASTE

55 Technical assistance. The Bureau of Solid Waste Management provided money for research, planning, and demonstration. Before the 1970 reorganization it was one of five bureaus under the Environmental Control Administration, which was one of three divisions of the Consumer Protection and Environmental Health Services (the others being the National Air Pollution Control Administration and the Pure Food and Drug Administration) in the Public Health Service of HEW. Appropriations rose from $4.4 million in fiscal 1966 to $17.5 million in fiscal 1969, in each year falling short of authorizations by $2 to $4 million.

The costs of waste handling in the United States have been estimated as at least $4.5 billion a year. The publicly paid share represents the third most expensive item on the public service budget, after schools and highways. (See Ayres and Kneese, p. 669). In addition, there is the cost of land engrossed for dumps. Senator Muskie has guessed that about 7000 square miles have been covered or damaged by garbage in the past 30 years. (Remarks reported in *Environmental*

*Science and Technology,* vol. 3 (June 1969), p. 517.) This does not, of course, represent net loss, since sanitary landfill properly located can create sites for industry or housing. Proper landfill, however, remains the exception, and incalculable esthetic damage and threats to health must be reckoned one of the significant costs of the usual insanitary dump. Finally, the dump is permanent burial ground of potentially useful materials, whose removal from the scene will presumably be reflected eventually in higher costs of harder-to-recover natural resources. (For a carefully documented view that depletion of high-grade resources so far has not led to higher costs, see Harold J. Barnett and Chandler Morse, *Scarcity and Growth: The Economics of Natural Resource Availability* (Baltimore: Johns Hopkins Press, 1963).

56 Into the sun. *National Observer,* November 25, 1968.

56 Collection and transport. The President in his message on the environment February 10, 1970, said: "I have ordered a redirection of research under the Solid Waste Disposal Act to place greater emphasis on techniques for recycling materials, and on the development and use of packaging and other materials which will degrade after use . . ." *New York Times,* February 11, 1970.

56 No more money. See *Conservation Foundation Newsletter,* February, 1970, p. 10.

56 High-quality scrap). *Cleaning Our Environment: The Chemical Basis for Action* (Washington: American Chemical Society, 1969), p. 181.

57 Such as Ur. See Gideon Sjoberg, *The Preindustrial City* (New York: Free Press, 1960), p. 35.

57 Somewhere else. One of the comparatively economical methods of reducing sulphur dioxide emissions from power plants, by adding limestone in combustion, increases the amount of ash to be removed by two to four times. Half the capital and operating costs of secondary treatment plants may go into handling the residual sludge. For example, three treatment plants in Chicago produce more than 900 tons

of sludge (dry weight) a day. To dispose of that costs $14.5 million a year, 46 per cent of the whole water treatment bill.

57 "Growing public concern." U.S., Congress, Senate, first report of the Secretary of HEW to Congress, *Progress in the Prevention and Control of Air Pollution,* 90th Cong., 2d sess., June 28, 1968, p. 1.

57 To the states. Appropriations were, of course, smaller. Beginning with $186,000 in 1955, spending rose to about $11 million by 1963. The states did still less. California spent half as much each year as all the rest of the states combined, and even the Californian effort was hardly equal to the challenge. Nominal air pollution control programs existed in 15 states in 1963, but they had no staff or money even to collect necessary information much less take action.

57 "Pollution problems." *Progress in the Prevention and Control of Air Pollution,* 1968, p. 1.

58 "Was negligible." U.S., Congress, House, second report by the Committee on Government Operations, *Federal Air Pollution Research and Development,* 91st Cong., 1st sess., March 13, 1969, p. 3.

58 Abatement and control. Estimated spending for 1969 was $24.7 million for research and demonstration, and $22.7 million for abatement and control out of total appropriations of more than $88 million. That contrasted, however, to an authorization of $185 million.

58 Highly suspect. U.S., Congress, House, Subcommittee on Science, Research and Development of the Committee on Science and Astronautics, *Environmental Quality: Hearings,* 90th Cong., 2d sess., January 17–19, 31; February 1–2; March 12–14, 1968, pp. 128–129.

59 To warm them. Personal communication from Dr. J. Y. Wang of San Jose State College.

59 The streets can take. George B. Morgan, Guntis Ozolins, and Elbert C. Tabor, "Air Pollution Surveillance Systems," *Science,* vol. 170 (October 16, 1970), pp. 289–296.

59 Than in 1967. *Science,* vol. 163 (June 24, 1969), p. 374.

59 Power-generating plants. *New York Times,* June 4, 1969.

60 Out of every two. U.S., Congress, Senate, staff report to the Committee on Public Works, *A Study of Pollution — Air*, 88th Cong., 1st sess., September 1963, p. 11.

60 To cause plant damage. Philip A. Leighton, "Geographic Aspects of Air Pollution," *Geographical Review*, vol. 66 (April 1966), pp. 163, 166–167.

60 Could be enforced. *Environmental Quality*, pp. 72–73, 583–586. Motor vehicles contribute 60 per cent by weight of all air pollutants, as compared with 14 per cent for power plants, 17 per cent for other industry and 9 per cent for heating and waste incineration. See Abel Wolman, "Air Pollution: Time for Appraisal," *Science*, vol. 159 (March 29, 1968), p. 1439. Automobiles are responsible for 90 per cent of the carbon monoxide (which has been shown to impair human functioning at concentrations that are common on city streets in rush hours), 60 per cent of the hydrocarbons (key ingredients in photochemical smog), 50 per cent of the oxides of nitrogen (which are also important in the formation of smog and appear to affect cell chemistry in mice, though in ways and with consequences not understood), virtually all the lead whose concentration in air in large part from burning leaded gasoline is estimated to be at least one thousand times what it would be were it not for man's activities. (See *Cleaning Our Environment*, p. 42; Robert U. Ayres, "Air Pollution in Cities," *Natural Resources Journal* (University of New Mexico), vol. 9 (January 1969), p. 5.

61 Mechanics, and drivers. U.S., Senate, second report of the Secretary of HEW to Congress, *Progress in the Prevention and Control of Air Pollution*, 91st Cong., 1st sess., March 4, 1969, p. 39; U.S., Congress, Senate, staff report to the Committee on Commerce, *The Search for a Low-emission Vehicle*, 91st Cong., 1st sess., 1969, p. 4.

62 Health Association. *New York Times*, March 12, 1970.

62 Cancer-causing agents. *A Study of Pollution — Air*, p. 17; *The Search for a Low-emission Vehicle*, p. 2.

62 Make man healthier. For a flat assertion that dirty air makes a man sicker, and an excellent review of the literature on

smogging and health, see Lester B. Love and Eugene P. Seskin, "Air Pollution and Human Health," *Science,* vol. 169 (August 21, 1970), pp. 723ff.

62 Be an accessory. Studies of second-grade school children in Cincinnati recently showed that the lungs of those who lived in the more polluted parts of the city worked significantly less well and that the difference in function was measurable even when the difference in average exposure was as little as 20 per cent, other things being apparently equal. (See *Progress in the Prevention and Control of Air Pollution,* second report, p. 18.) Young children as apparently much more subject to asthma and eczema where the air is heavily polluted (*New York Times,* June 15, 1970).

63 City people breathe. At Hazelton Laboratories in Falls Church, Virginia. See *Environmental Quality,* p. 137.

63 Proof before acting. Federal programs of research and control have been unconscionably dilatory and hobbled by patchwork institutions. In 1968 Washington spent less than $7.5 million for research on all aspects of air pollution, including its effect on human health. Much-publicized increases in appropriations since then still leave the federal effort way below the minimum standard required to reverse deterioration. Standards set for air purity and automobile emissions appear to be commands of Canute; enforcement procedures are either unworkable or nonexistent. The Department of HEW admitted recently that after passing on prototype automobile smog control devices it is thereafter without power to see to it that such devices are used and continue to work. The new Environmental Protection Agency may have more power. On the broader front, the system of interstate airsheds in which the states are charged with maintaining air quality with federal intervention authorized only if they do not act is not on the face of it the most obviously effective political mechanism.

States and localities have not rushed to fill their role as the primary enforcers. In 1961 only 17 states and 85 localities had air pollution control agencies. Together they spent $10 million. Nine years later amid unprecedented public clamor all but four states had adopted programs, but the number of local agencies had not even doubled. The 46 states and 142 local agencies in 1969 together spent only $47.3 million, including federal assistance.

63 Minor dangers. *Environmental Quality,* p. 178.

64 And industrial wastes. Secondary treatment means that after the gross solids in sewage have been screened and settled, the effluent (in which, of course, there are still suspended and dissolved solids) is put through filters or digesters — there are several different techniques — which essentially imitate the filtration and biological digestion processes that would occur in natural waters if the raw sewage were dumped in the river. By controlling and speeding up these natural processes, secondary treatment can spare the stream bacteria up to 90 per cent of the work they would otherwise have to perform in breaking down organic compounds in the water into their organic components. Since bacteria in degrading organics use up oxygen dissolved in the water, the quality of the effluent can also be stated in terms of how much oxygen it would take to purify it. Secondary treatment thus can be said to remove up to 90 per cent of the biological oxygen demand (BOD), generally figured as the demand over a five-day period. To reduce BOD further requires more sophisticated processes of filtration and chemical treatment. Costs rise exponentially as absolute purity is approached.

65 Acceptable water purity. U.S., Congress, Senate, report of the Department of the Interior to Congress, *The Cost of Clean Water,* 90th Cong., 2d sess., January 10, 1968; also *Environmental Science and Technology,* vol. 3 (March 1969), p. 213.

65 Prove insufficient. Out of 146 million city dwellers in the United States in 1966 at least 32 million were not served even by sewers; another 32 million put their sewage through primary treatment only. New treatment plants thus had to be constructed for 64 million people. During the five

years of construction, facilities would have to be installed for about 17 million more people who would in that time collect in cities by birth or migration. Existing systems, of course, at the same time had to be maintained, and antiquated equipment replaced. Capital outlays needed just for taking care of the sewage of the urban newcomers were estimated at $2.2 billion by 1973. To keep existing plants in working order meanwhile would take about $1.2 billion. In short, the five-year charge for holding our own came to at least $3.4 billion.

Actually the holding costs would be much higher. Besides agricultural pollution, storm run-off is increasingly important both because it contains a considerable load of pollutants itself and because in heavy rains it overwhelms city treatment plants so that they are obliged to dump raw sewage. Separation of storm drains and sewers has been proposed, at an estimated cost of $20 billion to $30 billion, a probably prohibitive cost for a solution that might not accomplish the purpose. Studies have shown that water flushed from city streets can contain more suspended solids, coliform bacterial (the classic indicator of feces in water), organics, nitrogen and phosphorus than that flushed through the plumbing of the city's buildings. (See *Cleaning Our Environment*, p. 99.) Treatment plants big enough to handle the run-off from peak storms clearly would have large unused capacity most of the year and would therefore be grossly uneconomic. The cost of providing them for Washington, D.C., alone has been reckoned at $2 billion. (See U.S., Congress, House, report of the Subcommittee on Science, Research and Development of the Committee on Science and Astronautics, *Managing the Environment*, 90th Cong., 2d sess., 1968, p. 27.

65 Clean them up. The arithmetic is inexorable. For the heart of the program, the construction of municipal treatment plants and auxiliary facilities, Interior Department experts conservatively estimated $8 billion would have to be spent over five years. Congress under the 1966 Act authorized federal matching grants to begin in fiscal 1968 at $450

million, rise to $700 million in fiscal 1969, and to $1 billion in fiscal 1971, making a four-year total of $3.4 billion. Under the matching provisions, ranging from 30 to 55 per cent federal to local money, this amount might have been barely sufficient. But the money was not appropriated. Congress voted $203 million in fiscal 1969. For fiscal 1970 the Administration asked only another $214 million (21 per cent of the authorized figure). But by that time Congress was feeling political pressures and in a calculated rebuke appropriated $800 million. Even so, the three-year outlay fell short of estimated need by almost a billion dollars. In his 1970 message (see Note to p. 56) the President, calling for "total mobilization by all of us," proposed a four-year $10 billion program to construct sewage treatment plants. Of this, $4 billion would be federal money but it would be spent over a period of nine years. The outlay for fiscal 1971 would be only $40 million, as contrasted to $1.25 billion under the superseded congressional authorization. The net effect of the new program as a whole would be to appropriate for seven years (paid out in twelve) a total of $5,417,000 instead of $3,400,000 which Congress said in 1966 it wanted to spend in four years. (The new "accelerated" program thus averaged a commitment of $774 million a year as compared to the old "slower" $850 million a year.) The President also wanted the federal share cut from the old maximum of 55 per cent that applied for nearly all large cities to 50 per cent. Considering the original understatement of need and the unexpectedly rapid rate of inflation, the new attack was in fact even feebler than it looked. In recognition of that fact Congress went ahead at the end of 1970 to vote $1 billion authorized under the old law.

65 Wastes from industry. "Examination into the Effectiveness of the Construction Grant Program for Abating, Controlling, and Preventing Water Pollution," report to Congress by the Comptroller General of the United States (Washington, D.C.: General Accounting Office, November 1969).

66 Prevent a recurrence. For details of the Santa Barbara incident see Malcolm F. Baldwin, "The Santa Barbara Oil Spill," in Malcolm F. Baldwin and James K. Page, Jr., eds., *Law and the Environment* (New York: Walker & Co., 1970).

67 "No less than $500,000,000." Milton Katz, "The Function of Tort Liability in Technology Assessment," *University of Cincinnati Law Review,* vol. 38 (Fall 1969), pp. 645ff.

67 The continental shelf. Ibid, p. 650.

68 Or suspend licenses. *New York Times,* March 24, 1970.

68 "Acts of God"). *The Congressional Record,* March 2, 1970, p. S-4395.

68 Federation, Ltd. *New York Times,* April 27, 1970.

69 Had 4300 in 1968. "Oil Pollution of the Sea," *Harvard International Law Journal,* vol. 10 (Spring 1969), pp. 317–318.

CHAPTER 7. TO KILL A GOOSE

71 Costly techniques. The federal government in fiscal 1967 (the latest year for which comprehensive figures have been gathered and published) spent nearly $100 million for research on pests, pesticides and pest control. This represents a spectacular increase in the post–Rachel Carson era from the $280,000 authorized by the first pesticide research act passed in 1958, but most of it went into the quest for better chemical agents. Since that is also the object of virtually all industry-financed research, we are still working hardest at improving the poisons.

72 Was powerfully suggested. U.S., Congress, House, report of the Committee on Government Operations, *Deficiencies in Administration of Federal Insecticide, Fungicide and Rodenticide Act,* 91st Cong., 1st sess., November 13, 1969.

73 In humane form. See, for instance, Aldo Leopold, *A Sand County Almanac,* enlarged ed. (New York: Oxford University Press, 1966).

74 And park development. States match those funds at least 50–50, but on the other hand fully two thirds up to 1968

went for development rather than purchase. The four-year federal and state total for acquisition under the fund was thus a little over $400 million. In 1970 the President authorized expenditures of $357 million, representing accumulated and unspent past and current funds.

75 Possibly $85 billion. Marion R. Clawson, R. Burnell Held and Charles H. Stoddard, *Land for the Future* (Baltimore: Johns Hopkins Press, 1960), p. 191.

For more than thirty years the Bureau of Sport Fisheries and Wildlife has been buying bird and wild animal habitat with duck stamp money and revenue from taxing firearms and ammunition. In 1962, in order to buy more marshes for waterfowl, before they were all drained and filled, Congress authorized the Migratory Bird Conservation Account, for which a total of more than $53 million has now been appropriated. More than one million acres of marshes have been bought or protected by easement. Appropriated sums are considered advances against hunting stamp revenues to be repaid beginning in fiscal 1977.

75 Overlaps BOR's. HUD's Open Space program began in fiscal 1962 with grants of $3.1 million under legislation requiring state and local governments to put up at least 70 per cent of the land costs. To the end of 1964 about 100,000 acres were purchased with this grant aid at a total cost of more than $121 million, of which the federal share was $32 million. In that year Congress liberalized the act, raised federal matching to 50 per cent, and authorized assistance to acquire and clear built-up city land.

## PART II — THE ANTAGONISTS

### CHAPTER 8. NATURAL SYSTEMS

82 Evolving system. Theodosius Dobzhansky, *Mankind Evolving: The Evolution of the Human Species* (New Haven: Yale University Press, 1962), p. 89.

84 And trypanosome. Charles Elton, *The Ecology of Animals,* 3d ed. (London: Methuen, 1950), pp. 21–22.

84 Its lifelong home. Paul R. Ehrlich and Richard W. Holm, *The Process of Evolution* (New York: McGraw-Hill, 1963), p. 84.

84 Greedy and competitive. Theodor Rosebury, *Life on Man* (New York: Viking, 1969).

84 Packages of sea water. Marston Bates, *The Forest and the Sea* (New York: Mentor, 1960), p. 24.

85 Only after death. See the extremely lucid description of this whole process of energy capture and cycling in Garrett Hardin, *Biology: Its Principles and Implications,* 2d ed. (San Francisco: W. H. Freeman, 1966), pp. 223ff.

85 Over without loss. Kenneth E. F. Watt, *Ecology and Resource Management* (New York: McGraw-Hill, 1968), p. 36.

86 To talk about. Norbert Wiener, *The Human Use of Human Beings* (New York: Avon Books, 1967). Reprint of the 1954 edition.

86 "Heat death." See Hardin, p. 238.

86 Becomes irreversible. See Harold F. Blum, *Time's Arrow and Evolution* (Princeton: Princeton University Press, 1951).

87 Of living things. All from Hardin, p. 237.

87 They used to grow. Robert H. MacArthur and Joseph H. Connell, *The Biology of Populations* (New York: Wiley, 1966), pp. 178–179.

87 Calcium washed away. Eugene P. Odum, "The Strategy of Ecosystem Development," *Science,* vol. 164 (April 18, 1969); see also G. M. Woodwell, "Effects of Pollution on the Structure and Physiology of Ecosystems," *Science,* vol. 168 (April 24, 1970).

CHAPTER 9. THE COEXISTENCE PROCESS

88 Time's arrow. Sir Arthur Eddington's term, cited in Harold F. Blum, *Time's Arrow and Evolution* (Princeton: Princeton University Press, 1951), pp. 5–6.

88 Niches in the environment. George Gaylord Simpson, *The*

*Meaning of Evolution,* 2d ed. (New Haven: Yale University Press, 1967), p. 242.

89 Some vital force. Henri Bergson called it "élan vital." See his *Creative Evolution* (New York: Modern Library, 1944).

90 In the Maine woods. Robert H. MacArthur, "Population Ecology of Some Warblers of Northeastern Coniferous Forests," *Ecology,* vol. 39 (1958), pp. 599–619.

90 Could not live at all. In G. E. Hutchinson, *The Ecological Theater and the Evolutionary Play* (New Haven: Yale University Press, 1965), pp. 35–36.

91 No need to change. John J. Christian, "Social Subordination, Population Density, and Mammalian Evolution," *Science,* vol. 168 (April 3, 1970), pp. 84–90.

91 Form to be. William H. Telfer and Donald Kennedy, *The Biology of Organisms* (New York: Wiley, 1965), p. 12.

91 Is not clear. Simpson, pp. 38–39.

92 Kills the specialist. Simpson, p. 204.

95 Under differing conditions. Robert H. MacArthur and Joseph H. Connell, *The Biology of Populations* (New York: Wiley, 1966), p. 66.

96 (Or trophic) chain. Kenneth E. F. Watt, *Ecology and Resource Management* (New York: McGraw-Hill, 1968), p. 42.

96 Cause and effect. Lawrence B. Slobodkin, "Aspects of the Future of Ecology," *Bioscience,* vol. 18 (January 1968).

97 Great scientific interest. See, for instance, C. S. Holling, "Diversity and Stability in Ecological Systems," *Brookhaven Symposia in Biology,* no. 22 (Brookhaven, N.Y.: Brookhaven National Laboratory, 1969).

97. Would be its own species. See discussion in MacArthur and Connell, p. 182.

97 141 species. Ibid., p. 37.

97 Of North America. Marston Bates, *The Forest and the Sea* (New York: Mentor, 1960), p. 86.

98 Number of species. See David Pimentel, "Population Regulation and Genetic Feedback," *Science,* vol. 159 (March 29, 1968), p. 1433.

98 Readjustment and rebuilding. Watt, p. 42.

100 Time lags in the system. C. S. Holling, "Stability in Ecological and Social Systems," in *Brookhaven Symposia*. I am chiefly indebted to Dr. Holling for the whole analysis of stability in natural systems.

100 In the plains of Africa. See, for instance, Robert Ardrey, *The Territorial Imperative: A Personal Inquiry into the Animal Origins of Property and Nations* (London: Collins, 1967); and Konrad Lorenz, *On Aggression,* trans. Marjorie Kerr Wilson (New York: Harcourt, 1966).

100 To current stimuli. The basic naiveté of the naive formulations of what man owes to his animal past is their assumption that evolutionary learning proceeded up to a critical point and then stopped, leaving a kind of high-water mark forever. The ape who learned to kill (if he did) could also learn to live at peace if the latter skill better suited changed environmental conditions.

100 Has a "memory." Holling, p. 131.

102 Wood into crops. See MacArthur and Connell, pp. 14ff.; also see Chapter 10 of this book.

103 Inhibit reproduction. V. C. Wynne-Edwards, *Animal Dispersion in Relation to Social Behavior* (Darien, Conn.: Hafner, 1962); J. J. Christian, "The Adreno-Pituitary System and Population Cycles in Mammals," *Journal of Mammalogy,* vol. 31; John B. Calhoun, "Population Density and Social Pathology," *Scientific American,* vol. 206.

103 Have those switches. Watt, p. 85.

103 "Man himself." E. C. Pielou, *An Introduction to Mathematical Ecology* (New York: Wiley, 1969), p. 2.

CHAPTER 10. THE NONCONFORMING SPECIES

107 For the dwindling habitat. Sir Wilfrid E. LeGros Clark, *Man-Apes or Ape-Men? The Story of Discoveries in Africa* (New York: Holt, 1967).

107 To escape predators. Charles F. Hockett and Robert Ascher,

"The Human Revolution," in M. F. Ashley Montague, ed., *Culture: Man's Adaptive Dimension* (New York: Oxford University Press, 1968), p. 30.

107 As has sometimes been done. See, for instance, Robert Ardrey, *African Genesis: A Personal Investigation into the Animal Origins and Nature of Man* (New York: Atheneum, 1961).

108 Further manual skills. "Observations on the Ecology and Social Behavior of the Mountain Gorilla," in F. Clark Howell and François Bourlière, eds., *African Ecology and Human Evolution* (Chicago: Aldine, 1963).

108 Trim it to serve. Clark, pp. 113–114.

109 Ever more rapidly. J. T. Robinson, "Adaptive Radiation in the Australopithecus and the Origin of Man," in Howell and Boulière, p. 411.

110 Biological change. Irven De Vore and S. L. Washburn, "Baboon Ecology and Human Evolution," in Howell and Boulière, p. 337.

111 As great good. W. M. S. Russell, *Man, Nature and History* (London: Alden, 1967), p. 10.

112 Smokey the Bear. Ibid., p. 25.

112 Paleolithic man. The terms "paleolithic" and "neolithic" are in disfavor among at least some archeologists because they artificially and dubiously mark a cultural watershed by a change in tool-making technique (from chipped to polished stone). The words remain useful, however, to distinguish the period before domestication (paleolithic) from that following. That is the sense in which they are used here.

112 Different actors. See, for instance, Kenneth E. F. Watt, *Ecology and Resource Management* (New York: McGraw-Hill, 1968), pp. 57–58.

113 Now roam in Africa. At the end of the Pleistocene age (between 11,000 and 8000 years ago) scores of genera of large mammals suddenly and simultaneously died out on three continents, most dramatically in North America which lost at least 33 genera. Not only did they die out with spectacular

speed — 3000 years is a geological blink — but they were not replaced with animals of comparable size or feeding habits. One of the giant sloths of North America was built like a giraffe and similarly browsed in parkland trees. The camelops was like the dromedary and has gone from here without replacement. The horse which evolved here became extinct too at that time and was only reestablished by import much later from Europe. Demise of the saber-toothed tiger left us without a king-size cat. See P. S. Martin and H. E. Wright, Jr., eds., *Pleistocene Extinctions: The Search for a Cause* (New Haven: Yale University Press, 1967); Karl J. Narr, "Early Food-Producing Populations," in William L. Thomas, Jr., ed., *Man's Role in Changing the Face of the Earth* (Chicago: University of Chicago Press, 1956); C. Vance Haynes, Jr., "The Earliest Americans," *Science*, vol. 166 (November 7, 1969), pp. 709–715. The thesis of Pleistocene "overkill" is swallowed whole in the census of endangered species compiled by the International Union for the Conservation of Nature. See James Fisher, Noel Simon and Jack Vincent, *Wildlife in Danger* (New York: Viking, 1969), p. 15.

114 "And eat it too." Quoted by Lewis Lapham, "Alaska: Politicians and Natives, Money and Oil," *Harper's* (May 1970), p. 88.

### CHAPTER 11. THE AGRICULTURAL REVOLUTION

116 An assembly line. See Richard B. Lee, "!Kung Bushman Subsistance: An Input-output Analysis," in Andrew P. Vayda, ed., *Environment and Cultural Behavior* (New York: Natural History Press, 1969.

116 "Think about for so long." Carl Sauer, *Agricultural Origins and Dispersals* (New York: American Geographical Society, 1952), p. 9.

117 Drying out of the climate. V. Gordon Childe, *Man Makes Himself*, 4th ed. (New York: Mentor, 1965) and Childe,

*New Light on the Most Ancient East,* 4th ed. (New York: Norton, 1969).

117 "In the word 'domestication.' " Childe, *New Light,* p. 25.

118 Was not ever designed. Karl W. Butzer, *Environment and Archeology* (Chicago: Aldine, 1964); Carl Sauer, *Agricultural Origins;* and Sauer, "The Agency of Man on the Earth," in William L. Thomas, Jr., ed., *Man's Role in Changing the Face of the Earth* (Chicago: University of Chicago Press, 1956); Kent V. Flannery, "The Ecology of Early Food Production in Mesopotamia," in Vayda; William T. Sanders and Barbara J. Price, *Mesoamerica: The Evolution of a Civilization* (New York: Random House, 1968); Robert McC. Adams, *The Evolution of Urban Society: Early Mesopotamia and Prehispanic Mexico* (Chicago: Aldine, 1966); Robert J. Braidwood, *Prehistoric Man,* 7th ed. (Glenview, Ill.; Scott, Foresman, 1967); Sir Wilfrid E. Legros Clark, *Man-Apes or Ape-Men? The Story of Discoveries in Africa* (New York: Holt, 1967); Charles A. Reed, "Animal Domestication in the Prehistoric Near East," in J. R. Caldwell, ed., *New Roads to Yesterday: Essays in Archeology* (New York: Basic Books, 1966).

119 Part in the process. Reed, pp. 193–194.

119 Easy range of its home. Braidwood, p. 110.

119 For about a year. Estimate in Lester R. Brown, *Seeds of Change* (New York: Praeger, 1970), p. 142.

119 Grain and fish. Adams, pp. 38–39.

120 Food collecting. The terms and distinctions are those of Robert Braidwood. See Braidwood, pp. 91–94.

120 And composite tools. Braidwood and Bruce Howe, "Southwestern Asia Beyond the Lands of the Mediterranean Littoral," in Braidwood and Gordon R. Willey, eds., *Courses Toward Urban Life: Archeological Considerations of Some Cultural Alternates* (Chicago: Adline, 1962), pp. 141–142.

120 Trade thus developed. Flannery, p. 293.

121 Was transplanting. Braidwood and Willey, p. 142.

121 Pattern of development. Sanders and Price, p. 120.

122 On him for survival. Flannery, citing Hans Helbaek.
122 Another 3000 years. Braidwood and Willey, pp. 346–347.
122 Farm communities. Ibid., p. 115.
123 "Control the environment." Ibid., p. 348.
125 Of dead matter. Eugene P. Odum, "The Strategy of Ecosystem Development," *Science*, vol. 164 (April 18, 1969).

### CHAPTER 12. COUNTRY ECOLOGY

127 "A burned clearing." For an excellent nontechnical account of swiddening see W. M. S. Russell, *Man, Nature and History* (London: Alden, 1967), pp. 6off.
128 Some from cuttings. "Hanunóo Agriculture," FAO Development Paper No. 12 (1957).
129 Erosion of heavy rain. Carl Sauer in William L. Thomas, Jr., ed., *Man's Role in Changing the Face of the Earth* (Chicago: University of Chicago Press, 1956), p. 57.
129 Or temporarily possible. Russell, p. 84; also Karl W. Butzer, *Environment and Archeology* (Chicago: Aldine, 1964), p. 348; D. E. Dumond, "Swidden Agriculture and the Rise of the Maya Civilization" and Clifford Geertz, "Two Types of Ecosystems," in Andrew P. Vayda, ed., *Environment and Cultural Behavior* (New York: Natural History Press, 1969), p. 15.
129 Clues to ancient life. V. Gordon Childe, *Man Makes Himself*, 4th ed. (New York: Mentor, 1965).
130 Into Imperata grass. Geertz, p. 15.
130 Tribal energy. Andrew P. Vayda, "Expansion and Warfare Among Swidden Agriculturists," in Vayda, pp. 202–216.
131 Remained exceptional. Robert McC. Adams, *The Evolution of Urban Society: Early Mesopotamia and Prehispanic Mexico* (Chicago: Aldine, 1966), pp. 55–56.
131 Population pressure. William T. Sanders and Barbara J. Price, *Mesoamerica: The Evolution of a Civilization* (New York: Random House, 1968), pp. 146–147.
132 Returned to swiddening. Pierre Gourou, "The Quality of Land Use of Tropical Cultivators," in Thomas, p. 345.

132 Irrigated agriculture. Karl A. Wittfogel, "The Hydraulic Civilizations," in Thomas.

133 Management chores. Russell, p. 97.

134 Mirror the process. See criticisms of the Wittfogel thesis in Adams; Robert J. Braidwood and Gordon R. Willey, eds., *Courses Toward Urban Life: Archeological Considerations of Some Cultural Alternates* (Chicago: Aldine, 1962); and Gideon Sjoberg, *The Preindustrial City* (New York: Free Press, 1960). Sanders and Price offers some defense.

135 Ended in disaster. Frederick E. Smith, "Today the Environment, Tomorrow the World," *Bioscience*, vol. 19 (April 1969), p. 318.

135 Irrigation project itself. Lord Ritchie-Calder, "Mortgaging the Old Homestead," *Foreign Affairs*, vol. 48 (January 1970).

136 "Country ecologists." Personal communication.

136 Not the same as the most. Kenneth E. F. Watt, *Ecology and Resource Management* (New York: McGraw-Hill, 1968), p. 6.

CHAPTER 13. HOME IS THE CITY

140 That preceded it. See, for instance, Lewis Mumford, *The City in History: Its Origins, Its Transformations, and Its Prospects* (New York: Harcourt, 1961), p. 31.

140 "Of the family or clan." Ibid., p. 10.

141 Structure of a state. Cited in Gordon R. Willey, "Mesoamerica," in Robert J. Braidwood and Gordon R. Willey, eds., *Courses Toward Urban Life: Archeological Considerations of Some Cultural Alternates* (Chicago: Aldine, 1962), p. 96.

142 No evidence of crowding. Robert McC. Adams, *The Evolution of Urban Societies: Early Mesopotamia and Prehispanic Mexico* (Chicago: Aldine, 1966), pp. 44–45; Braidwood and Willey, pp. 350–351.

143 Exception to the rule. Gideon Sjoberg, *The Preindustrial City* (New York: Free Press, 1960), p. 41.

144 To the nonproducers. Adams, p. 46.

144 "As esthetically enchanting." Mumford, p. 8.
144 Also god and priest. Sjoberg, pp. 34–35; also Adams, p. 129.
145 Until another harvest. Adams, pp. 122–124.
145 "Civilized exploitation." Mumford, p. 36.
148 Each other's production. For more formal language ("cities as nodes of human interaction") see Harvey S. Perloff, ed., *The Quality of the Urban Environment* (Baltimore: Johns Hopkins Press, 1969), p. 11.
148 Space of the country. Mumford, pp. 313, 336.

CHAPTER 14. THE CITY MEANS BUSINESS

150 "Transactional civilization." Cited in H. Wentworth Eldredge, ed., *Taming Megalopolis*, vol. 1 (New York: Anchor Books, 1967), p. 442.
151 Uptowns and suburbs. See Edgar M. Hoover and Raymond Vernon, *Anatomy of a Metropolis* (New York: Anchor Books, 1962), p. 255. First published 1959 by Harvard University Press.
151 Having no natural limits. Cited in Lewis Mumford, *The City in History: Its Origins, Its Transformations, and Its Prospects* (New York: Harcourt, 1961), p. 412.
152 Like used cars. Brian J. L. Berry and Elaine Neils, "Location, Size, and Shape of Cities as Influenced by Environmental Factors: The Urban Environment Writ Large," in Harvey S. Perloff, ed., *The Quality of the Urban Environment* (Baltimore: Johns Hopkins Press, 1969), p. 297; Hoover and Vernon, p. 183; Britton Harris, "Quantitative Models of Urban Development; Their Role in Metropolitan Policy-Making," in Perloff, pp. 393–394.
153 Before we all are. Cited in Lord Ritchie-Calder, "Mortgaging the Old Homestead," *Foreign Affairs*, vol. 48 (January 1970), p. 219.
153 A total of 310 million. Marion Clawson, R. Burnell Held and Charles H. Stoddard, *Land for the Future* (Baltimore: Johns Hopkins Press, 1960), p. 117.

153 Fell to 250,000. Hoover and Vernon, pp. 192–193.
154 Of urban sprawl. George J. Stolnitz, "The Changing Profile of Our Urban Human Resources," in Perloff, p. 194.
154 "Megalopolis"). See his book by that name.
154 Shaping new patterns. Most notably Melvin W. Webber in "Order in Diversity; Community Without Propinquity," in Lowdon Wingo, Jr., ed., *Cities and Space: The Future Use of Urban Land* (Baltimore: Johns Hopkins Press, 1966). For the opposite view see Bertram M. Gross, "The City of Man; a Social Systems Reckoning," in William R. Ewald, Jr., ed., *Environment for Man; the Next Fifty Years* (Bloomington: Indiana University Press, 1967). As of 1962 the 212 metropolitan areas in the United States embraced 18,442 independent governmental units. See Julius Margolis, "The Demand for Urban Public Service," in Perloff, p. 529.
155 Gottman has argued. As in "Why the Skyscraper?" in Eldredge, pp. 429ff.
155 Complex management structures. John Kenneth Galbraith, *The New Industrial State* (Boston: New American Library, 1967).
155 And technical services. Hoover and Vernon, p. 95.
156 Adds to these a hotel. Irving Hoch, "The Three-Dimensional City; Contained Urban Space," in Perloff, p. 119.

CHAPTER 15. ARE SLUMS NECESSARY?

158–159 Streets by day. Cited in Scott Greer, *The Emerging City; Myth and Reality* (New York: Free Press, 1962), p. 171.
159 As far back as 1905. Wilfred Owen, "Transport: Key to the Future of Cities," in Harvey S. Perloff, ed., *The Quality of the Urban Environment* (Baltimore: Johns Hopkins Press, 1969), p. 206.
159 As the old got buried. Gideon Sjoberg, *The Preindustrial City* (New York: Free Press, 1960), p. 35.
159 Refuse on site. Gordon R. Willey, "Mesoamerica," in Robert J. Braidwood and Gordon R. Willey, eds., *Courses Toward*

*Urban Life: Archeological Considerations of Some Cultural Alternates* (Chicago: Aldine, 1962), pp. 94–95; also Emrys Jones, *Towns and Cities* (New York: Oxford University Press, 1966), p. 22.

159 Also, alas, temporarily. Sjoberg, pp. 93–95.

163 "Rise in land values." Lewis Mumford, *The City in History: Its Origins, Its Transformations, and Its Prospects* (New York: Harcourt, 1961), p. 426.

163 Sell out and move. William L. Baldwin, "Economic Aspects of Business Blight and Traffic Congestion," in H. Wentworth Eldredge, ed., *Taming Megalopolis*, vol. 1 (New York: Anchor Books, 1967), p. 418.

163 Joblessness and decay. Brian J. L. Berry and Elaine Neils, "Location, Size, and Shape of Cities as Influenced by Environmental Factors: The Urban Environment Writ Large," in Harvey S. Perloff, ed., *The Quality of the Urban Environment* (Baltimore: Johns Hopkins Press, 1969), p. 301.

163 Rich men's ledgers. Wilbur R. Thompson, "Urban Economics," in Eldridge, p. 176.

164 "Living conditions." Baldwin, p. 428.

167 Planners heartily agree. See, for instance, Stephen Carr, "The City of the Mind," in William R. Ewald, Jr., ed., *Environment for Man; the Next Fifty Years* (Bloomington: Indiana University Press, 1967); cf. Leonard J. Duhl, "The Human Measure; Man and Family in Megalopolis," in Lowdon Wingo, Jr., ed., *Cities and Space: The Future Use of Urban Land* (Baltimore: Johns Hopkins Press, 1966), pp. 146–147.

CHAPTER 16. A PASSION TO CONSUME

170 C. S. Holling. "Stability in Ecological and Social Systems," *Brookhaven Symposia in Biology*, no. 22 (Brookhaven, N.Y.: Brookhaven National Laboratory, 1969).

171 Other human activities. See Karl Polanyi, *The Great Transformation* (New York: Rinehart, 1944). This is a brilliant analysis of the transformation wrought by the Industrial

Revolution that deserves to be much better known than it is.

173 "Other types of contact." Melville J. Herskovits, *Economic Anthropology: The Economic Life of Primitive Peoples* (New York: Norton, 1965), pp. 158–159. First published in 1952 by Knopf.

174 "Support those of another." Raymond W. Firth, *Economics of the New Zealand Maori*, 2d ed. (Wellington, New Zealand: Government Printer, 1959), p. 493.

174 "Take off." See, for instance, Walt W. Rostow, *The Stages of Economic Growth* (Cambridge: Cambridge University Press, 1960).

175 Motive power of the system. For instance, Campbell R. McConnell, *Economics: Principles, Problems and Policies*, 3d ed. (New York: McGraw-Hill, 1966), p. 45; Lorie Tarshis, *Modern Economics: An Introduction* (Boston: Houghton Mifflin, 1967), p. 69; Lowell C. Harriss, *The American Economy: Principles, Practices and Policies*, 6th ed. (Homewood, Ill.: Irwin, 1968), p. 33; George L. Bach, *Economics*, 6th ed. (Englewood Cliffs, N.J.: Prentice-Hall, 1968), pp. 18, 458.

175 "Condition of utopia." Paul A. Samuelson, *Economics: An Introductory Analysis*, 5th ed. (New York: McGraw-Hill, 1961), p. 675; compare Rendigs Fels, *An Introduction to Economics*, 2d ed. (Boston: Allyn & Bacon, 1966), p. 5. Economics, Fels writes, is "not concerned with studying goals."

176 "Measure of social merit." John Kenneth Galbraith, *The New Industrial State* (New York: The New American Library, 1967), p. 49.

177 Turns out food or cigarettes. Bach, p. 45.

181 For the social welfare. Kenneth J. Arrow, *Social Choice and Individual Values* (New York: Wiley, 1951), pp. 83–86; also Ezra J. Mishan, *Welfare Economics: Five Introductory Essays* (New York: Random House, 1964), pp. 6, 88–89; and Mishan, *The Costs of Economic Growth* (London: Staples, 1967), p. 115.

182 Equally national needs. Galbraith, p. 176ff.

182 For innovation. Joseph A. Schumpeter, *The Theory of Economic Development* (New York: Oxford University Press, 1961). First published in German in 1911.

183 They must grow. Besides Schumpeter, see Bach, pp. 458, 465–467; Samuelson, p. 675; Robert L. Heilbroner, *The Great Economists: Their Lives and Their Conceptions of the World* (London: Eyre & Spottiswood, 1955), p. 134.

183 As Galbraith has shown. John Kenneth Galbraith, *American Capitalism: The Concept of Countervating Power* (Boston: Houghton Mifflin, 1956).

183 Expanded production. Galbraith, *The New Industrial State,* pp. 199–200.

### CHAPTER 17. AMERICAN DREAMS

186 Regained in heaven. Erich Kahler, "Culture and Evolution," in *Culture: Man's Adaptive Dimension,* M. F. Ashley Montague, ed. (New York: Oxford University Press, 1968).

186 To make their own way. Ludwig Edelstein, *The Idea of Progress in Classical Antiquity* (Baltimore: Johns Hopkins Press, 1967); Morris Ginsberg, *The Idea of Progress: A Revaluation* (Boston: Beacon Press, 1953).

186 Unoccupied homesites. Daniel J. Boorstin, *The Americans: The Colonial Experience* (New York: Random House, 1958), p. 155.

187 American process of growth. Ibid., p. 418.

187 "Having been conceived." Boorstin, *The Americans: The National Experience* (New York: Random House, 1965), p. 219.

188 The heroic virtues. Howard Mumford Jones, *O Strange New World* (New York: Compass, 1967), pp. 179ff. First published in 1964.

189 Promised to prosper them. Carl Bridenbaugh, *Vexed and Troubled Englishmen, 1590–1642* (New York: Oxford University Press, 1968), pp. 401–402.

190 Came out of the forest. Frederick Jackson Turner, *The Frontier in American History* (New York: Holt, 1920).

191 Private and public welfare. Boorstin, *The Americans: The National Experience*, p. 72.

192 Asserted jurisdiction. Ibid., pp. 65–66.

192 Material prosperity. Francis X. Sutton, Seymour E. Harris, Carl Kaysen and James Tobin, *The American Business Creed* (Cambridge; Harvard University Press, 1956), p. 26.

192 "Considered socially useful." Gordon Harrison, *Road to the Right* (New York: Morrow, 1954), p. 165; see Louis Hartz, *Economic Policy and Democratic Thought: Pennsylvania, 1776–1860* (Cambridge: Harvard University Press, 1948); Oscar Handlin, "Laissez-Faire Thought in Massachusetts, 1790–1880," *Journal of Economic History Supplement* (December 1943); Sidney Fine, *Laissez-Faire and the General-Welfare State: A Study of Conflict in American Thought, 1865–1901* (Ann Arbor, Michigan: University of Michigan Press, 1956), p. 23.

193 And First World Wars. The classic study is Richard Hofstadter, *Social Darwinism in American Thought, 1860–1915* (Philadelphia: University of Pennsylvania Press, 1944).

193 350,000 copies. Fine, p. 42.

195 *"Laissez-faire* principle." Ibid., p. 353.

195 And game commissions. Ibid., pp. 354–361.

196 "Power might exist." Alexander Mackay quoted in Jones, p. 310.

PART III — EARTHKEEPING

CHAPTER 18. A PRICE ON EVERYTHING

199 "Other than it is." Preface to Raymond W. Firth, *Economics of the New Zealand Maori*, 2d ed. (Wellington, New Zealand: Government Printer, 1959).

202 Into watercourses. See, for instance, Allen V. Kneese and Blair T. Bower, *Managing Water Quality: Economics, Technology, Institutions* (Baltimore: Johns Hopkins Press, 1968).

204 Benefits of clean air. Marion Clawson and Jack L. Knetsch,

*Economics of Outdoor Recreation* (Baltimore: Johns Hopkins Press, 1966); Jack L. Knetsch and Robert K. Davis, "Comparisons of Methods for Recreation Evaluation," in Allen V. Kneese and Stephen C. Smith, eds., *Water Research* (Baltimore: Johns Hopkins Press, 1966), pp. 125–142; Ronald C. Ridker, *Economic Costs of Air Pollution: Studies in Measurement* (New York: Praeger, 1967).

CHAPTER 19. ALL THERE IS

207 He had to destroy. David Lowenthal, ed., *Man and Nature* (Cambridge: Harvard University Press, 1965), p. 36. See Lowenthal, *George Perkins Marsh, Versatile Vermonter* (New York: Columbia University Press, 1958).

208 Of an American dream. The most interesting scholarly account of the classic American conservation movement is Samuel P. Hays, *Conservation and the Gospel of Efficiency* (Cambridge: Harvard University Press, 1959); see also Frank E. Smith, *The Politics of Conservation* (New York: Random House, 1966); and Stewart L. Udall, *The Quiet Crisis* (New York: Holt, 1963).

209 "For the individual." Roderick Nash, *The American Environment: Readings in the History of Conservation* (Reading, Mass.: Addison-Wesley, 1968), p. 38.

209 Progressive movement. See, for instance, George E. Mowry, *Theodore Roosevelt and the Progressive Movement* (Madison, Wisconsin: University of Wisconsin Press, 1946).

209 Throughout most of our history. Morton and Lucia White, *The Intellectual Versus the City* (Cambridge: Harvard University Press, 1962).

210 "Urban and industrial." Quoted in Nash, p. 195.

210 Yet be put off. Ibid., pp. 37–38.

211 To make it work. See Gordon Harrison, *Road to the Right* (New York: Morrow, 1954), pp. 265–282.

212 One-crop staples. Russell Lord, *The Care of the Earth: A History of Husbandry* (New York: Mentor, 1963), p. 222.

212 Flood and erosion. For a summary of New Deal conservation actions see Ernest S. Griffith, "Main Lines of Thought and Action," in Henry Jarrett, ed., *Perspectives on Conservation: Essays on America's Natural Resources* (Baltimore: Johns Hopkins Press, 1958).

212 Eloquently of the land ethic. Aldo Leopold, *A Sand County Almanac*, enlarged ed. (New York: Oxford University Press, 1966).

213 "And frequently uncertain." Grant McConnell, "The Conservation Movement — Past and Present," in Ian Burton and Robert W. Kates, eds., *Readings in Resource Management and Conservation* (Chicago: University of Chicago Press, 1965), p. 189.

213 From which it obtruded. See especially Hans H. Landsberg, Leonard L. Fischman and Joseph L. Fisher, *Resources in America's Future* (Baltimore: Johns Hopkins Press, 1963).

### CHAPTER 20. THE MEEK TAKE HEART

216 Play by its rules. This is the revolution of which Charles A. Reich dreams in his *The Greening of America* (New York: Random House, 1970).

217 "Considered." Joseph L. Sax, *Defending the Environment: A Strategy for Citizen Action* (New York: Knopf, 1971), pp. 131–134.

219 "Deception." Malcolm F. Baldwin and James K. Page, Jr., eds., *Law and the Environment* (New York: Walker, 1970), p. 58.

220 To become law. Personal communication from Helen Fenske, assistant commissioner of conservation, state of New Jersey.

226 Highest in history. Ray F. Smith, "Patterns of Crop Protection in Cotton Ecosystems," talk given at Cotton Symposium on Insect and Mite Control Problems and Research in California, March 12–13, 1969, Hotel Claremont, Berkeley, California.

227 Nuisance. For instance in a symposium sponsored by the

International Minerals and Chemical Corporation, the achievement of a "pest-free environment through chemicals" was hailed as the millenial threshold of a "revolution in crop production thinking." See T. J. Army and F. A. Greer, "Photosynthesis and Crop Production Systems," in A. San Pietro et. al., eds., *Harvesting the Sun: Photosynthesis in Plant Life* (New York: Academic Press, 1967), p. 322.

232 What *they* want. On the inherent limitations of regulatory agencies see Sax.

# Index

Adams, Robert, 145
Adaptation, 91, 94–95, 230; conditioned by past experiences, 99–101
Africa, 29, 153
Agricultural Adjustment Administration, 211–212
Agriculture, 116–125, 126; theories on invention of, 117–118; preconditions for invention of, 118–120; and swiddening, 127–133; and water management, 133–135
Agriculture, U.S. Department of, 71–72; Pesticides Regulation Division (PRD), 71
Air pollution, 53, 57–63, 75, 201; and the automobile, 58–61; and health, 62–63; from pesticides, 72. *See also* Pollution
Airports, 54, 229
Air Quality Act (1967), 58; and inversion emergencies, 60
Alaska, 114–115
Ames, Edward A., viii
Antipoverty programs, 180
Aquinas, St. Thomas, 151–152
Arctic Ocean, 19
Arizona, 71

Army Corps of Engineers, *see* Corps of Engineers, U.S. Army
Arrow, Kenneth, 181
Asia, 29, 118, 122
Audubon societies, 220
*Australopithecus,* 107–108
Automobiles, 24, 56, 59, 60, 158, 164, 229; federal standards for emissions, 58, 60–61; and substitute for internal combustion engine, 61; and suburbanization, 154

Badaga tribe, India, 172–173
Bates, Marston, 21, 84, 96, 97
Beckett, Samuel, 20
Birdsell, Joseph R., 42
Birth control, 6, 45. *See also* Contraception
Birthrate, 6, 29, 31, 32, 45; urban compared to rural, 153
Boeing Corporation, 178
Boone, Daniel, 190
Boorstin, Daniel J., 187, 191
Boston, 160
Boy Scouts, 21
Braidwood, Robert J., 120–122
Bridenbaugh, Carl, 188–189

Bureau of Mines, U.S., 76
Bureau of Outdoor Recreation (BOR), Department of Interior, 74, 75
Bureau of Solid Waste Management, 56
Bureau of Sport Fisheries and Wildlife, 74
Bureaucracy, 76, 155; unresponsiveness of, 35
Butzer, Karl, 117

Caesar, Julius, 158
Calcutta, 37
Calhoun, John, 103
California, 51, 58, 60; and DDT, 71; suburbanization in, 154
Cancer: and air pollution, 62–63; and water pollution, 63
Cañete Valley, Peru, 225–227
Carbon dioxide, atmospheric concentration of, 7–8
Childe, V. Gordon, 117, 139–141
China, 38, 39, 118, 132–134, 142
Chlorinated hydrocarbons, 70–71, 95. See also DDT
Christian, John J., 90, 103
City, 40–41, 139–148, 209–210; early man's disposition toward, 140–141; characteristics of, 141, 151–152; in early civilization centers, 142; compared with settled village agriculture, 142; and the temple, 143; and civic life, 143–146; and division of labor, 147–148; industrial, 149–156; central business district, 151, 153, 155, 166; and public transportation, 152; tendency toward suburbanization and conurbation, 153–155; and natural production-consumption cycle, 157; and traffic, 158–159; and waste, 159–160; and neighborhood rehabilitation, 162; and community action, 163–165
City planning, 166–169
Civilian Conservation Corps, 212
Clawson, Marion, 74–75, 204
Clean Air Act (1963), 57–58
Clean Water Restoration Act (1966), 58, 64; program, 65
Climate, 13; and the SST, 178
Community action, 163–165
Competition, 89–91; for space, 102–103
Congress, U.S., 3, 53, 56; and air pollution, 57, 58; Muskie bill, 61; and water pollution, 64–65; and oil pollution, 68; and recreation areas, 74–75
Conklin, Harold C., 128
Consensus, social, 181
Conservation, history of in U.S., 207–214
Consolidated Edison Company, 217–218
Consumption, 39, 170–185; and effluent charge, 201–203
Continuous Air Monitoring Program — CAMP, 58–59
Contraception, 31, 44, 46
Conurbation, 154, 166
Coolidge, Calvin, 211
Cornell University, 46
Corps of Engineers, U.S. Army, 11, 76, 221, 231
Cost-benefit analysis, social, 203–205, 221–225
Cotton, Stephen, 24, 25
Crowding, strains produced by, 35, 37, 40–41; historical perspective

of, 41–42; and population control, 43–48
Cultural invention, 133–134
Cultural practices, as population control mechanism, 30–31

Dams, 221–222
Darwin, Charles, 97–98, 110
Davis, Kingsley, 40, 152–153
Day, Lincoln H., 46
DDT, 70–72, 224–225; use of in Cañete Valley, 225–226
DeCarlo, Charles, 20
Degradation, environmental, 6, 10; and population pressures, 21–22; and the SST, 178–179
Delhi, 159
Denmark, 72
Density, population, 103, 133–134
Disease, 30, 42
District of Columbia Court of Appeals, 71
Diversity, 96–97; and evolution of agriculture, 119–120
DNA, 94
Domestication, 121–126; and urbanization, 139
Donora, Pennsylvania, 57
Dreiser, Theodore, 210
Ducks Unlimited, 220

Earth Day (April 22, 1970), 24, 216
Ecology, 126–138; and effective action, 215–232
Edinburgh, 148
Education, 35, 43–44; and population growth, 46–47
Effluent charge, 201–202, 205; conservationists' objection to, 202–203
Egypt, 131, 133
Ehrlich, Paul, 28

Electricity, 51. See also Power consumption
Elton, Charles, 41, 83
Emerson, Ralph Waldo, 210
Emlen, John T., 108
Energy: in organism-environment system, 84–85
Energy consumption, 38–39; U.S., 51
Entropy, 85–86
Environment: man's interaction with, 20–21, 92–93, 103, 104–115; as political issue, 22; bandwagon effect, 23–24; restoration of quality, 49–50; coexistence in, 88–103; man's management of, 135–138, 207–214; social cost-benefit analysis, 203–205, 221–225
Environmentalism, 18
Environmental Protection Agency (EPA), 54, 67, 76; and Pesticides Regulation Division (PRD), 71
Environmental Quality Improvement Act (1970), 77
Europe, 122
Evolution, 81–82, 88, 194; and succession, 82–84, 89; and environment, 83–84, 89; and competition, 89; and specialization, 90–93; and adaptation, 91, 94–95; and diversity, 96–97; conditioned by past experience, 99–101; and spatial needs, 102–103
Extinction, 91–93

Family planning, 45–46
Famine, specter of, 34, 35
Federal government, see Government
Federal Power Commission, 76, 217–219

Federal Water Quality Administration, 65–66
Federal Wildlife Conference (1936), 212
Felling, William E., viii
Ferkiss, Victor, 18
Fertilizers, 19, 50; run-off from, and water pollution, 64
Fire, man's control of, 110–113, 122
Firth, Raymond W., 174
Fish, 53, 64, 67
Fisher, Joseph L., viii
Flannery, Kent, 120
Flour beetles (Tribolium), 30
Food, 6, 19; as population control mechanism, 29, 34–36; and production of energy, 51
Ford Foundation, vii, 213
Forest Service, U.S., 73, 74
Fox Plaza Building, San Francisco, 156
France, 33
Frejka, Tomas, 32
Freud, Sigmund, 101
Fundamentalism, economic, 199

Galbraith, J. Kenneth, 155, 176, 181–183
Gallup poll, 45
Galveston, Texas, 13, 14
Galveston Bay, exploitation of, 11–15, 19
Garbage, 55, 159. See also Waste
Gasoline consumption, 51
General Accounting Office, U.S., 65; and Pesticides Regulation Division, 71
Geological Survey, 68
Girl Scouts, 21
Gottman, Jean, 150, 154, 155, 156
Gourou, Pierre, 131

Government, federal, 53–54; overlapping authority, 54; and pollution control, 57–69; and recreation areas, 73–77
Grand Canyon, 221
Great Britain, 72
Great Depression, 211
Great Society, 163
Great Swamp, New Jersey, 220
Greeley, Horace, 187
"Green revolution," 34, 36
Gross national production, 177, 179–181
Growth, 177–181, 207; and profits, 182–183; limits to, 184–185
Guatemala, 42
Gulf of Mexico, 68

Hancock (John) Tower, Chicago, 156
Hanunóo people, 128
Harappa, 143
Harding, Warren G., 210, 211
Harvard University, 135
Health: and air pollution, 62–63; and water pollution, 63
Health, Education, and Welfare, U.S. Department of, 58; and inversion emergencies, 60
Herskovits, Melville J., 172
Hetch-Hetchy Valley, San Francisco, 220–221
Hickel, Walter J., 22, 68
Highways, 54, 221
Highway Trust Fund, 228
Historic sites, 74
Holling, C. S., viii, 100, 170–171
Holyrood Abbey, Edinburgh, 148
Hoover, Edgar, 155
Hoover, Herbert, 211
Horst, Oscar, 42
Housing, 6, 34

Housing and Urban Development (HUD), U.S. Department of, 75
Houston, Texas, 12, 13
Houston Ship Channel, 12
Howells, William Dean, 210
Hudson Highlands, 218
Hudson River, 66
Hudson River Valley, 217
Hutchinson, G. Evelyn, 31
Hydrology, continental, 19

Idealism, American, 188
Income, per capita, 38
India, 38–39, 142, 167
Indochina, 132
Indonesia, 43, 130
Industrialization, 210; and population growth, 29
Industrial Revolution, 194
Indus Valley, 118, 131, 132
Insects, 225–227; and immunity to DDT, 70–71
Interior, U.S. Department of, 12, 64, 66–67, 76; purchase of land to protect game, 73; Bureau of Outdoor Recreation (BOR), 74
Internal Revenue Service, 229
Inversions, see Temperature
Iron and steel industry, processing of scrap, 56
Irrigation, 132–135
Izaak Walton League, 220

Jacobs, Jane, 41, 167
Japan, 33; population density, 37
Jericho, 119

Katz, Milton, 67
Keynes, John Maynard, 183
Kirtland warbler, 83
Kneese, Allen, viii, 202

Knetsch, Jack, 204
Koch, Janet, viii
Kota tribe, India, 172–173
Kurumba tribe, India, 172–173

Labor, division of, 146–148
Laissez-faire, U.S., 192–193, 195, 207, 210–211
Lakeshores, national, 74
Land, 72–73; and Mam Indians, 42–43; public, 73; and federal policy, 73–77
Land and Water Conservation Fund, 73–75
Land use, 54
Latin America, 29
Legislation, 3, 53. See also Congress, U.S.
Lemmings, 30, 41
Leopold, Aldo, 212
Levittown, 154
Lewis, Sinclair, 208
Litter, 26, 159
London, 57, 159
Los Angeles, 57, 59; emergency plans for temperature inversions, 60; and reduction of automobile traffic, 60

MacArthur, Robert, 90
McConnell, Grant, 213
Mam Indians, Guatemala, 42–43
Man, 104–115; interaction with his environment, 20–21, 92–93, 103, 104; origins of, 104–109; and missing link, 105–106; and use of tools, 108–109; as food gatherer, 109–110; his control of fire, 110–113; continued patterns of response after change in environmental conditions, 114; and invention of agriculture, 116–125;

Man (*contd.*)
  as environmental manager, 135–136
Management, environmental, 136–138, 207–214, 225–230
Manhattan, 37, 153; Lower East Side, 153
Marina City, Chicago, 156
Marsh, George Perkins, his *Man and Nature*, 207–208
Marshall, John, 192
Marshall, Robert, 212
Marshlands, 220
Mass transportation, *see* Transportation
Massachusetts, wetlands protection law, 220
Materials Policy Commission, *see* Paley Commission
Mayans, 130–131
Megalopolis, 154
Mesoamerica, 118, 119, 121, 122, 142, 145; and swiddening, 131; development of cities in, 143; and waste, 159
Mesopotamia, 118, 119, 120, 122, 134, 142, 145; and overpopulation, 131
Methemoglobinemia (blue-baby syndrome), 63
Metropolis, 154
Meuse Valley, 57
Michigan, 71
Middle East, 142
Migration, 111, 189–190, 230; in population control, 41–43
Miller, Richard, 90
Mindoro Island, 128
Mississippi-Missouri-Ohio river system, 63
Mississippi River, 73
Mohenjo-Daro, 143

Monitoring, environmental, 53
Monuments, national, 74
Mortality rates, 29, 31, 42
Motor vehicle emissions, federal standards for, 58, 60–61
Mumford, Lewis, 140, 144, 145, 148, 163
Muskie, Senator Edmund, 61
Mutants, 90–91, 94

Nash, Roderick, 209
National Center for Atmospheric Research, 59–60
National Environmental Policy Act (1969), 76–77
National forests, 73
National parks, 21, 73, 74
National wildlife refuges, 212
Natural resources, 49; and federal budget, 75
Natural systems, 13, 19, 73, 81–87; alterations in, 81–83; stability in, 96; conditioned by past experience, 99–101; spatial needs, 102–103; nonconforming species, 104–115; management of, 225–230
Nature: man's insulation from, 20–21; in American dream, 186
Nature Conservancy, The, 213, 220
Netherlands, 37, 38
New Deal, 211, 215
New Jersey, 220
New York City, 217, 223; problems of waste disposal, 52; reduction in sulphur dioxide content in smog, 59; emergency plans for temperature inversions, 60; and pulmonary emphysema, 62; traffic in, 159
New York Metropolitan Region, 38

New York Tuberculosis and
Health Association, 62
Nile River Valley, 132, 133
Nixon, Richard M., 3, 5, 49
Norris, Frank, 210
North Africa, 118
North America, 43, 122
North Queensland, Australia, 97
Nuclear power, for excavation, 16,
19

Ocean pollution, 53; from pesti-
cides, 72. See also Pollution
Oil, 23; pollution from, 66–69
Open Space Program (HUD), 75
Osborne, Fairfield, his Our Plun-
dered Planet, 212–213
Outer Continental Shelf Lands
Act, 66
Outward Bound program, 21
Overcrowding, see Crowding

Packaging, 52, 203
Pakistan, 34–35, 135
Paley Commission, 213
Park Service, U.S., 74
Parks, 53. See also National parks
Peru, 118
Pest control, agricultural, 70–72,
225–227; and DDT, 70–71. See
also DDT
Pesticides, 19, 50, 53; run-off, and
water pollution, 64, 201; and
regulation, 71
Petroleum industry, 72
Philippines, 130
Planning, 166–169
Ploughshare program, 16, 19
Politics (politicians): and environ-
mental issues, 22; and water pol-
lution, 64–65

Pollution, 8, 75, 170, 200–201, 224–
226; of bay areas, 11–12; from
fertilizer or pesticide run-off, 50;
and EPA, 54; from heat, 64;
from oil, 66–69. See also Air
pollution; Water pollution
Population, 6–7, 21–22, 37; projected growth, 27–28; past up-
surges in, 28–29; control mechanisms, 29–31, 34–36, 41–43;
exponential growth, 31–32;
problems inherent in control,
32–34; and problem of food, 34–
36; density (crowding), 37–38;
demands on resources and energy, 38–39; and the city, 40–41;
and migration, 41–43; checking
of growth, 44–45; pessimism
concerning success of control,
45–48; California, 51; density
limits, 103; and Mayan civilization, 130
Poverty, 180
Power consumption, 51, 176–177;
and Storm King Mountain con-
troversy, 217–220
Priorities, environmental, 24–25,
222–223
Progress, 186–187
Progressive movement, 209–211,
215
Protection, environmental, 75
Prudential Center, Boston, 156
Public domain, 73–75
Public Health Service, 55; and
lung cancer in densely popu-
lated urban areas, 62
Public services, 35
Pulmonary emphysema, 62

Ramapithecus, 107

Reclamation, 56
Recreation, outdoor, 21, 53, 74, 203
Recreation areas, national, 74
Recycling, 56
Red River Gorge, Kentucky, 221
Reed, Charles, 119
Resources: demands made upon, 38–39, 50–51; transformation of, 213–214
Resources for the Future, 74, 213
Ridker, Ronald G., 204
Road building, 228. *See also* Highways
Roberts, Walter Orr, 59
Roosevelt, Franklin D., 215
Roosevelt, Theodore, 208, 209, 213, 215
Ruhr Valley, 202
Rutgers University, 55–56

Salt marshes, 11–12, 220
Salvage, 56–57
Samuelson, Paul, 175
San Francisco, 13
Sanitation, 23–24
Santa Barbara Channel, 66, 67, 68
Santa Clara County, California, 58–59
Sauer, Carl, 116, 117, 118–119
Scenic Hudson Preservation Conference, 217
Schaller, George B., 108
Schumpeter, Joseph A., 182
*Science* magazine, 11, 12
Seashores, nation, 74
Self-interest, 181, 188
Senate Interior Committee, U.S., 54
Sewage, 13, 159; treatment plants, 66

Sierra Club, 217, 221
Simpson, George Gaylord, 88, 91
Sive, David, 218–219
Skyscrapers, 155–156
Slums, 41, 153, 157–169; attempts at clearance, 161–162; rehabilitation, 162; created by affluence, not poverty, 163; and social action, 163–164
Smallpox, 30, 42
Smith, Adam, 181
Smog, 24, 57, 222. *See also* Air pollution
Social Darwinism, 193–195
Soil Erosion Service (later Soil Conservation Service), 211
Solid Waste Disposal Act (1965), 55
Southeast Asia, 118, 130, 137
Soviet Union, 18–19, 167
Space needs, 102–103
Specialization, 90–93, 101
Speciation, 90–92
Spencer, Herbert, 186, 193, 194
SST, *see* Supersonic transport plane
State, U.S. Department of, 35
Stegner, Wallace, 209–210
Storm King Mountain, 217–220
Streisand, Barbra, 26
Student Conservation Association, 21
Suburbs, 153–154
Succession, 82–84, 89
Sumerian civilization, 134, 143, 144
Sumner, William Graham, 193
Supersonic transport plane (SST), 178; and human welfare, 179
Sviridoff, Mitchell, viii
Swamp, 221–222
Sweden, 72

Swiddening, 127–133; and the Mayans, 130; in Mesoamerica, 131

Taboos, 30–31
Tawney, R. H., 199
Technology, 8–9; and progress, 16–18; and costs, 17, 18; and population growth, 28–29
Teilhard de Chardin, Pierre, 89
Teller, Dr. Edward, 16–17
Temperature: air, 7–8; water, 12–13; inversions, 59–60; adaptation to, 94
Tennessee Valley Authority, 211
Territoriality, 109–110; and space needs, 102–103
Tigris-Euphrates River Valley, 132
Toda tribe, India, 172–173
*Torrey Canyon*, tanker, 23, 68–69
Traffic, 158–159
Transportation, 6, 228; nineteenth century, 152
Transportation, U.S. Department of, 76
Trash, 55, 159
Trinity River, 11
Truman, Harry S, 213
Turkey, 119
Turner, Frederick Jackson, 190

Udall, Stewart, 65, 73
Underdeveloped nations, 39, 224–225; and use of DDT, 72
Unindustrialized nations, 29
United Nations, population projection, 28
United States, 186–196; population density, 38; demands upon the environment, 39, 50–51; need to restore environment, 49–54; accumulation of waste, 51–52; projected city populations (2000), 153; frontier life, 189–192, 207–210; and laissez-faire dogmas, 192–193, 195, 207, 210–211; awakening concerning conservationism, 207–214
Ur, 159
Urban development, 152–153
Urbanization, 40, 139–148. See also City
Utilities, 54

Value judgments, 174–175
Vernon, Raymond, 155
Vietnam, 22, 178
Villages, 142–143
Vogt, William, his *Road to Survival*, 212–213
Von Neumann, John R., 18

Waste, solid: disposal, 6, 12, 27, 53, 55–69, 75, 201; accumulation of, 51–52; agricultural, 52; growth rate, 52–53; and EPA, 54; federal research into disposal, 55; new methods of collection and transport, 56; and salvage and recycling, 56–57; an urban problem, 159–160; and effluent charge, 201–202
Water pollution, 53, 63–69, 75, 201; and health, 63; and esthetics, 63–64; and politics (cost of cleanup), 64–65; and Federal Water Quality Administration, 65–66; from oil spills, 66–69
Watt, Kenneth, 136
Weather, 7–8, 19
White House Council for Environmental Quality, 77
Whitman, Walt, 210
Wilderness areas, 228; national, 74

Wilderness Society, 212
Wildlife, 54, 67
Williams, Roger, 187
Wilson, Woodrow, 210
Wisconsin, 71

Wittfogel, Karl, 132, 133, 134
Wynne-Edwards, V. C., 103

Yellowstone National Park, 73
Yucatan, 130